CENSUS OF INDIA 1891

Census of India 1871-1951, 9 Sets In 384 Bindings (9788121258876) Rs. 700000

Census of India 1891, 28 Vols. In 49 Bindings (978-81-212-7129-5) Rs. 125000

1. General Report (9788121269834) Rs. 1450
2. General Tables For British Provinces And Feudatory States (9788121269810) Rs. 2710 (Vol. I)
3. General Tables For British Provinces And Feudatory States (9788121269797) Rs. 950 (Vol. II)
4. Assam - Report (9788121269773) Rs. 2390 (Vol. I, V.1)
5. Assam - Tables (9788121269759) Rs. 2210 (Vol. II, V.2)
6. Assam - Provincial Tables (9788121269735) Rs. 1310 (Vol. II, V.3)
7. The Lower Provinces of Bengal and their Feudatories - The Report (9788121269711) Rs. 1660 (Vol. III)
8. The Lower Provinces of Bengal and their feudatories - The Administrative Tables (9788121269698) Rs. 4200 (Vol. IV)
9. The Lower Provinces of Bengal and their feudatories - The Caste Tables (9788121269674) Rs. 2600 (Vol. V, Pt. 1)
10. Lower Provinces of Bengal - The Provincial Tables (9788121269650) Rs. 1980 (Vol. V, Pt. 2)
11. Berar or the Hyderabad Assigned Districts (9788121269636) Rs. 3360 (Vol. VI)
12. Bombay and Its Feudatories - Report (9788121269612) Rs. 4010 (Vol. VII, Pt. 1)
13. Bombay And Its Feudatories - Imperial Tables (9788121269599) Rs. 790 (Vol. VIII, Pt. 2)
14. Imperial Series - Burma Report (9788121269575) Rs. 2320 (Vol. IX-V.1)
15. Imperial Tables - Burma Report (9788121269551) Rs. 3360 (Vol. X-V.2)
16. Provincial Tables Burma Report (9788121269537) Rs. 3510 (Vol. X-V.3)
17. Provincial Tables Burma Report (9788121269513) Rs. 3630 (Vol. X-V.4)
18. The Central Provinces And Feudatories - The Report (9788121269490) Rs. 2290 (Vol. XI, Pt. 1)
19. The Central Provinces And Feudatories - Imperial tables and supplementary returns (9788121268936) Rs. 2010 (Vol. XII)
20. Madras The Report On The Census (9788121269476) Rs. 2870 (Vol. XIII)
21. Madras - Tables I to XVII-C, British Territory (9788121269452) Rs. 3490 (Vol. XIV)
22. Madras - Tables A TO E, British Territory. Tables for feudatory States and A Caste Index (9788121269438) Rs. 2820 (Vol. XV)
23. The North Western Provinces and Outh - Report and Provincial Tables (9788121268912) Rs. 3100 (Vol. XVI, Pt. 1)
24. The North - Western Provinces and Oudh- Imperial Tables (9788121269414) Rs. 2000 (Vol. XVII, Pt. 2)
25. The North - Western Provinces and Oudh- Imperial Caste Tables (9788121269391) Rs. 3020 (Vol. XVIII, Pt. 3)
26. Punjab and Its Feudatories - The Report on the Census (9788121269377) Rs. 2710 (Vol. XIX, Pt. 1)
27. Punjab and Its Feudatories - Imperial Tables and Supplementary Returns for the British Territory (9788121269353) Rs. 1370 (Vol. XX, Pt. 2)
28. Punjab and Its Feudatories - Imperial Tables and Supplementary Returns for the Native States, Together With A Caste Index (9788121269339) Rs. 4910 (Vol. XXI, Pt. 3)
29. Report on The Census of The Districts of Ajmere-Merwara (9788121269056) Rs. 720 (Vol. XXII)
30. His Highness The Nizam's Dominions - Report (9788121269315) Rs. 2240 (Vol. XXIII, Pt. 1)
31. His Highness The Nizam's Dominions - Report (9788121269292) Rs. 2410 (Vol. XXIII, Pt. 2)
32. His Highness The Nizam's Dominions - Imperial And Supplementry Tables and Caste Index (9788121269278) Rs. 3390 (Vol. XXIII, Pt. 3)
33. Baroda - Report (9788121269254) Rs. 3810 (Vol. XXIV, Pt. 1)
34. Baroda - Tables (9788121269230) Rs. 2620 (Vol. XXIV, Pt. 2)
35. Mysore - Report (9788121269216) Rs. 2590 (Vol. XXV, Pt. 1)
36. Mysore - Imperial Tables (9788121269193) Rs. 1600 (Vol. XXV, Pt. 2)
37. Mysore - Tables (9788121269179) Rs. 5320 (Vol. XXV, Pt. 3)
38. Mysore - Supplementary Tables (9788121269155) Rs. 3590 (Vol. XXV, Pt. 4)
39. Mysore- Supplement to the Mysore census report of 1891 being a list of villages in the Mysore province and : comparing the population as per Censuses of 1891, 1881 & 1871 (9788121279024) Rs. 5350 (Vol. XXV, Pt. 5)
40. Rajputana - The Report, Imperial Tables And Supplementary Returns (9788121269131) Rs. 2330 (Vol. XXVI, Pt. 1)
41. Rajputna - The Provincial Tables and Remarks (9788121269117) Rs. 550 (Vol. XXVI, Pt. 2)
42. Central India (9788121269094) Rs. 2000 (Vol. XXVII)
43. Kashmir State - The Report on the census and Imperial and supplementary Tables (9788121269070) Rs. 2290 (Vol. XXVIII)
44. The Census of Calcutta (9788121269032) Rs. 890
45. Report on the census of Cochin (9788121269018) Rs. 790 (Pt. 1)
46. Report on the census of Cochin - The Final Census Tables with Appendices (9788121268998) Rs. 910 (Pt. 2)
47. Report on the Census of Coorg (9788121268974) Rs. 730
48. Report on the census of Travancore -Report (9788121274029) Rs. 4220 (Vol. I)
49. Report on the census of Travancore -Appendix (9788121268950) Rs. 5300 (Vol. II)

Owing to the antiquity and rarity of this book, certain pages are regrettably absent, and readability is compromised due to the blurring of the original text. If you possess any insights regarding the availability of these missing sections, kindly inform us. Your assistance is crucial in ensuring the completion of this significant work for the benefit of future generations.

CENSUS OF INDIA, 1891

BOOK-47

REPORT

ON THE

CENSUS OF COORG

H. A. STUART

GYAN

Published by

Gyan Publishing House
5, Ansari Road
Daryaganj, New Delhi-110002
Phone: 011-47034999, 9811692060
E-mail: books@gyanbooks.com

Distribution Network
gyanbooks.com
India, USA, Canada, UK, Australia

ISBN: 978-81-212-7129-5 (Set) 28 Vols. In 49 Bindings
978-81-212-6897-4 (PB) Book-47

First Published, 1893

2nd Impression 2024

Printed at: Gyan Press, Delhi.

CENSUS OF INDIA 1891

CENSUS OF INDIA, 1891.

REPORT

ON THE

CENSUS OF COORG.

BY

H. A. STUART,
OF THE INDIAN CIVIL SERVICE,
FELLOW OF THE ROYAL STATISTICAL SOCIETY,
MEMBER OF THE ROYAL ASIATIC SOCIETY, ETC.,
PROVINCIAL SUPERINTENDENT OF CENSUS OPERATIONS FOR MADRAS AND COORG.

CALCUTTA:
OFFICE OF THE SUPERINTENDENT OF GOVERNMENT PRINTING, INDIA.
1893.

PREFACE.

THE completion of the Census Report of Coorg has been delayed, as I felt myself bound to give my first efforts to Madras. It would perhaps be better, in many ways, to entrust the administration of the Coorg Census to a local officer in future, and this would allow of the tables and report being issued at a much earlier date.

This report is somewhat brief, but I have, I hope, noticed all the salient features in the census statistics, and given explanations where they were required. The absolute numbers dealt with are so small that in many cases it was not safe to draw from them deductions which are permissible enough when the facts are more varied as in a large population. Matters are further complicated, too, by the high proportion of immigrants among the people of Coorg.

I am glad of this opportunity to acknowledge the assistance rendered to me throughout by Mr. Brooke Leggatt, the First Assistant Commissioner and District Magistrate. Without his cordial co-operation the success which attended the taking of the census would have been impossible.

H. A. STUART,
Superintendent of Census Operations.

OOTACAMUND,
22nd March 1893.

REPORT

ON THE

CENSUS OF COORG, 1891.

CHAPTER I.

PHYSICAL DESCRIPTION, AREA, DENSITY, TOWNS, VILLAGES AND HOUSES.

(TABLES I, III, IV AND V.)

Physical Description.

1. The tiny province of Coorg lies on the summits of the Western Ghâts and is bounded on the west by South Canara, on the south-west and south by Malabar, and on the north and east by the Mysore State. The country is one of hill and dale and forest, the mountain peaks rising to a height of nearly 6,000 feet above sea level, while the cultivated and inhabited parts have an altitude of from 3,000 to 3,500 feet. The main drainage of the country is towards the east, the most considerable of the rivers being the Kâveri, which rises at a place called Tale Kâveri, on the extreme edge of the ghâts. There are many minor streams and the water-supply is everywhere abundant throughout the year. There are no natural lakes of any size.

Rainfall.

2. The physical configuration of Coorg gives the greater part of it an exceptionally heavy rainfall during the time of the south-west monsoon, the dense rain clouds of which are arrested by the mountain summits and discharge their copious showers with but little intermission from June to August. The average annual fall during the prevalence of the summer monsoon is over 100 inches and the total annual fall exceeds 120 inches. The country round Frazerpet, however, on the extreme east of the province, gets comparatively little rain from the south-west monsoon, as the elevation is lower.

Civil Administration.

3. The government of Coorg is administered by a Chief Commissioner, an office which is now held in conjunction with that of Resident in Mysore. The principal executive officer is the Commissioner, who combines the functions of Civil and Sessions Judge and head of the revenue administration. One Assistant Commissioner performs the double duty of District Magistrate and head of the police, while the second Assistant is a judge for the trial of civil suits. The country is divided into six taluks and each is directly administered by a native officer called a Subedar. Each taluk again is sub-divided into *náds* or *hoblis*, the head of which is styled a Parpettegar.

Taluk.	Area in square miles.
Mercára	216·30
Padinalknád	399·90
Yedenalknád	201·45
Kiggatnád	410·45
Nanjarájpatna	263·89
Yelusavirashíme	90·82
Total	1,582·81

Revenue and Expenditure.

4. The gross receipts of the province in 1890-91, the year of the census, amounted to R8,71,964, and the net receipts to R6,20,995. The expenditure from this net income amounted to R3,71,514, and there was thus a surplus of about two and a half lakhs of rupees. The principal sources of income are the land revenue, excise on spirits and drugs, state forests and stamps; and the chief items of expenditure are civil establishments, public works and education.

Trade.

5. The imports, including R2,47,500 of treasure, are valued at R17,20,170 and the exports at R27,78,800. The grain imported is of the estimated value of R2,00,000, and the imports of salt are put at the same figure, while a sum of R2,17,150 is entered for provisions. The only other considerable items of import are live stock, manufactured piece goods, oils, liquors, and sugar and saccharine produce. The exports consist almost entirely of coffee, the value of which is entered as R25,55,400. Wood comes next with R1,03,700, and then cardamoms and spices, valued at R53,600.

Area and Population.

6. The area of Coorg is 1,583 square miles or a little less than the size of Hampshire. There are eight English counties with an area larger than that of Coorg.

The population of Coorg is 173,055 or about the same as that of Buckinghamshire in 1881. There are only five English counties with a population less than that of Coorg.

It is perhaps unnecessary to state that Coorg is much the smallest of all Indian provinces both as regards area and number of inhabitants. The average sub-division of a Madras district has a larger area and a greater population.

Density, Areality and Proximity.

7. There are in Coorg 109 persons to each square mile. There are 5·85 acres to each individual, and the mean distance between each person is 181 yards. The marginal table shows that Coorg is more sparsely populated than most parts of India.

Province.	Persons per square mile.	Acres per person.	Proximity in yards.
Coorg	109	5·85	181
Madras	252	2·54	119
Bengal	471	1·36	87
Bombay	151	4·24	154
N.-W. P. and Oudh	436	1·47	91
Punjab	189	3·39	138
Burma	45	14·21	282
Mysore	177	3·62	142

In the South Canara district of Madras which borders on Coorg, there are 271 persons to the square mile, but in the Nilgiris, a district which resembles Coorg in many respects, the number is only 104. The density of the population in Coorg is not one-fourth of that of England and Wales, but it is not much less than that of Scotland, where there are only 132 persons to the square mile. We must in fact take into consideration the very mountainous nature of the country, for the density is probably as high as in most districts of similar character.

Towns and Villages.

8. The total number of towns and inhabited villages is 497, which is six less than the number in 1881; but it is not clear whether the number for that year includes uninhabited villages also. The average population of each is 348, but for villages alone the mean number of inhabitants is 320. The average area of each, that is the area of the parish, so to speak, not that of the inhabited site alone, is 3·19 square miles, and the mean distance between each site is 1·92 miles. The people of Coorg, however, like those of Malabar and parts of Canara, live in

isolated homesteads, and the Coorg village is merely a revenue expression denoting the area lying within certain boundaries. This must be borne in mind in considering the statistics given in Table III, which shows the number and population of towns and villages of different sizes. From that table we find that 45·5 per cent. of the villages contain less than 200 inhabitants, 78·1 per cent. have less than 500 inhabitants, and in the case of 95·6 per cent. the population is below 1,000. Put in another way, 11·2 per cent. of the population live in villages with less than 200 inhabitants, 44·1 per cent. in villages with less than 500 inhabitants and 77·8 per cent. in villages whose population is less than 1,000 persons. These statistics relating to towns and villages are compared with those for Madras in the following tables :

Number of towns and villages in each group out of 1,000.

Province.	1—199.	200—499.	500—999.	1,000—1,999.	2,000—2,999.	3,000—4,999.	5,000 and over.	Total.
Coorg .	455	326	175	36	4	2	2	1,000
Madras .	402	243	184	115	33	16	7	1,000

Number of persons in 1,000 living in each class of village or town.

Province.	1—199.	200—499.	500—999.	1,000—1,999.	2,000—2,999.	3,000—4,999.	5,000 and over.	Total.
Coorg .	112	329	337	126	29	26	41	1,000
Madras .	53	131	211	258	127	98	122	1,000

Towns.

9. The five places noted on the margin have been shown as towns in the census tables, because they are all under some form of Municipal Government, but even the largest has a smaller population than many a village of the Madras Presidency, while Frazerpet, Somvárapet and Kodlipet can have very little of an urban character. It will be noticed that the population of all except Frazerpet has decreased since 1881. The decline is considerable only in the case of the Mercára, where the difference is attributed to the withdrawal of the regiment formerly stationed there. The decrease in the other cases is probably more apparent than real, and is attributable to the same causes as have affected the population as a whole. These will be noticed in the next chapter.

Towns.	Population. 1891.	Population. 1881.	Variation.
Mercára .	7,034	8,383	−1,349
Virájendrapet .	4,447	4,576	−129
Frazerpet .	1,710	1,310	+400
Somvárapet .	1,510	1,528	−18
Kodlipet .	810	856	−46

Urban and Rural population.

10. The total population of these five so-called towns is 15,511, so the urban population is 8·96 per cent. of the total. In Madras the proportion is 9·56 per cent., but there a town is something very different from the tiny municipalities of Coorg. A curious feature of the Coorg urban population is that the number of persons to an occupied house in towns is considerably less than in villages, an anomaly which is partially due to the rural population being frequently found in large family houses containing several generations of the same parent stock.

	Number of persons per occupied house. In Towns.	Number of persons per occupied house. In Villages.
Coorg . .	4·89	6·67
Madras . .	5·60	5·28

The annexed statement shows the distribution between town and country of the followers of each religion. It will be seen that Musalmans and Christians affect a town life much more than Hindus, a feature which is also observed in Madras, and is due to the preference for trading shown by the followers of the cross and the crescent.

Religion.	Proportion in		Percentage of Urban and Rural population following each main religion.	
	Towns.	Villages.	Urban.	Rural.
Hindus	6·81	93·19	68·84	92·78
Musalmans	28·56	71·44	23·32	5·74
Christians	32·93	67·07	7·20	1·45
Others	65·36	34·64	0·64	0·03

11. The number of occupied houses is 26,806 and the average number of inmates of a house is 6·46. In 1881 the average was 7·98, but the definition of a house seems to have differed on the two occasions. I do not, however, think that the difference can have had any great effect in the case of ordinary dwelling houses, and I believe that a great part of the decrease in the average number of occupants indicates a real improvement. The averages for other provinces of India are given in the marginal statement. In Canara the average is 5·57, in Malabar 5·87, and excluding Madras city, there is only one district (S. Arcot) of the Madras Presidency in which the average is higher than that of Coorg.

Houses.

	Number of persons per occupied house.
Coorg	6·46
Madras	5·31
Bombay	5·59
North-West Provinces and Oudh	5·70
Punjab	6·67
Mysore	5·53

The average space to each house is 37·79 acres and the mean distance between each is 460 yards. The corresponding figures for the Madras Presidency are 13·47 acres and 274 yards.

CHAPTER II.

THE MOVEMENT OF THE POPULATION.

(TABLE II.)

Decrease of the population.

12. The population of Coorg on the 17th February 1881 was 178,302: on the 26th February 1891 it was 173,055. The population has thus decreased by 5,247 or 2·94 per cent.

Year.	Population.		
	Total.	Males.	Females.
1881	178,302	100,439	77,863
1891	*173,055*	*95,907*	*77,148*
Variation	—5,247	—4,532	—715
Variation per cent.	—2·94	—4·51	—0·92

The explanation of this striking exception to the general increase of population throughout India is to be found in the fact that a very high proportion of the population of Coorg consists of immigrant labourers who come from Mysore and the neighbouring Madras districts to work on the coffee plantations. As soon as the preliminary compilation brought to notice that there had been a decrease instead of an increase of the people, I addressed the district Magistrate on the subject, and he informed me that he attributed the decrease to the fact that a large number of these immigrant labourers had returned to their homes in Malabar, South Canara and Mysore by the date of the Census, while in 1881, when the Census was taken nine days earlier in the year and the coffee season was later than in 1891, these people were enumerated in Coorg. This view is fully borne out by the statistics. Taking first those relating to birthplace we get the following results :—

Year.	Born in Coorg.			Born elsewhere.		
	Total.	Males.	Females.	Total.	Males.	Females.
1881	103,437	53,235	50,202	74,865	47,204	27,661
1891	*120,110*	*61,571*	*58,539*	*52,945*	*34,336*	*18,609*
Variation	+16,673	+8,336	+8,337	—21,920	—12,868	—9,052

Thus the indigenous population has increased by 16·12 per cent. or at the rate of 1·502 per cent. per annum, and the decrease is entirely confined to the immigrant population, which is 29·28 per cent. less now than in 1881. In that year the native-born population constituted only 58·01 per cent. of the total: in

1891 the percentage was 69·42. If we turn to the figures of the principal indigenous caste, *viz.*, the Kodagu or Coorg race, we find that there has been an increase of 20·63 per cent. Between 1871 and 1881 the Coorgs increased by only 2·44 per cent. Unfortunately it is not possible to compare the figures for other castes found only in Coorg, as in the 1881 tables these have been lumped together in a single group, which also includes some immigrant castes, or castes partly immigrant and partly native. Nor can I obtain any trustworthy results from a comparison of the occupation statistics, owing to the widely different systems of classifying and tabulating which were followed in 1881 and on the present occasion.

Coorgs.

Year.	TOTAL.	Males.	Females.
1891	32,611	16,527	16,084
1881	27,033	13,701	13,332
Variation	5,578	2,826	2,752

13. Further evidence in support of the view of Mr. Leggatt, the District Magistrate, is afforded by the age tables, which show a great increase in the population under 5, a state of things which is incompatible with a declining population. There is also an increase of more than 8 per cent. in the population over 40, and the decrease is confined to the numbers between the ages of 5 and 39. I should not have expected the falling off to appear at the early ages, but many immigrants evidently bring all except their very young children with them.

Age Statistics.

POPULATION UNDER 5.		
Year.	Males.	Females.
1891	10,677	11,226
1881	8,430	8,768
Increase	2,247	2,458

14. It is clear from the figures that have been given that the native population of Coorg is a progressive one, and it further appears that its rate of growth is high when compared with that found in other parts of India. Mysore, Madras and Bombay suffered heavily from the famine of 1877-78, and the recovery from its effects has raised the rates of increase. Coorg was unaffected by that famine, and yet its indigenous population has increased at a rate less only than that found in Mysore.

The population a progressive one.

Increase per cent. since 1881.

Madras	15·58
Mysore	18·09
Bombay	14·49
Bengal	6·89
N.-W. P. and Oudh	6·34
Punjab	10·74
Assam	12·19

Moreover, there is no reason to suppose that there is any real falling off in the numbers of immigrants, for between 1880-81 and 1890-91 the area under coffee has advanced by 15,491 acres or 32·79 per cent., while the acreage under rice, the only other widely cultivated crop, has also advanced. In 1881 there were 1,584 immigrants to every acre under coffee, and if this ratio had been maintained we should have had 99,410 immigrants in 1891 and the total population would have been 219,520, or 23·12 per cent. in excess of that of 1881. It is not, however, permissible to assume that the ratio between the acreage under coffee and the number of immigrants is a fixed one or even approximately permanent, but I think that it may be asserted with confidence that the ratio between indigenous and immigrant population, during the months that the latter is present, cannot

Cultivation of Coffee and Rice.

Year.	Coffee.	Rice.
	Acs.	Acs.
1890-91	62,741	74,497
1880-81	47,250	72,881
Variation	+ 15,491	+ 1,616

have decreased since 1881, seeing how greatly the cultivation of coffee has advanced. On this hypothesis the normal population of Coorg, that is, the population during the months when the labourers are at work on the coffee estates, would be 207,051. This may be taken to be the minimum normal population and that given above (219,520) as the maximum. The actual number will lie somewhere between these two.

15. I give below the birth and death statistics for the ten official years which approximate most nearly to the period between the two enumerations :

Birth and Death Statistics.

Registered Births and Deaths in Coorg.

Year.	Births.	Deaths.	Excess of Births over Deaths.
1881-82	2,829	3,192	—363
1882-83	2,798	3,112	—314
1883-84	2,394	3,879	—1,485
1884-85	2,652	2,689	—37
1885-86	3,118	2,956	+162
1886-87	2,505	3,626	—1,121
1887-88	2,582	3,461	—879
1888-89	2,963	3,461	—498
1889-90	2,917	4,087*	—1,170
1890-91	2,719	4,515†	—1,796
TOTAL	27,477	34,978	—7,501

In every year but one (1885-86) the deaths exceed the births and the total excess amounts to 7,501. In a country like Coorg, however, in which nearly half the population is immigrant, the birth and death statistics are of little use for the purpose of ascertaining the growth of the population. It is evident that the registration is defective, for both birth and death rates are much lower than those found elsewhere. On the other hand it must be remembered that a high proportion of the immigrant population consists of males who are unmarried or have not brought their wives with them. These, therefore, contribute nothing or very little to the births, while they are included in the population on which the birth rates are calculated; and as the deaths among these labourers help to swell the number of deaths it is intelligible that the latter should exceed the number of births. The Administration Reports do not give details of sex in the death returns, so I am not able to say how far the statistics support this view by showing an excess of male deaths.

16. In the case of a population so small as that of Coorg it is hardly necessary to give information for any area smaller than the whole province, but as the subject dealt with in this chapter presents unusual features, I give the figures for each taluk in the annexed table.

Taluk figures.

In Yelusavirashíme, Padinalknád and Kiggatnád there has been an increase. The decrease is greatest in Mercára, then comes Yedenalknád, and lastly Nanjarájpatna. I believe that coffee is most extensively grown in Mercára and Yedenalknád, so we should expect to find the decrease at a maximum in these two taluks. I have, however, no taluk statistics of coffee cultivation, so I cannot pursue this subject further. It may be, too, that the coffee season was earlier in some taluks than in others.

* No epidemic; better registration.

† Influenza epidemic.

Comparative Statement of Population.

Taluk.	Population by Census of 1881.			Net gain or loss by subsequent transfer.			Population in 1881 of present limits.			Population in 1891.			Variation.			Per cent. of Variation.		
	Total.	Males.	Females.	Total.	Males.	Females.	Total.	Males.	Females.	Total.	Males.	Females.	Total.	Males.	Females.	Total.	Males.	Females.
Yelusavirashíme	16,411	8,174	8,237	...	...	...	16,411	8,174	8,237	16,639	8,345	8,294	+228	+171	+57	1·39	2·09	0·69
Nanjarájpatna	26,984	13,886	13,098	−744	−479	−265	26,240	13,407	12,833	25,059	13,059	12,000	−1,181	−348	−833	−4·50	−2·60	−6·49
Mercára	34,088	20,275	13,813	−827	−389	−438	33,261	19,886	13,375	27,722	16,381	11,341	−5,539	−3,505	−2,034	−16·65	−17·63	−15·21
Padinalknád	28,219	16,342	11,877	...	...	...	28,219	16,342	11,877	30,615	17,036	13,579	+2,396	+694	+1,702	8·49	4·25	14·33
Yedenalknád	41,370	24,771	16,599	−977	−639	−338	40,393	24,132	16,261	38,213	22,295	15,918	−2,180	−1,837	−343	−5·40	−7·61	−2·11
Kiggatnád	31,230	16,991	14,239	+2,548	+1,507	+1,041	33,778	18,498	15,280	34,807	18,791	16,016	+1,029	+293	+736	3·05	1·58	4·82
Total	178,302	100,439	77,863	...	...	...	178,302	100,439	77,863	173,055	95,907	77,148	−5,247	−4,532	−715	−2·94	−4·51	−0·92

CHAPTER III.

RELIGION.

TABLES VI, A AND B.

Comparison with 1881.

17. In the following statement the statistics relating to religion are compared with those for 1881 :

Statement showing the number of persons returning each of the principal religions in 1881 and 1891.

Religion.	Number of persons returning it.		Variation.	Percentage of variation.
	1881.	1891.		
Hindu	162,489	156,845	— 5,644	— 3·47
Musalman	12,541	12,665	+ 124	+ 0·99
Christian	3,152	3,392	+ 240	+ 7·61
Jain	99	114	+ 15	+ 15·15
Parsi	21	39	+ 18	+ 85·71

Comparison with other Provinces.

18. It will be of interest to compare the proportion under each religion with similar statistics for other provinces :

Statement showing the distribution according to Religion of 10,000 of the population in each Province.

Province.	Hindus.	Musalmans	Christians.	Buddhists.	Jains.	Sikhs.	Animistic.	Parsis.	Others.
Coorg	9,063·30	731·85	196·01	...	6·59	...	...	2·25	...
Madras	8,984·25	631·85	243·02	0·29	7·70	0·03	132·75	0·07	0·04
Assam	5,472·27	2,709·55	30·76	14·05	2·50	0·15	1,770·67	...	0·05
Bengal	6,338·21	3,285·28	26·75	26·51	0·99	0·06	321·62	0·02	0·56
Bombay	7,772·79	1,857·08	84·20	0·36	127·51	0·43	113·28	39·21	5·14
Burma	225·60	332·69	158·79	9,056·69	...	4·16	221·48	0·13	0·46
Central Provinces	8,188·94	275·96	12·03	0·30	45·11	0·16	1,476·36	0·72	0·42
Mysore	9,384·05	511·72	77·14	0·01	26·86	0·06	...	0·07	0·09
North-West Provinces	8,608·91	1,353·08	12·46	0·30	18·04	2·42	...	0·07	4·72
Punjab	3,710·90	5,575·44	25·68	2·76	18·92	666·10	...	0·17	0·03

Hinduism.

19. In the report on the Census of the Madras Presidency I have attempted to show that the Hinduism of its Dravidian population is nothing more than a thin veneer of Puranic beliefs overlying a great mass of demonolatry, combined with the worship of tutelar deities of human origin. Mr. Rice's excellent account of the religion of the Coorg Hindus* brings out the same facts very clearly, and the expression Hindu must, therefore, be understood as indicating only a partial and

* Gazetteer of Mysore and Coorg, vol. III, pp. 258 *et. seq.*

not very living belief in the gods of the Brahman pantheon. This is the Hinduism which is professed by over 90 per cent. of the inhabitants of Coorg. There are 12 Hindus to one Musalman, and 46 to one Christian. The Musalmans are relatively more numerous than in Madras or Mysore, while only Madras has a higher proportion of Christians. It will be noticed that the apparent decrease in the population is entirely confined to Hindus.

20. The marginal statement gives statistics for each of the principal Hindu sects. According to these figures Saivism is the predominant creed, and the same feature is found in the southern half of the Madras Presidency. The Saivism of both Coorg and Madras, however, is but little removed from the demon worship of the primitive Dravidians, and the sect returned merely indicates the particular class of Brahmanic deity to which formal veneration is occasionally paid. The real worship of all classes except the Bráhmans and a few higher castes is reserved for the devils, the tutelar deities and the ancestral spirits. Of the 17,516 persons shown under 'Others' in the above statement 16,666 made no return of sect at all. The remaining 850 returned caste names for the most part.

Hindu Sects.

Sect.	Number of persons returning it.		
	Total.	Males.	Females.
Saivite	1,08,987	60,274	48,713
Vaishnavite	21,531	11,681	9,850
Mádhva	258	135	123
Lingáyat	8,553	4,124	4,429
Others	17,516	9,843	7,673

21. The numbers returning each sect of Christians are given in Table A. The total number of Christians is 3,392, and of these 2,588 are Roman Catholics. In the marginal statement the figures are compared with those of 1881. In this statement members of the Church of Scotland and of the Free Church are included in Presbyterians. In the 1881 returns 152 persons are shown as "Others, Basel Mission": these have here been treated as Lutherans. At the recent Census 152 persons returned their sect as Protestant: there were none under this vague term in 1881, nor were there in that year any Christians who did not return their sect. In the 1891 table—Table A—it will be noticed there are 2 persons who returned their sect as Heathen: similar absurdities are found in the Madras return and no doubt in those of other provinces also. 'Sarveswaranamatha' is returned as their sect by three individuals. This expression means 'the religion of the Omnipresent Deity.' Table A also shows how many of the Christians are foreigners, how many Eurasians and how many natives. The Native Christians number 2,931, or 86·41 per cent. of the total. Of the Native Christians again, 2,460, or 83·93 per cent., are Roman Catholics; 71 are members of the Church of England; 46 are Presbyterians; 130 have returned themselves as Protestants simply, and 173 have made no return. The foreign Christians number 249, and of these 174 are members of the Church of England and only 16 are Roman Catholics. The Eurasian Christians number 212, and 112 of them are Roman Catholics and 60 are members of the Church of England.

Sects of Christians.

Sect.	Number.	
	1891.	1881.
Roman Catholic	2,588	2,508
Church of England	305	392
Protestant	152	...
Presbyterian	65	35
Wesleyan	49	51
Lutheran	29	152
Unsectarian	11	...
Baptist	1	14
Others	10	...
Not stated	182	...
Total	3,392	3,152

CHAPTER IV.

AGE AND SEX.

(TABLE VII.)

Age.

Age-Distribution.

22. In the following statement I give the age-distribution of 10,000 persons of each sex according to the Census of 1881 and that of 1891, and I also add the corresponding figures for Madras and Mysore. The two sets of figures for Madras are respectively those based on the actual returns and those founded on the returns as adjusted by me :—

Distribution by Age of 10,000 persons of each sex.

Age-period.	MALES.					FEMALES.				
	Coorg, 1891.	Coorg, 1881.	MADRAS, 1891.		Mysore, 1891.	Coorg, 1891.	Coorg, 1881.	MADRAS, 1891.		Mysore, 1891.
			Actual.	Adjusted.				Actual.	Adjusted.	
0	221	205	330	370	...	286	280	338	380	...
1	151	130	171	330	...	197	173	178	340	...
2	251	136	315	307	...	330	187	327	320	...
3	263	182	352	295	...	354	249	365	305	...
4	228	186	314	283	...	288	237	316	290	...
TOTAL (0—4)	1,114	839	1,482	1,585	1,385	1,455	1,126	1,524	1,635	1,471
5—9	1,146	1,113	1,391	1,275	1,364	1,388	1,421	1,346	1,285	1,414
10—14	941	1,133	1,084	1,110	922	988	1,166	923	1,085	835
15—19	988	1,152	828	975	867	1,031	1,101	783	960	792
20—24	1,093	1,144	820	870	850	1,121	1,177	973	860	943
25—29	1,277	1,310	821	770	902	1,104	1,184	865	770	905
30—34	1,032	1,078	828	690	830	818	855	885	700	825
35—39	767	781	592	615	700	540	546	505	620	614
40—44	605	575	670	545	656	529	480	661	545	600
45—49	364	311	365	465	440	269	256	305	455	379
50—54	314	275	427	385	413	327	291	460	375	442
55—59	131	96	177	300	220	115	99	157	290	213
60 and over	228	193	515	415	451	315	298	613	420	567
TOTAL	10,000	10,000	10,000	10,000	10,000	10,000	10,000	10,000	10,000	10,000

In 1881 the proportions at all periods from 10 to 39 were higher than in 1891, and this I ascribe to the greater number of immigrant labourers present in the former year. A comparison of the figures for 1891 with those for other provinces shows that there was still a considerable body of these labourers in 1891. For an ordinary population that is not declining and is not affected by immigration or emigration, the numbers at each age should show a steady decrease. In Coorg, however, the maximum number is found at the age 25—29, and in 1881 this was the case with both sexes. In 1891 the female figures show a closer resemblance to the normal state of things, for the female immigrants are less numerous than the male, and comparatively few were present at the enumeration of 1891. For the reasons I have given in the Report on the Madras Census, the ages as returned cannot be accepted as correct, but the error is sufficiently constant to enable us to draw certain broad conclusions, the most important of which in the case of Coorg is that the immigrant population present at the Census of 1891 was much less than in 1881, a fact which has perhaps been sufficiently insisted upon.

23. It is not necessary to recapitulate in this volume the errors which vitiate the return of age, but I give below a statement showing the exact ages returned by 1,000 persons enumerated in all parts of the province :—

Errors in the returns.

Statement showing the numbers at each age in 1,000 of the population.

Age.	Males.	Females.	Age.	Males.	Females.
Infant . . .	13	13	29 . . .	1	2
1 . . .	11	8	30 . . .	33	27
2 . . .	10	13	31 . . .	...	1
3 . . .	10	11	32 . . .	10	5
4 . . .	22	11	33 . . .	3	...
5 . . .	13	5	34 . . .	2	1
6 . . .	18	13	35 . . .	24	20
7 . . .	9	6	36 . . .	6	1
8 . . .	18	17	37 . . .	1	2
9 . . .	8	8	38 . . .	7	1
10 . . .	18	23	39 . . .	2	2
11 . . .	3	1	40 . . .	24	30
12 . . .	14	14	41 . . .	...	...
13 . . .	2	6	42 . . .	1	2
14 . . .	18	14	43 . . .	2	1
15 . . .	9	8	44 . . .	4	1
16 . . .	24	16	45 . . .	13	8
17 . . .	2	4	46 . . .	1	...
18 . . .	17	20	47 . . .	1	...
19 . . .	1	2	48 . . .	4	4
20 . . .	28	31	49 . . .	1	...
21 . . .	...	3	50 . . .	14	13
22 . . .	10	12	51 . . .	1	...
23 . . .	5	3	52 . . .	1	3
24 . . .	10	10	53 . . .	2	...
25 . . .	23	39	54 . . .	...	1
26 . . .	7	4	55 . . .	4	2
27 . . .	5	3	56 . . .	...	1
28 . . .	24	10	57 . . .	...	3

Statement showing the numbers at each age in 1,000 of the population—contd.

Age.	Males.	Females.	Age.	Males.	Females.
58	1	...	80	...	4
59	1	...	81	...	...
60	4	8	82	...	...
61	...	1	83	...	...
62	...	...	84	...	...
63	...	...	85	...	...
64	...	1	86	...	...
65	...	...	87	...	...
66	...	...	88	...	...
67	...	...	89	...	...
68	...	...	90	...	...
69	...	...	91	...	...
70	2	4	92	...	1
71	...	...			
72	...	...			
73	...	...			
74	...	...			
75	...	...			
76	...	...			
77	...	...			
78	...	...			
79	...	...	TOTAL	522	478

The partiality for round numbers is most noticeable. This can be discounted to some extent by grouping the ages for all persons over 5 in decennial periods with the multiple of ten in the centre. The high proportion of males between 15 and 34 is now very marked. The figure for the 35—44 period also is higher than it would be normally, while that at the next two periods is lower. The presence of large additional numbers at the middle ages of course affects *pro tanto* the proportions at the beginning and end of life. In the case of females the proportions at 15—34 are also higher than the normal, but the difference is not on the whole so great as among males for there are relatively fewer female immigrants. The number of foreign women labourers over 35 must be small.

Number in 10,000 in each decennial period after age 4.

Age.	Males.	Females.
0—4	1,114	1,455
5—14	2,087	2,376
15—24	2,081	2,152
25—34	2,309	1,922
35—44	1,372	1,069
45—54	678	596
55 and over	359	430

24. For the Madras Presidency I have taken 15 as the age at which both males and females on an average cease to be dependent, and I have put the end of working life at 44 for females and 59 for males. Adopting the same ages for Coorg, we find that 65·71 per cent. of the males and 51·43 per cent. of the females are 'supporters.' These proportions are higher than in any other province owing to the presence of many foreign adult labourers in Coorg. They are lower than the proportions of 1881 as there were then more of these immigrants present. They approximate very closely to the figures for the Nilgiris, a district which resembles Coorg in many respects, and especially in requiring a large amount of foreign labour for the cultivation of special products.

Useful and dependent ages.

Percentage of Supporters.

	Males.	Females.
Coorg (1891)	65·71	51·43
Coorg (1881)	67·22	53·43
Madras	55·28	46·72
Nilgiri District	65·66	51·00
Mysore	58·78	46·79
Bombay	56·74	46·76
Bengal (1881)	54·01	45·82
N.-W. P. and Oudh	56·99	47·03

Proportion of the Sexes.

25. In the population of Coorg there are only 804 females to 1,000 males. In 1881 the corresponding number was 775. The marginal table shows the proportion in other provinces. In the Nilgiri District the ratio is 777 to 1,000, and the reason for the low proportion of females in this district and in Coorg is the predominance of males in the large body of immigrant labourers. This conclusion is strongly supported by the statistics showing the proportion at the different ages, for the preponderance of males is greatest between 25 and 44. It is, however, greater than would be expected at the later ages, and there has no doubt been some omission to return females. This error is found in the returns for the greater part of India and not in Coorg alone, and is due to a sentiment common to most oriental races. The following statement, which gives the proportion for each of the principal castes, shows that the excess of males is not confined to the immigrant castes :—

Proportion of the sexes.

Number of Females to 1,000 Males.

Province.	Number of Females.
Coorg	804
Madras	1,022
Mysore	990
Bengal	1,011
Bombay	931
N.-W. P. and Oudh	930
Punjab	854
Assam	968
Burma	857
England and Wales (1881)	1,055
France (1881)	1,005
Germany (1881)	1,043
Italy (1881)	995

Number of Females per 1,000 Males at different ages.

Age.	Number of Females.
0	1,046
1	1,048
2	1,056
3	1,082
4	1,018
TOTAL 0-4	1,051
5-14	916
15-24	832
25-34	670
35-44	626
45-54	707
55 and over	963
TOTAL	804

Caste.	Number of Females per 1,000 Males.	Number of Wives per 1,000 Husbands.	Caste.	Number of Females per 1,000 Males.	Number of Wives per 1,000 Husbands.
Kodagu	973	1,010	Máppilla	492	452
Gauda	903	971	Dévánga	956	964
Vakkaliga	742	649	Kuruba	848	859
Holeya	755	720	Sheik	786	802
Pále	502	477	Native Christian	853	795
Yerava	926	980	Lingáyat	983	865
Bráhmans	859	817			

Among Kodagus or Coorgs the proportion of females is fairly high, and the wives exceed the husbands in number. The only other caste in this statement that is essentially a Coorg caste is Yerava, and among these the husbands exceed the wives. This indicates an omission of wives and no doubt of other females also. There is not a single caste of any size in which the females exceed the males.

The proportions for people of each religion are given on the margin, but these figures throw but little light on the question. They indicate, however, that Musalmans either omit to return their females to a greater extent than followers of other religions, or that they less frequently bring their womenkind with them. Probably both causes are at work.

Religion.	Number of Females per 1,000 Males.
All Religions	804
Hindus	823
Musalmans	603
Christians	816
Others	937

Distribution by civil condition of 10,000

Province.	Sex.	All ages.			0—14.		
		Unmarried.	Married.	Widowed.	Unmarried.	Married.	Widowed.
1	2	3	4	5	6	7	8
Coorg	Males	5,315	4,297	388	9,915	83	2
	Females	4,234	4,101	1,665	9,643	341	16
Madras	Males	5,390	4,267	343	9,846	150	4
	Females	3,720	4,358	1,922	8,994	974	32
Bengal (1881)	Males	4,651	4,946	403	9,165	810	25
	Females	2,937	4,913	2,150	7,454	2,438	108
Bombay	Males	4,727	4,801	472	9,401	579	20
	Females	3,193	5,151	1,656	7,898	2,057	45
Punjab	Males	5,264	4,107	629	9,563	421	16
	Females	3,750	4,877	1,373	8,827	1,147	26
N.-W. Provinces and Oudh	Males	4,503	4,864	633	9,070	907	23
	Females	3,070	5,254	1,676	8,114	1,851	35
Assam	Males	5,622	3,968	410	9,915	77	8
	Females	4,138	4,162	1,700	9,113	853	34
Mysore	Males	5,390	4,140	470	9,930	70	...
	Females	3,640	4,250	2,110	9,050	930	20
England and Wales (1881)	Males	6,193	3,463	344	10,000	...	...
	Females	5,928	3,314	758	10,000	...	...
Scotland (1881)	Males	6,628	3,044	328	10,000	...	...
	Females	6,285	2,896	819	10,000	...	...
Ireland (1881)	Males	6,871	2,750	379	10,000	...	...
	Females	6,344	2,698	958	10,000	...	...
Prussia (1881)	Males	6,242	3,435	323	10,000	...	...
	Females	5,794	3,325	881	10,000	...	...
German Empire (1881)	Males	6,213	3,449	338	10,000	...	...
	Females	5,809	3,321	870	10,000	...	...
Austria (1881)	Males	6,151	3,554	295	10,000	...	...
	Females	5,771	3,416	813	9,998	2	...
Hungary (1881)	Males	5,603	4,090	307	10,000	...	...
	Females	4,941	4,050	1,009	9,985	14	1
Sweden (1881)	Males	6,233	3,411	356	10,000	...	...
	Females	5,958	3,233	809	10,000	...	...

persons of each sex at each Age-period.

15—24.			25—39.			40—49.			50 and over.		
Unmarried.	Married.	Widowed.	Unmarried.	Married.	Widowed.	Unmarried.	Married.	Widowed.	Unmarried.	Married.	Widowed.
9	10	11	12	13	14	15	16	17	18	19	20
7,365	2,547	88	1,814	7,738	448	385	8,616	999	212	7,787	2,001
2,150	7,353	497	251	7,679	2,070	142	4,515	5,343	67	1,803	8,130
6,891	3,049	60	1,360	8,368	272	310	9,041	649	192	7,991	1,817
1,255	8,244	501	241	7,931	1,828	181	5,181	4,638	136	2,047	7,817
4,377	5,437	186	823	8,753	424	233	8,979	788	159	8,074	1,767
290	8,872	838	69	7,686	2,245	39	4,976	4,985	30	2,212	7,758
4,496	5,349	155	1,073	8,495	432	404	8,611	985	306	7,410	2,284
548	9,074	378	152	8,429	1,419	115	5,819	4,066	88	2,449	7,463
4,763	4,966	271	1,399	7,833	768	721	7,721	1,558	635	6,345	3,020
690	8,911	399	79	8,297	1,624	51	5,750	4,199	54	2,946	7,000
3,779	5,981	240	1,260	8,090	650	638	8,096	1,266	485	6,871	2,644
360	9,277	363	96	8,644	1,260	64	6,304	3,632	55	2,847	7,098
6,973	2,895	132	1,611	7,888	501	367	8,682	951	225	7,959	1,816
1,305	8,071	624	212	7,789	1,999	102	4,979	4,919	71	2,155	7,974
7,150	2,800	50	1,800	7,810	390	450	8,510	1,040	270	7,390	2,340
970	8,500	530	280	7,470	2,250	200	4,510	5,290	130	1,920	7,950
...	...	...	...	...	...	...	...	...	...	...	...
...	...	...	...	...	...	...	...	...	...	...	...
9,275	716	9	3,431	6,366	203	1,457	8,016	527	1,140	7,069	1,791
8,623	1,360	17	3,274	6,339	387	2,001	6,680	1,319	1,961	4,282	3,757
9,660	334	6	5,221	4,636	143	2,095	7,471	434	1,388	6,848	1,764
9,107	877	16	3,767	5,832	401	1,869	6,760	1,371	1,514	4,408	4,078
9,634	363	3	3,086	6,799	115	893	8,762	345	676	7,512	1,812
8,702	1,282	16	2,355	7,283	362	1,030	7,663	1,307	855	4,981	4,164
9,649	348	3	3,148	6,735	117	944	8,712	344	765	7,400	1,835
8,754	1,231	15	2,411	7,241	348	1,134	7,632	1,234	1,092	4,896	4,012
9,541	456	3	3,230	6,665	105	1,194	8,516	290	962	7,482	1,556
8,202	1,775	23	2,626	7,029	345	1,484	7,321	1,195	1,388	4,909	3,703
8,331	1,653	16	1,337	8,501	162	470	9,091	439	353	7,806	1,841
5,416	4,461	123	741	8,475	784	375	7,467	2,158	269	4,750	4,981
9,645	352	3	3,861	6,017	122	1,256	8,383	361	784	7,536	1,680
9,109	884	7	3,661	6,121	218	1,816	7,308	876	1,311	5,344	3,345

CHAPTER V.

CIVIL CONDITION.

TABLES VIII AND E.

Statistics of Civil Condition for Hindus, Musalmans and Christians,

26. The following statement shows the civil condition of 10,000 persons of each sex at each of certain age-periods. The figures are given for the whole population and for Hindus, Musalmans and Christians separately:—

Statement showing the distribution, by civil condition, of 10,000 persons of each sex at each age-period.

Age-period.	Religion.	Males.				Females.			
		Unmarried.	Married.	Widowed.	Total.	Unmarried.	Married.	Widowed.	Total.
All Ages	All Religions	5,315	4,297	388	10,000	4,234	4,101	1,665	10,000
	Hindus	5,342	4,254	404	10,000	4,280	4,077	1,643	10,000
	Musalmans	4,994	4,787	219	10,000	3,612	4,513	1,875	10,000
	Christians	5,421	4,171	408	10,000	4,196	3,933	1,871	10,000
0—14	All Religions	9,915	83	2	10,000	9,643	341	16	10,000
	Hindus	9,913	85	2	10,000	9,646	338	16	10,000
	Musalmans	9,931	69	...	10,000	9,535	447	18	10,000
	Christians	9,943	57	...	10,000	9,814	186	...	10,000
15—24	All Religions	7,365	2,547	88	10,000	2,150	7,353	497	10,000
	Hindus	7,270	2,635	95	10,000	2,209	7,290	501	10,000
	Musalmans	8,167	1,799	34	10,000	1,170	8,360	470	10,000
	Christians	8,081	1,919	...	10,000	2,453	7,236	311	10,000
25—39	All Religions	1,814	7,738	448	10,000	251	7,679	2,070	10,000
	Hindus	1,770	7,758	472	10,000	250	7,666	2,084	10,000
	Musalmans	2,055	7,725	220	10,000	151	8,084	1,765	10,000
	Christians	2,516	7,035	449	10,000	601	7,067	2,332	10,000
40—49	All Religions	385	8,616	999	10,000	142	4,515	5,343	10,000
	Hindus	367	8,572	1,061	10,000	137	4,549	5,314	10,000
	Musalmans	390	9,109	501	10,000	122	4,244	5,634	10,000
	Christians	1,031	8,162	807	10,000	427	4,017	5,556	10,000
50 and over	All Religions	212	7,787	2,001	10,000	67	1,803	8,130	10,000
	Hindus	198	7,731	2,071	10,000	72	1,883	8,045	10,000
	Musalmans	336	8,542	1,122	10,000	23	1,093	8,884	10,000
	Christians	345	7,069	2,586	10,000	...	1,040	8,960	10,000

Of youths under 15 very few are married, but the proportion of the married is higher for Hindus than for persons of the other two religions. The proportion of married is lower than in most parts of India, and the difference is greater still in the case of girls under 15. It will be observed that the relative number of married girls and widows at this age is greater for Musalmans than for Hindus and Christians, but the absolute numbers are very small.

At the next age-period (15—24), the proportion of single males and females is still comparatively high, and it is evident that early marriage is less common in Coorg than elsewhere. Again, we find that Musalman females exhibit a greater tendency to marriage than their co-religionists, but the Hindus have a higher proportion of widows.

At the 25—39 period, the unmarried males constitute only 18·14 per cent. of the males at these ages. The proportion of widowers is higher than in Madras, Bengal, Bombay or Mysore. The females are nearly all married, but the proportion of single women is appreciably higher for Christians than for others.

Of the women at these ages as many as 20·70 per cent. are widows, a proportion that is exceeded only in Bengal and Mysore. It is clear that the custom of compulsory widowhood prevails largely in Coorg. It is curious to find the proportion higher for Christians than Hindus, but the number of Christians is comparatively small.

At the next period (40—49), the proportion of widowers is higher than in Madras, Bengal, Bombay or Assam, and the proportion of widows is higher than in any other part of India, being 53·43 per cent. of the total female population between the ages of 40 and 50. The proportion is higher for Musalmans and Christians than for Hindus.

At the last period (50 and over), the difference in the civil condition of the two sexes is most marked. Out of every 100 males 2 are single, 78 are married, and 20 are widowers; out of every 100 females 1 is single, only 18 are married, and no less than 81 are widows. In the case of Musalman women, only 11 are wives and 89 are widows, while of Christians 10 are married and 90 widowed. The proportion of widowed at these ages is high everywhere, but in no province is it so high as in Coorg.

Age of persons in each civil condition.

27. The next statement shows the distribution by age of 10,000 persons in each civil condition :—

Statement showing the distribution by age of 10,000 persons of each sex in each civil condition.

Age-period.	Males.				Females.			
	Unmarried.	Married.	Widowed.	All Civil Conditions.	Unmarried.	Married.	Widowed.	All Civil Conditions.
0—4	2,084	10	5	1,114	3,413	17	5	1,455
5—9	2,146	12	...	1,146	3,247	32	5	1,388
10—14	1,738	39	11	941	2,062	270	27	988
15—19	1,655	246	89	988	893	1,530	157	1,031
20—24	1,230	988	382	1,093	200	2,330	485	1,121
25—29	698	2,017	1,035	1,277	82	2,284	799	1,104
30—34	255	1,971	1,277	1,032	37	1,466	1,211	818
35—39	97	1,553	1,236	767	27	861	1,053	540
40—44	51	1,211	1,481	605	21	606	1,628	529
45—49	19	732	1,013	364	6	271	930	269
50—54	13	599	1,282	314	5	195	1,471	327
55—59	5	244	616	131	2	63	534	115
60 and over	9	378	1,573	228	5	75	1,695	315
Total	10,000	10,000	10,000	10,000	10,000	10,000	10,000	10,000

It will be seen that comparatively few males are married before they are 20 years old, while very few females remain unmarried after that age. Of the widowers 15·22 per cent. are under 30, while only 14·78 per cent. of the widows are below that age. In fact, there is not nearly so much difference between the ages of the widowers and widows as would have been expected, but as we have already seen, the proportion of widows far exceeds that of widowers.

Further statistics of widowed.

28. The following statement shows the proportions of the widowed among those who have been married. It brings out in a very marked way the difference between the two sexes :—

Proportion of married and widowed in a total (of both civil conditions) of 10,000 of each sex.

Religion.	Married.		Widowed.		Total.	
	Males.	Females.	Males.	Females.	Males.	Females.
All Religions	9,171	7,113	829	2,887	10,000	10,000
Hindus	9,133	7,128	867	2,872	10,000	10,000
Musalmans	9,563	7,064	437	2,936	10,000	10,000
Christians	9,109	6,776	891	3,224	10,000	10,000

Mean age of the married.

29. The mean age of the married males is 36·21 years; that of the married females is 28·32 years. The average difference, therefore, between the age of husband and wife is 7·89 years. The considerably younger average age of the wife accounts in part for the greater degree of the widowed state among females. In Madras the average age of husbands is 39·06 years and that of wives 28·98 years.

Proportion of the sexes in each civil condition.

30. The next statement gives the number of females to 1,000 males for each age and civil condition separately :—

Statement showing the average number of females per 1,000 males of the same age and civil condition.

Ages.	Unmarried.	Married.	Widowed.	Total.
0—14	608	3,938	7,833	963
15—24	243	2,401	4,714	832
25—39	89	639	2,978	644
40—49	244	347	3,539	662
50 and over	285	210	3,678	905
All Ages	641	768	3,447	804

The low proportion of wives to husbands at age 25 and upwards is partly due to the fact that many of the immigrant labourers are married men who have not brought their wives with them; but even without this disturbing factor, the wives would be less numerous than the husbands at these ages, as the wife is nearly always considerably younger than the husband. For the same reason the wives under 25 are much more numerous than the husbands.

Wives at reproductive ages.

31. Taking 15 to 39 as the period of child-bearing, we have the following interesting statistics :—

Percentage of wives at reproductive ages.

Province or Country.	Wives at child-bearing age in	
	10,000 of the total population (both sexes).	10,000 women of child-bearing age.
Coorg	1,548	7,527
Madras	1,637	8,068
Bombay	1,698	8,699
Bengal	1,617	8,168
N.-W. Provinces and Oudh	1,708	8,903
Punjab	1,707	8,585
England and Wales	1,133	4,914

The proportion of married women of child-bearing ages to the total population is lower than in other provinces, but the difference is less than would have been expected considering the large excess of males. The lower proportion of married among women at the reproductive period of life must be due to the greater prevalence of widowhood in Coorg.

Marriage statistics for different castes.

32. The following statement, based upon Table E, shows the distribution, by civil condition, of 10,000 persons of each caste, containing not less than 2,000 members. As age is an important factor in the statistics for females, I have, in the case of that sex, given the distribution for each age-group shown in the table :

Distribution, by civil condition, of 10,000 persons of each sex at each age in certain castes.

Caste.	Males. All Ages.			Females. All Ages.			Females. 0—9.			Females. 10—14.			Females. 15—39.			Females. 40 and over.		
	Unmarried.	Married.	Widowed.	Unmarried.	Married.	Widowed.	Unmarried.	Married.	Widowed.	Unmarried.	Married.	Widowed.	Unmarried.	Married.	Widowed.	Unmarried.	Married.	Widowed.
Kodagu	6,283	3,385	332	5,208	3,511	1,281	9,983	17	...	9,734	266	...	794	8,328	878	38	3,439	6,523
Ganda	5,549	4,074	377	4,190	4,379	1,431	9,834	166	...	8,218	1,766	16	625	8,086	1,289	23	3,831	6,146
Vakkaliga	5,188	4,436	376	3,853	3,879	2,268	9,951	49	...	9,242	671	87	686	7,182	2,132	172	2,271	7,557
Holeya	5,180	4,492	328	3,935	4,286	1,779	9,934	59	7	8,283	1,685	32	806	7,459	1,735	173	3,043	6,784
Pále	4,214	5,277	509	3,817	5,007	1,176	9,940	60	...	8,211	1,789	...	1,134	8,078	788	...	4,035	5,965
Yerava	5,156	4,365	479	4,489	4,620	891	9,957	36	7	8,319	1,653	28	3,257	6,268	475	205	5,170	4,625
Bráhmans	4,839	4,370	791	2,924	4,160	2,916	9,835	132	33	4,235	5,647	118	160	7,940	1,900	..	1,343	8,657
Máppilla	4,760	5,139	101	3,867	4,724	1,409	9,979	21	...	8,372	1,454	174	454	8,578	968	181	2,760	7,059
Déwánga	5,659	3,728	613	3,553	3,761	2,686	9,858	106	36	8,049	1,707	244	601	6,805	2,594	46	2,212	7,742
Kuruba	5,069	4,577	354	4,269	4,633	1,098	9,950	50	...	9,452	514	34	1,206	7,896	898	67	4,888	5,045
Sheik	5,273	4,420	307	3,396	4,515	2,089	9,945	55	...	8,306	1,694	...	504	8,300	1,196	67	2,367	7,566
Native Christian	5,374	4,317	309	3,932	4,029	2,039	9,934	66	...	9,421	579	...	1,146	7,234	1,620	98	2,390	7,512
Lingáyat	5,619	3,782	599	4,202	3,329	2,469	9,937	42	21	9,119	829	52	1,096	6,611	2,293	33	1,572	8,395

The low proportion of the married among Kodagus, between 10 and 15, shows that marriage before puberty is rare with them. It is also fairly uncommon among the Kurubas, Native Christians, Vakkaligas and Lingáyats. It is, of course, most extensively practised by Bráhmans. The proportion of widows at 15 to 39 affords some indication of the extent to which the prohibition of the marriage of widows prevails. It is absolutely fordidden among Bráhmans and it is not usual, even if not prohibited, among Dévángas, Lingáyats and Vakkaligas. Among Yeravas, Kodagus, Kurubas and Páles it is both allowed and practised to a not inconsiderable extent.

CHAPTER VI.

INFIRMITIES.

TABLES XII TO XV AND XIIA TO XVA.

33. The following statement gives the number of persons returned as afflicted with one of the four infirmities, regarding which statistics are collected at the Census; the figures of 1881 are added for comparison :—

Statistics of infirmities for 1881 and 1891.

Number of infirm persons compared with 1881.

Infirmity.		Total.	Males.	Females.
INSANITY	1891	44	25	19
	1881	*37*	*23*	*14*
	Variation	+7	+2	+5
	Percentage of variation	**+18·92**	**+8·70**	**+35·71**
DEAF-MUTISM	1891	126	77	49
	1881	*175*	*109*	*66*
	Variation	—49	—32	—17
	Percentage of variation	**—28·00**	**—29·36**	**—25·76**
BLINDNESS	1891	86	47	39
	1881	*162*	*92*	*70*
	Variation	—76	—45	—31
	Percentage of variation	**—46·91**	**—48·91**	**—44·29**
LEPROSY	1891	23	12	11
	1881	*43*	*25*	*18*
	Variation	—20	—13	—7
	Percentage of variation	**—46·51**	**—52·00**	**—38·89**

One person in every 3,933 is insane, one in every 1,373 is a deaf-mute, one in every 2,012 is blind, and one in every 7,524 is a leper.

The returns show an increase of insanity and a decrease of deaf-mutism, blindness and leprosy. The percentage variations are high, but the absolute figures are so small that much importance cannot be attached to percentages. Though the returns of both years are undoubtedly imperfect, there is no reason to suppose that the degree of error was greater in 1891 than in 1881, and the general improvement shown by the later enumeration may be accepted as a real improvement.

34. The number of insane persons is 44 or 254 in a million. The annexed table shows the extent of insanity in other parts of India and in some European countries. It will be seen that the degree of insanity in Coorg is not high. In most countries this malady is much more common among males than among females, but in Coorg the difference in the figures for the two sexes is slight.

Insanity.—Comparison with other provinces.

Province.	Number of insanes in 10,000 of the population.		
	Total.	Males.	Females.
Coorg	2·54	2·61	2·46
Madras	2·16	2·53	1·79
Assam	5·52	6·16	4·84
Bengal (1881)	4·44	5·31	3·57
Bombay (1881)	4·71	6·05	3·29
Burma	8·91	9·76	8·26
Central Provinces (1881)	2·19	2·84	1·53
North-West Provinces and Oudh	1·19	1·58	0·77
Punjab	3·02	3·76	2·16
Mysore	2·20	2·53	1·87
England and Wales (1881)	...	31	33
Scotland (1881)	...	38	39
Ireland (1881)	...	38	34
Italy (1881)	...	8	6
Austria (1881)	...	22	19
Hungary (1881)	...	22	18
United States of America (1881)	...	35	32

Age-distribution.

35. The next statement gives the age-distribution of the insane population.

Distribution, by age, of 100 persons of each sex who are insane.

Age.	Males.	Females.
0—4	...	...
5—9	4	5
10—14	16	21
15—19	20	5
20—24	...	11
25—29	8	27
30—34	8	5
35—39	4	...
40—44	20	16
45—49	4	5
50—54	8	...
55—59	4	5
60 and over	4	...
Total	100	100

Number of insanes in 10,000 persons of each age and sex.

Age.	Males.	Females.
0—4	...	...
5—9	0·91	0·93
10—14	4·43	5·25
15—19	5·28	1·26
20—24	...	2·31
25—29	1·63	5·87
30—34	2·02	1·58
35—39	1·36	...
40—44	8·62	7·36
45—49	2·87	4·83
50—54	6·64	...
55—59	7·96	11·25
60 and over	4·57	...
Total	2·61	2·46

The figures are somewhat irregular, but this must be expected when the total figures are so small. The most noticeable features are the absence of any insane persons among the population under five, and the high proportion at the 15—19 period for males and at the 10—14 period in the case of females. In Madras the percentage steadily rises up to the 30—34 period and then begins to decline. The second part of the above statement shows that insanity is most common in the case of males at the 40—44 age-period, and in the case of females at the 55—59 period. In Madras the proportion is highest for males at 30—34 and for females at 45—49.

Caste of insanes.

36. Table XII-A gives the caste of the insane persons: 10 of them are Kodagus or Coorgs and 7 are Holeyas, but in no other case does the number exceed 4. The Coorgs have one insane

person in every 3,261, the Holeyas one in every 3,441, and the Gaudas one in every 3,331. The proportions for the other castes are of little value as the numbers are so small. Thus there are 62 Jains and one is insane, but it would be absurd to suppose that this is the normal rate of insanity among members of that community.

Deaf-mutism: comparison with other provinces.

37. The total number of deaf-mutes is 126, or 728 in a million. The following table gives the proportions in other provinces and countries. Deaf-mutism is slightly more prevalent in Coorg than in Mysore, and slightly less prevalent than in Madras. In the adjoining district of South Canara, there are 532 deaf-mutes per million and in Malabar only 185.

Province or Country.	Number of Deaf-mutes in 10,000 of the Population.		
	Both Sexes.	Males.	Females.
Coorg	7·28	8·03	6·35
Madras	7·57	8·67	6·50
Assam	8·55	9·52	7·52
Bengal (1881)	12·47	15·47	9·50
Bombay (1881)	7·21	8·42	5·91
Burma	5·06	5·53	4·69
Central Provinces	5·81	6·61	5·00
N.-W. Provinces and Oudh	7·01	8·73	5·16
Punjab	9·70	11·49	7·61
Mysore	7·01	7·80	6·22
England and Wales (1881)	...	6	5
Scotland (1881)	...	3	2
Ireland (1881)	...	8	7
Italy (1881)	...	6	5
Austria (1881)	...	15	11
Hungary (1881)	...	14	12
United States of America (1881)	...	7	6

In all countries this affliction appears to be more common among males than females, and Coorg is no exception to this rule.

Age-distribution of deaf-mutes.

38. The subjoined statement gives particulars of the age-distribution of the deaf-mutes.

Distribution, by age, of 100 deaf-mutes of each sex.

Age.	Males.	Females.
0—4	...	6
5—9	12	10
10—14	16	17
15—19	17	2
20—24	18	17
25—29	10	8
30—34	10	10
35—39	6	10
40—44	5	2
45—49	3	8
50—54	3	4
55—59	...	4
60 and over	...	2
Total	100	100

Number of deaf-mutes in 10,000 persons of each age and sex.

Age.	Males.	Females.
0—4	...	2·67
5—9	8·19	4·67
10—14	13·30	10·50
15—19	13·73	1·26
20—24	13·36	9·26
25—29	6·53	4·70
30—34	8·09	7·92
35—39	6·80	12·02
40—44	6·90	2·45
45—49	5·74	19·31
50—54	6·64	7·92
55—59	...	22·50
60 and over	...	4·12
Total	8·03	6·35

The infirmity is most common among males between the ages of 10 and 25, but in the case of females the greatest degree of prevalence is at the 55—59 period. The male statistics correspond with those for Madras, but in that province the age of greatest prevalence is 20—24 for males and 15—19 for females. The Coorg statistics for females are very irregular, but, as I have already explained, this must be expected when the absolute figures dealt with are so small.

Caste of deaf-mutes.

39. The Holeyas have the largest number of deaf-mutes (23) and the Coorgs come next with 21. Among the Kurubas there are 15 and among the Vakkaligas 9.

40. The total number of blind persons is 86 or 497 in a million. The proportion is much lower than in any other province of India or in any European country for which I have statistics. In Travancore, however, the proportion is somewhat lower. It will be noticed that in Coorg blindness is more common among females than among males. This feature is also found in most of the Indian provinces, but of European countries Ireland alone has a greater degree of blindness among females than among the opposite sex.

Blindness: Comparison with other provinces.

Number of blind persons in 10,000 of the population.

Province.	Total.	Males.	Females.
Coorg	4·97	4·90	5·06
Madras	10·22	10·05	10·39
Assam	10·65	10·75	10·54
Bengal (1881)	14·13	13·74	14·52
Bombay (1881)	26·59	23·95	29·41
Burma	19·73	17·19	22·87
Central Provinces (1881)	21·87	18·58	25·23
North-West Provinces and Oudh	23·43	22·82	24·09
Punjab	35·17	33·79	36·78
Mysore	10·62	10·76	10·47
England and Wales (1881)	...	9	8
Scotland (1881)	...	9	8
Ireland (1881)	...	11	12
Italy (1881)	...	8	7
Austria (1881)	...	10	8
Hungary (1881)	...	13	13
United States of America (1881)	...	10	9

Age-distribution.

41. The following statement gives age statistics for the blind:—

Distribution, by age, of 100 blind persons of each sex.

Age.	Males.	Females.
0—4	6	10
5—9	11	5
10—14	6	13
15—19	11	3
20—24	2	5
25—29	15	3
30—34	6	...
35—39	6	5
40—44	15	20
45—49	9	10
50—54	9	8
55—59	0	5
60 and over	4	13
Total	100	100

Number of blind persons in 10,000 of the population of each sex at each age.

Age.	Males.	Females.
0—4	2·81	3·56
5—9	4·55	1·87
10—14	3·33	6·56
15—19	5·28	1·26
20—24	0·95	2·31
25—29	5·71	1·17
30—34	3·03	...
35—39	4·08	4·81
40—44	12·07	19·63
45—49	11·47	19·31
50—54	13·28	11·89
55—59	...	22·50
60 and over	9·14	20·58
Total	4·90	5·06

The age-distribution differs considerably from what is found elsewhere. In Madras, for example, 30 per cent. of the blind males and 38 per cent. of the blind females are not less than 60 years of age: in Coorg the proportions are only 4 and 13 per cent., respectively. This is no doubt in part due to the peculiar age constitution of the people of Coorg, where the relative numbers in early middle life are much higher than in Madras, but this is not a complete explanation; for the prevalence of blindness is not so high among persons of 60 years of age and upwards as at some of the earlier age-periods. There is, however, a sudden increase in the degree of blindness at age 40, and the figures for this and the subsequent periods are markedly higher than for ages below forty. This is especially the case with females.

Blindness in different castes.

Coorg.

42. Table XIV-A shows the caste of the blind. Among Coorgs one in every 2,508 is blind, among Vakkaligas one in every 2,071, among Holeyas one in

every 1,720, among Gaudas one in every 1,666, and among Yeravas one in every 1,184. The other figures are small.

Leprosy: Comparison with other provinces.

43. There are only 23 lepers or 133 in a million. This is a lower proportion than that found in any other Indian province. In Madras, there are 354 lepers in every million, and in the South Canara district as many as 867. In Mysore, it is true, there are only 165, but Mysore differs widely in climate from Coorg, and in a tract with such a heavy rainfall I expected to find the disease more common. It must be admitted, however, that our census of lepers is very imperfect, and the omission of a few individuals would largely affect the proportion for a population so small as that of Coorg.

No. of Lepers in 10,000 of the population.

PROVINCE.	Total.	Males.	Females.
Coorg	1·33	1·25	1·43
Madras	3·54	5·36	1·76
Assam	12·28	18·19	6·02
Bengal (1881)	8·09	12·20	4·02
Bombay (1881)	6·14	8·74	3·36
Burma	8·37	11·69	5·14
Central Provinces (1881)	5·58	7·60	3·52
N. W. Provinces	3·60	5·74	1·30
Punjab	2·09	2·95	1·07
Mysore	1·65	2·19	1·10

Age-distribution.

44. I give the age-distribution of the lepers; but as the total number is only 23, these figures are of very little value, and it is not necessary to discuss them. One curious feature in the returns, however, is that while in every other province leprosy is shown by the census to be much more common among males than females, the reverse is the case in Coorg, where the proportions are 125 lepers out of every million males and 143 out of every million females.

Distribution, by age, of 100 Lepers of each sex.

AGE.	Males.	Females.
0—4	8	...
5—9	...	18
10—14	...	...
15—19	...	9
20—24	17	9
25—29	...	9
30—34	17	18
35—39	25	...
40—44	25	18
45—49	...	...
50—54	8	19
55—59	...	...
60 and over	...	...
TOTAL	100	100

Number of Lepers in 10,000 persons of each sex and age.

AGE.	Males.	Females.
0—4	0·94	...
5—9	...	1·87
10—14	...	...
15—19	...	1·26
20—24	1·91	1·16
25—29	...	1·17
30—34	2·02	3·17
35—39	4·08	...
40—44	5·17	4·91
45—49	...	...
50—54	3·32	7·92
55—59	...	...
60 and over	...	...
TOTAL	1·25	1·43

Leprosy in different castes.

45. The statistics given in Table XV-A show that 8 of the 23 lepers belong to the Yerava caste, a forest tribe now largely employed as labourers. Possibly these people are less unwilling than their more civilized neighbours to admit the existence of leprosy, but the proportion (one leper in every 1,776) is not so high as is found in many Madras castes. No other caste has returned more than two lepers.

CHAPTER VII.

EDUCATION.

Tables IX and C.

Education statistics.

46. The following is an abstract of the education statistics for the population taken as a whole :—

	Total Males.	Total Females.	Percentage, 1891.		Percentage, 1881.	
			Males.	Females.	Males.	Females.
Pupils	4,155	605	4·36	0·79	4·25	0·55
Literates	10,679	671	11·22	0·88	8·80	0·46
Illiterates	80,399	75,297	84·42	98·33	86·95	98·99
Not stated	674	575	Distributed.		...	...
Total .	95,907	77,148	100·00	100·00	100·00	100·00

There has been an improvement in the decade, but some of this must be ascribed to the smaller number of labourers, mostly illiterate, who were present at the enumeration of 1891.

Education by age and religion.

47. The next statement gives the education statistics combined with particulars of age and religion :—

Age.	Instruction.	All Religions.		Hindus.		Musalmans.		Christians.	
		Males.	Females.	Males.	Females.	Males.	Females.	Males.	Females.
All ages	Learning . . .	4·36	0·79	4·43	0·71	2·97	0·66	6·89	4·98
	Literate . . .	11·22	0·88	10·12	0·63	17·29	0·95	34·49	11·55
	Illiterate . . .	84·42	98·33	85·45	98·66	79·74	98·39	58·62	83·47
	Total .	100·00	100·00	100·00	100·00	100·00	100·00	100·00	100·00
5—9	Learning . . .	15·42	3·44	14·80	3·04	17·75	3·21	36·60	25·42
	Literate . . .	0·33	0·19	0·25	0·11	0·76	0·68	3·09	2·83
	Illiterate . . .	84·25	96·37	84·95	96·85	81·49	96·11	60·31	71·75
	Total .	100·00	100·00	100·00	100·00	100·00	100·00	100·00	100·00
10—14	Learning . . .	21·24	2·93	21·68	2·66	13·50	2·41	32·23	17·01
	Literate . . .	2·94	0·99	2·65	0·91	5·79	0·96	6·61	4·08
	Illiterate . . .	75·82	96·08	75·67	96·43	80·71	96·63	61·16	78·91
	Total .	100·00	100·00	100·00	100·00	100·00	100·00	100·00	100·00
15—24	Learning . . .	2·90	0·12	3·02	0·09	1·32	0·20	4·63	1·26
	Literate . . .	15·70	1·86	14·79	1·53	20·49	1·31	35·15	18·87
	Illiterate . . .	81·40	98·02	82·19	98·38	78·19	98·49	60·22	79·87
	Total .	100·00	100·00	100·00	100·00	100·00	100·00	100·00	100·00
25 and over.	Learning . . .	0·03	0·01	0·03	0·01	0·05	0·00	0·00	0·15
	Literate . . .	16·16	0·87	14·57	0·49	22·61	1·15	51·62	15·73
	Illiterate . . .	83·81	99·12	85·40	99·50	77·34	98·85	48·38	84·12
	Total .	100·00	100·00	100·00	100·00	100·00	100·00	100·00	100·00

The lowest proportion of illiterate is found amongst the Christians, of whom nearly half the males and a quarter of the females can read and write. The

Musalmans are more educated than the Hindus, but the difference in the case of the females is small. The relation between the different religions was much the same in 1881 :—

Percentage of Pupils, Literates, and Illiterates in 1881, for each religion.

Religion.	Males.			Females.		
	Learning.	Literate.	Illiterate.	Learning.	Literate.	Illiterate.
Hindus	4.21	7.70	88.09	0.46	0.20	99.34
Musalmans	3.87	14.11	82.02	0.75	0.64	98.61
Christians	8.11	40.34	51.55	4.50	12.86	82.64

Turning now to the age figures we find that, out of 20,006 boys between the ages of 5 and 14, which may be taken as the school-going period, only 3,566, or 17.82 per cent., are at school; and out of 18,328 girls of the above ages only 583, or 3.18 per cent., are being educated. Taking a smaller period, namely 5—9, the proportions are 15.42 per cent. for boys and 3.44 per cent. for girls. Of the population over 15, one in every 6 males and one in every 83 females is able to read and write. Female education, indeed, is practically non-existent except among the Christians.

48. The following statement gives the percentage of illiteracy among every caste with a strength of not less than 200 :—

Diffusion of education.

Percentage of illiterates among castes with a population of 200 and over.

Caste.	Males.	Females.	Caste.	Males.	Females.
Kshatriya	64.34	100.00	Agasa	97.90	100.00
Kodagu	64.00	96.05	Madivála	95.72	100.00
Maráthi	92.31	99.80	Golla	90.32	99.33
Náyar	82.51	67.36	Heggade	87.77	99.34
Rájput	64.89	97.97	Kuruba	99.42	99.97
Banta	89.00	98.48	Gániga	90.63	98.46
Gauda	86.73	99.49	Koyava	91.91	100.00
Vakkaliga	94.22	99.90	Kumbára	97.93	100.00
Vellála	57.89	90.47	Uppara	98.10	100.00
Adiyán	100.00	100.00	Besta	98.38	100.00
Holeya	99.16	99.92	Bóyi	96.47	100.00
Pále	99.92	100.00	Toreya	98.39	100.00
Kudiya	100.00	100.00	Billava	96.16	100.00
Yerava	99.95	99.99	Dívar	93.58	100.00
Bráhman Havig	32.49	96.36	Tiyyan	85.27	96.55
„ Sivalli	33.67	97.73	Mádiga	99.67	100.00
All Bráhmans	30.10	94.41	Odde	100.00	100.00
Jangam	68.62	99.59	Gauriga	98.92	100.00
Padárti	55.96	100.00	Korama	97.40	100.00
Kaniya	49.59	100.00	Médara	100.00	100.00
Banajiga	71.89	97.77	Bédar	94.53	98.94
Labbai	54.61	100.00	Pathán	83.80	98.52
Máppilla	85.56	99.05	Saiyad	80.54	98.40
Naváyat	53.67	93.33	Sheik	76.34	97.64
Vaisya	38.24	99.15	European	7.55	15.79
Akkasále	80.85	99.40	Eurasian	26.32	34.02
Áyiri	78.37	100.00	Native Christian	66.30	90.90
Pánchála	78.52	100.00	Konkani	72.58	97.95
Visvakarma	70.34	100.00	Lingáyat	80.58	99.60
Hajám	92.44	99.54	Musalman	85.83	99.82
Kollan	86.15	100.00	Pancháchára	84.71	100.00
Badagi	92.41	100.00	Saiva	81.74	100.00
Kóláyiri	94.09	100.00	Telugu	79.22	98.93
Bilimagga	80.28	99.81	Vírasaiva	65.30	99.77
Dévánga	72.07	98.87			

The Europeans show the greatest degree of education, but the majority of them are adults. The Eurasians come next with a very low proportion of illiterates in both sexes. Then come the Bráhmans and the so-called Vaisyas, but with them the education of females is very backward, more so indeed than among the Vellálas. The Coorg males are fairly educated, but only four in a hundred of their women can read and write. About half of the males of the Kaniya (Astrologer) caste are educated, but not a single one of their females is returned as a literate. All the Adiyáns, Kudiyas, Oddes, and Médaras are illiterate, and the Páles and Holeyas are not in a much better position.

The Labbais are the most educated of the Musalman sections, and the Máppillas the least. A comparatively large number of Native Christian males are educated, but the statistics for females are less satisfactory.

49. There are 10,679 male literates, and of these 717, or 6·71 per cent., can read and write English. Among females there are 671 literates and 102 of these, or 15·20 per cent., have a literary acquaintance with English. But these figures include the Europeans and Eurasians: if they be excluded, the number of English-knowing people is 518 males and 8 females. In other words, only one in every 185 males, and one in every 9,620 females, can read and write English. In Madras, the proportions are one in 255 for males and one in 7,056 for females. Of the eight females, six are Native Christians, one is an Armenian and the other is a Kodagiti. Of the 518 males, 249 are Kodagus, 95 are Bráhmans, 58 are Native Christians, 29 are Vellálas, 11 are Banajigas, and the rest are distributed over a number of castes. I should explain that the above figures do not include pupils who can read and write English.

Knowledge of English.

50. In the following statement the statistics of education in Coorg are compared with those for other provinces :—

Comparison with other provinces.

Statistics of education in different provinces.

Province.	Number in 10,000.					
	Males.			Females.		
	Learning.	Literate.	Illiterate.	Learning.	Literate.	Illiterate.
Coorg . .	**436**	**1,122**	**8,442**	**79**	**88**	**9,833**
Madras . .	330	1,158	8,512	33	67	9,900
Assam . .	175	581	9,244	13	22	9,965
Bengal (1881) .	300	590	9,110	11	18	9,971
Bombay (1881) .	319	792	8,889	23	41	9,936
Burma . .	587	3,908	5,505	49	240	9,711
N.-W. Provinces and Oudh .	98	517	9,385	4	17	9,979
Punjab . .	141	601	9,258	8	19	9,973
Mysore . .	246	807	8,947	26	47	9,927

It will be seen that the proportion of illiterate in Coorg is lower than in any other province except Burma, and this is true of both males and females.

There are, however, many districts in the Madras Presidency in which education is more advanced than it is in Coorg.

Comparison of Census statistics with those of the Educational Department.

51. According to the Coorg Administration Report for 1890-91, there were 4,059 male and 736 female pupils on the rolls of public and private schools on the 31st March 1891: according to the census the numbers are 4,155 males and 605 females. The difference in the case of males is comparatively small, but not so with females. In Madras and Bengal, however, the relative discrepancy is much greater, and it must, I think, be in part ascribed to the fact that the attendance at school of girls on the rolls is very irregular, and that many of them are, therefore, not regarded as pupils by the members of their families, who have accordingly returned them at the census as 'literate.'

CHAPTER VIII.

PARENT-TONGUE.

TABLE X.

Statistics.

52. The actual numbers returning each language as their parent-tongue will be found in Table X. The following statement gives the relative numbers :—

Language.	Percentage on total population.
A.—Coorg Languages—	
Kodagu or Coorgi	20·45
Yerava	1·50
Total, A.—Coorg Languages	**21·95**
B.—Madras Languages—	
Áré	0·04
Hindustáni	4·00
Kanarese	44·02
Konkani	1·23
Koraga	0·01
Kurumba	1·61
Lambádi	0·05
Malayálam	6·54
Tamil	9·40
Telugu	2·17
Tulu	6·99
Yerukala	0·04
Total, B.—Madras Languages	**76·10**
C.—Other Indian Languages—	
Gujaráti	0·07
Hindi	0·01
Maráthi	1·52
Others	0·01
Total, C.—Other Indian Languages	**1·61**
D.—Non-Indian Asiatic Languages—	**0·01**
E.—Non-Asiatic Languages—	
English	0·27
German	0·01
Portuguese	0·04
Others	0·01
Total, E.—Non-Asiatic Languages	**0·33**

The *Kodagu* or *Coorg* language is described by Dr. Caldwell as standing about midway between old Canarese and Tulu. *Yerava* is the tongue of the tribe of that name; it is a dialect of Malayálam.* *Áré* is in reality a form of Maráthi, differing so little from the standard that it cannot even be considered a dialect. The grounds on which it was shown separately in the table are given in the

* *Gazetteer of Mysore and Coorg*, Vol. III, p. 215. But according to Mr. Richter, the language resembles that of the Coorgs by whom it can be understood—*Compendium of Castes and Tribes found in Coorg*, p. 9.

volume on the Madras Census. *Konkani* is a dialect of Maráthi. *Koraga* I believe to be a dialect of Tulu; its character is briefly discussed in the Madras Report. *Kurumba* is a dialect of Kanarese. *Yerukala* or *Korava* is a dialect of Tamil.

Linguistic classification.

53. In the following statement the languages returned are arranged by linguistic families and groups, dialects being separated from languages:—

Family.	Group.	Language.	Dialect.	Population returning it. Total.	Males.	Females.
I.—Indian Languages.						
Aryan	Eranic	Pashtu	...	10	7	3
Do.	Indic	Gujaráti	...	126	90	36
Do.	Do.	Do.	Kach'hi	8	8	...
Do.	Do.	Gypsy dialects	Lambádi	79	60	19
Do.	Do.	Hindi	...	23	12	11
Do.	Do.	Do.	Hindustáni	6,919	3,841	3,078
Do.	Do.	Do.	Márvádi	1	1	...
Do.	Do.	Maráthi	...	2,621	1,530	1,091
Do.	Do.	Do.	Âré	73	58	15
Do.	Do.	Do.	Konkani	2,129	1,297	832
Do.	Do.	Sindhi	...	5	5	...
Dravidian	...	Kodagu	...	35,369	17,993	17,376
Do.	...	Kanarese	...	76,115	40,664	35,451
Do.	...	Do.	Kurumba	2,791	1,475	1,316
Do.	...	Malayálam	...	11,299	8,467	2,832
Do.	...	Do.	Yerava	2,587	1,339	1,248
Do.	...	Tamil	...	16,257	8,591	7,666
Do.	...	Do.	Yerukala	75	33	42
Do.	...	Telugu	...	3,751	2,163	1,588
Do.	...	Tulu	...	12,090	7,834	4,256
Do.	...	Do.	Koraga	9	4	5
II.—Languages foreign to India.						
Aryan	Eranic	Persian	...	1	1	...
Do.	Italic	French	...	8	3	5
Do.	Do.	Portuguese	...	71	41	30
Do.	Teutonic	English	...	474	288	186
Do.	Do.	German	...	17	12	5
Do.	Celtic	Celtic	...	1	1	...
Semitic	...	Arabic	...	4	3	1

54. In many cases the names of castes and tribes were entered in the parent-tongue column and much difficulty was experienced in determining whether the particular section had or had not a dialect of its own. The following statement shows how all entries not appearing in the table were dealt with :—

Difficulties in dealing with returns.

Parent-tongue returned in the schedule.	Language with which included in Table X.
Adiya	Malayálam.
Ándhra	Telugu.
Bálabund	Maráthi.
Bettakuruba	Kurumba.
Bhatkal	Konkani.
Christian Báshé	Konkani.
Dakhni	Hindustáni.
Danagar	Maráthi.
Drávida	Tamil.
Jamathi	Hindustáni.
Jénukuruba	Kurumba.
Kandhar	Pashtu.
Konga	Tamil.
Koracha	Yerukala.
Korama	Yerukala.
Kudiya	Kodagu.
Kumbar	Kanarese.
Maharáshtra	Maráthi.
Máppilla	Malayálam.
Méman	Kach'hi.
Musalman	Hindustáni.
Naváyat	Konkani
Náyar	Malayálam.
Oddar Básha	Telugu.
Sanketha	Tamil.
Thamidi	Yerukala.
Theya (*i.e.*, Tiyyar)	Malayálam.
Urudu	Hindustáni.

CHAPTER IX.

BIRTHPLACE.

TABLE XI.

55. The birthplace statistics are given in Table XI. In the following statement they are arranged somewhat differently so as to bring out more clearly the nature of the immigration into the province:—

Statistics.

Statement showing the distribution of Population by Birthplace.

Birthplace.		Population.			Percentage on Total Population.
		Total.	Males.	Females.	
A.—District of enumeration		120,110	61,571	*58,539*	69·42
B.—Contiguous Districts, etc.	Malabar	10,308	7,511	*2,797*	5·96
	South Canara	12,432	8,907	*3,525*	7·19
	Mysore	25,139	14,413	*10,726*	14·53
	Total	47,879	30,831	17,048	27·68
C.—Provinces and States in India.	Madras	3,749	2,480	*1,269*	2·17
	Bombay (British Territory)	783	664	*119*	0·45
	Other Provinces and States	319	209	*110*	0·18
	Total	4,851	3,353	1,498	2·80
D.—Countries in Asia beyond India		42	24	*18*	0·03
E.—Countries outside Asia		128	97	*31*	0·07
GRAND TOTAL		173,010	95,876	77,134	100·00

Of the total population, only 69·42 per cent. were born in the province, a proportion much lower than that found elsewhere. To find a parallel we have to turn to the figures of the Nilgiri District where the home-born population is only 59·31 per cent. But for the fact that the coffee season of 1891 was an early one, and many of the immigrant labourers had returned to their homes by the date of the census, the proportion of foreigners would have been even higher. In 1881 the proportion of foreigners was 41·99 per cent. as against 30·58 per cent. in 1891.

56. The immigrants, however, do not come from afar, for 13·15 per cent. out of the total of 30·58 per cent. were born in the adjoining British districts of Malabar and Canara and 14·53 per cent. in the neighbouring Mysore State; and of the remaining 4,851 from Provinces or States in India, 3,749 hail from the Madras Presidency. Bombay sends 783, and the numbers from other parts of India are altogether insignificant. The figures for countries beyond India are too small to call for notice.

Immigration chiefly from adjoining districts.

57. In the native population of Coorg there are 951 females to 1,000 males, but among the immigrants the ratio is 542 to 1,000. This great excess of males shows

Sex of immigrants.

that the immigration is one of labour. In most districts of Madras the immigrants are wives brought from across the border, and this is indicated by the predominance of females. Out of the 18,595 females who were enumerated in Coorg but born elsewhere, 10,726 are natives of Mysore, and some of these, no doubt, are wives of husbands permanently resident in Coorg.

58. I give in the marginal statement particulars of the residence at the time of the census of those natives of Coorg who were enumerated in other parts of India. The statement is not complete, as I have not received information for all provinces. Mysore and Madras are the only territories in which the Coorgs are at all numerous, and a considerable proportion of the natives of Coorg found there are probably children of Mysore and Madras parents who had gone to Coorg as labourers. The excess of females in the figures for Mysore indicates a slight degree of intermarriage between the people of that state and the inhabitants of Coorg.

Natives of Coorg enumerated elsewhere.

Natives of Coorg enumerated elsewhere.

Born in Coorg and enumerated in	Total.	Males.	Females.
Assam	...	...	...
Bombay	21	11	10
Burma	...	...	...
Madras	642	373	269
Madras Feudatories	13	10	3
Mysore	1,607	699	908
North-West Provinces	7	2	5
" Feudatories	...	...	...
Punjab	29	24	5
" Feudatories	5	4	1

CHAPTER X.

CASTES, TRIBES AND RACES.

59. As an account of the castes and tribes of Coorg was compiled so recently as 1887 by the Revd. G. Richter,[1] I do not propose to attempt any detailed notice of them. This is the less necessary, too, as most of the castes which appear in the tables are found in Madras, Mysore or elsewhere. The Kodagu or Coorg caste is in fact the only one of any considerable size which is confined to the province, and it numbers only 32,611 persons. I give below a list of the castes and tribes which appear to be peculiar to Coorg :

Detailed notice unnecessary.

Caste.	Strength.	Caste.	Strength.
Kápála	150	Vádári	27
Kodagu	32,611	Pále	4,045
Ayyambokkalu	4	Yerava	14,209
Binepatta	101	Mukkáti	23
Kárgóli	7	Áyiri	1,007
Kávudi	37	Kutuma	74

There are also a number of caste names returned by only one or two persons which are not found in other lists, but many of hese are probably not real castes at all. Such entries have been classified by the occupations returned at the census.

The classification of some of the castes is of doubtful accuracy. The *Kápálas*, for example, were formerly the watchmen and palace guards of the Coorg Rájas, but Mr. Richter says they are scarcely to be distinguished from the Páles or Páleyas, and that they originally came from Malabar.[2] The *Binepattas* again seem to have originally been mendicants[3]; they were classed as agriculturists on information furnished by the Commissioner of Coorg. *Kávudi* was originally classed as a barber caste (Malayálam *Kávutiyan*), but the Commissioner informed me they were agriculturists. He has possibly confused it with *Kavádi*, *Kávadi* or *Kavadi*, which I have classed as shepherds. *Vádári* is perhaps a mistake for *Vaddar* (*Odde*), but agriculture was returned as the occupation. *Agnáni*, "unenlightened," is a fairly common name for non-Christian pariahs, but as it was impossible to say whether they were Holeyas or Paraiyans, I was obliged to retain the name in the tables though it is not that of a distinct caste. Some of these Agnánis, it will be seen, have returned Christianity as their religion. *Ánekula* and *Bákuda* are, I believe, merely sub-divisions of Holeyas, but the former is also a sub-division of Vakkaliga and the latter of Pále. *Káládi* is, no doubt, the same as the *Káláti* of the Madras tables. *Máyila*, *Méra* and *Parava* are sub-divisions of Holeya. *Betta* is a sub-division of Kurumba, and ought to have been included with that caste. It would have been better, however, to have separated all the Betta Kurumbas and shown them in Group 4, but this

[1] *Ethnographical Compendium of the Castes and Tribes found in the Province of Coorg*, by the Revd. G. Richter, late Inspector of Schools in Coorg.
[2] Richter, *op cit*, p. 8,
[3] Richter, p. 16.

was not possible. *Magadava* (from *magga*, a loom) might perhaps have been clubbed with Bilimagga. *Golla* was classed as a shepherd caste as in the Madras tables, but the Gollas of Coorg appear to be mostly cow-keepers. *Heggades*, though now agriculturists, were formerly shepherds : the sub-divisions show this. Some of the *Kurumbas* are forest tribes like the Kurumbas of the Nilgiris and the Wynaad. *Biruva* was classified on information furnished by the Commissioner; the name is probably merely another form of Billava. Of the 14 castes, in Group 55, which have been left unclassified, *Bandâra* is possibly the same as Bhandâri, a Canara toddy-drawing caste, and *Kurchi* may be Korcha or Koracha, a Canarese name for Koravas or Yerukalas : another Canarese name for them is Korama.

Sub-divisions.

60. As explained in the Madras Census Report, the return of sub-divisions is imperfect. An index showing the sub-divisions returned by each caste is appended to the tables.

OCCUPATION STATISTICS.

Percentage of the numbers in each ORDER *on the Total Population.*

ORDER.	Percentage on total population.
I.—Administration	2·20
II.—Defence	...
III.—Foreign and Feudatory State Service	...
TOTAL, CLASS A.—GOVERNMENT	2·20
IV.—Provision and Care of Cattle	0·72
V.—Agriculture	72·00
TOTAL, CLASS B.—PASTURE AND AGRICULTURE	72·72
VI.—Personal, Household and Sanitary Services	2·39
TOTAL, CLASS C.—PERSONAL AND DOMESTIC SERVICES	2·39
VII.—Food and Drink	5·62
VIII.—Light, Firing and Forage	0·30
IX.—Buildings	0·38
X.—Vehicles and Vessels	0·02
XI.—Supplementary Requirements	0·19
XII.—Textile Fabrics and Dress	1·15
XIII.—Metals and Precious Stones	1·59
XIV.—Glass, Pottery and Stone Ware	0·49
XV.—Wood, Cane and Leaves, etc.	1·73
XVI.—Drugs, Gums, Dyes, etc.	0·01
XVII.—Leather, Horns, Bones and Grease	0·22
TOTAL, CLASS D.—PREPARATION AND SUPPLY OF MATERIAL SUBSTANCES	11·70
XVIII.—Commerce	0·37
XIX.—Transport and Storage	1·32
TOTAL, CLASS E.—COMMERCE	1·69
XX.—Learned and Artistic Professions	1·73
XXI.—Sport and Amusements	0·10
TOTAL, CLASS F.—PROFESSIONS	1·83
XXIII.—Indefinite	6·91
XXIV.—Independent of Work	0·56
TOTAL, CLASS G.—INDEFINITE OCCUPATIONS	7·47
TOTAL	100·00

CHAPTER XI.

OCCUPATIONS.

(TABLES XVIIA AND XVIIC.)

Introductory.

61. The distribution of the people according to their occupations or their means of subsistence is given in Table XVII. This table is divided into two parts. Part (A) gives the number of persons who follow each occupation in towns as well as in villages, with details of their sex and age. Part (C)[1] contains statistics of persons who combine agriculture with other occupations. These latter have been shown in Part (A) under their respective non-agricultural occupations. Every person who made any return is shown under the occupation which he exercises or upon which he depends for his means of subsistence. Thus, the item "Pleader" includes not only actual pleaders themselves but also their wives and children, for the latter depend upon that occupation for their support. In 1881 only the persons actually exercising a profession were shown under it, and this radical difference in the nature of the returns renders any general comparison of the statistics with those for 1881 impossible.

The Statistics examined.

62. The annexed statement shows the number of persons in every 10,000 of the population who follow each of the seven main classes of occupations. Taking the province, as a whole, 72·72 per cent., or nearly three-fourths, are dependent for their livelihood on pasture and agriculture, and a little over one-tenth on the preparation and supply of material substances. Indefinite occupations support 7·47 per cent. of the population, and personal services 2·39 per cent. Government employés with their families form 2·20 per cent., and the professions come next with 1·83 per cent. Commerce comes last with only 1·69 per cent.

Number of persons in each class in 10,000 of the total population.

Class.	TOTAL.	Town.	Country.
A	220	712	172
B	7,272	2,047	7,786
C	239	672	197
D	1,170	3,927	899
E	169	605	126
F	183	543	147
G	747	1,494	673
TOTAL	10,000	10,000	10,000

Proportions in towns and villages.

63. In the case of the rural population the proportions are practically the same as those for the whole province, but the proportions for the urban population differ considerably. About 39 per cent. of the inhabitants in towns, or nearly two-fifths, derive their support from the preparation and supply of material substances, and only one-fifth are dependent on Pasture and Agriculture. About 15 per cent. are engaged in indefinite occupations, and a little over 7 per cent. are Government employés and their dependents. Personal service stands next on the list with 6·72 per cent., and Commerce follows close with 6·05 per cent. The professions come last with but 543 followers in every ten thousand.

Proportions between the sexes.

64. The proportions between the sexes in each class are given in the marginal statement. The males preponderate in every class, and especially so in class E, where they are nearly four times as numerous as the females.

Number of females per 1,000 males.

Class		
Class A.	Government	655
„ B.	Pasture and Agriculture	850
„ C.	Personal and Household Services	919
„ D.	Preparation and Supply of Material Substances	678
„ E.	Commerce	251
„ F.	Professions	585
„ G.	Indefinite Occupations	840

[1] For most provinces there is a third part—Part B.—which gives the occupation statistics for each district. In Coorg there are no districts.

CLASS A.—GOVERNMENT.

Class A.—Government.

65. This class is divided into three orders: (1) Administration, (2) Defence, and (3) Foreign and Feudatory State Service. It contains 3,811 persons, nearly all of whom are engaged in the civil administration, the number of persons employed in the defence of the country and in Foreign State Service being only ten and one respectively. Of the 3,800 persons connected with the administration of the province, 1,946 are engaged in the service of the Imperial and Provincial Governments, 62 are in Municipal Service and the rest are village servants. Among village servants again, 1,207 persons are shown as non-agricultural village headmen. I doubt the accuracy of this, as nearly every village officer has some connection with the land.

CLASS B.—PASTURE AND AGRICULTURE.

Class B.—Pasture and Agriculture.

66. This class contains two orders: IV—Provision and Care of Cattle, and V—Agriculture.

Order IV.—Provision and Care of Cattle.

67. Order IV contains 1,249 persons, or 0·72 per cent. of the total population. Of these, 1,123 are herdsmen, 46 are sheep and goat-breeders, and 43 are farriers and gelders.

Order V.—Agriculture.

68. The next Order—Agriculture—is divided into four sub-orders, the proportional strength of each of which is shown in the margin. Land-owners and tenants form the large majority and constitute 60·03 per cent. of the total of the order. The number of non-cultivating land-occupants is only 2,688, while the cultivating occupants number 23,124. This is satisfactory, in so far as it shows that the majority of those who own land are also directly engaged in actual cultivation. Cultivating tenants number 48,867, and are nearly twice as numerous as land-occupants. Of the total number of labourers, 25,313 are field labourers and 21,756 farm-servants, *i. e.*, labourers employed throughout the year. Growers of special products and trees number 2,735, or 2·19 per cent. of the agricultural population. The majority of these are engaged in the planting industry, but the item 'Planters' includes Superintendents, Agents, Overseers, Maistries, etc. I give the details in the marginal statement, but the return is obviously imperfect, as the number of females who are actually planters themselves and not merely dependent on planters, cannot be so high as 635, while the number of 'dependent' females must be greater than 13. The mistake has arisen from the failure of the enumerators or the householders who filled up the schedule to distinguish between the terms 'planter' and 'planter dependent.' In 1881, the number of male coffee-planters was 208, so that

Agricultural population.

Sub-order.	Actual strength.	Percentage on total of order.
Interest in land	74,791	60·03
Agricultural labourers	47,069	37·78
Growers of special products and trees	2,735	2·19
Agricultural training and supervision	2	...
TOTAL	124,597	100·00

Statistics of Planters.

Name of occupation.	Population.		
	TOTAL.	Males.	Females.
Planters	1,429	794	635
Do. Dependent	60	47	13
Maistries	590	512	78
Overseers	15	7	8
Superintendents	17	9	8
Agents	165	75	90
Managers	7	5	2
Inspectors	2	1	1
Supervisors	1	1	...
TOTAL	2,286	1,451	835

after making all allowance for some under-statement in 1881 there has evidently been a considerable increase in the number of persons engaged in this industry.

Occupations combined with agriculture.

69. The total agricultural population of the province is 124,597 according to Table XVIIA. Adding to this the number of persons who combine agriculture with other occupations, we have 129,234 persons, or 74·68 per cent. of the population, who are either wholly or partially dependent for their livelihood on agriculture.

CLASS C.—PERSONAL SERVICES.

Class C.—Personal Services.

70. This class contains 4,139 persons, of whom 3,976 are engaged in personal and domestic service. Barbers number 711, washermen 1,390, cooks 706, and in-door servants 813. Among in-door servants the females predominate as would be expected.

CLASS D.—PREPARATION AND SUPPLY OF MATERIAL SUBSTANCES.

Class D.—Preparation and Supply of Material Substances.

71. This class comprises eleven orders, and the proportion borne by each of them to the total population is given below:—

Order.	Percentage on total population.
VII.—Food and Drink	5·62
VIII.—Light, Firing and Forage	0·30
IX.—Buildings	0·38
X.—Vehicles and Vessels	0·02
XI.—Supplementary Requirements	0·19
XII.—Textile Fabrics and Dress	1·15
XIII.—Metals and Precious Stones	1·59
XIV.—Glass, Pottery and Stone Ware	0·49
XV.—Wood, Cane and Leaves, etc.	1·73
XVI.—Drugs, Gums, Dyes, etc.	0·01
XVII.—Leather, Horns, Bones and Grease	0·22
TOTAL	11·70

Order VII.—Food and Drink.

72. Order VII.—Food and Drink—is by far the largest, nearly 6 per cent. of the entire population of the province being supported by it. It is divided into three sub-orders: (17) Animal Food, (18) Vegetable Food, and (19) Drink, Condiments and Narcotics. Persons engaged in the preparation and supply of vegetable food number 3,344. Of these, 2,274 are grain dealers and 684 are confectioners and sweetmeat makers or sweetmeat pedlars. The main items in sub-order 19 are toddy drawers and sellers (1,646), grocers and general condiment dealers (1,305), betel-leaf and areca-nut sellers (870) and coffee preparers and sellers (772). The keeper of the ordinary *chellara bazaar* has been classed as a grocer and general condiment dealer.

The only other orders in this class which have any considerable number of followers are:—

XII.—Textile Fabrics and Dress,
XIII.—Metals and Precious Stones, and
XV.—Wood, Cane and Leaves.

73. The first order comprises four sub-orders, of which sub-order 40—Cotton and sub-order 42—Dress, are the most important. Nearly all the persons shown in the former are cotton-weavers, while those in the latter are mainly tailors. It may be noted that of the 1,459 persons included in the latter sub-order, 983 or 67·37 per cent. were enumerated in towns.

Order XII.—Textile Fabrics and Dress.

74. The next order—Metals and Precious Stones—contains 2,745 persons, the majority of whom are gold and silver workers and blacksmiths. The former number 1,606 and the latter 822.

Order XIII.—Metals and Precious Stones.

75. The last order—Wood, Cane and Leaves—contains 2,985 persons, of whom 908 are carpenters, 333 are wood-cutters and sawyers, and 1,602 are basket-weavers and winnowing-pan makers.

Order XV.—Wood, Cane and Leaves.

CLASS E.—COMMERCE, TRANSPORT AND STORAGE.

76. This class is divided into two orders: XVIII—Commerce, and XIX—Transport and Storage. The former contains 638 persons, of whom more than one-half are general shop-keepers and contractors. In the latter there are 2,286 persons, 80 per cent. of whom are cart-owners and drivers. This is not strange, seeing that nearly all transport is by cart, Coorg having no railways or water communications.

Class E.—Commerce, Transport and Storage.

CLASS F.—PROFESSIONS.

77. There are two orders in this class: XX—Learned and Artistic Professions, and XXI—Sport and Amusements. The former contains 3,000 persons and the latter only 164. Among the former, persons engaged in religious services number 1,103; schoolmasters 466; private secretaries and clerks 548; vakils 128; and unqualified medical practitioners 159. The latter order is chiefly made up of exhibitors of trained animals (88) and *shikaris* (33).

Class F.—Professions.

CLASS G.—INDEFINITE OCCUPATIONS.

Class G.—Indefinite Occupations.

78. Class G contains two orders: XXIII—Indefinite, and XXIV—Independent of Work.

79. Persons engaged in indefinite occupations number 11,963, or 6·91 per cent. of the total population. Of these, 10,414 are general labourers, 955 are rice-pounders and huskers, and 277 are road labourers. Among rice-pounders and huskers, the females largely predominate, for this occupation is usually carried on by that sex. Many of the general labourers are probably in reality agricultural labourers.

Order XXIII.—Indefinite.

80. Order XXIV contains 963 persons, or 0·56 per cent. of the total population. It is divided into two sub-orders: 76—Property and Alms, and 77—Supported at the Public Charge. The only important item in the former is that relating to ordinary beggars, who number 716. The latter includes 113 pensioners, most of whom live in towns, and 118 prisoners. Among prisoners again, 18 were under trial at the time of the census, 4 were civil prisoners, and 96 were returned as convicts.

Order XXIV.—Independent of Work.

CHAPTER XII.

THE ADMINISTRATION OF THE CENSUS.

81. In connection with the taking of the census and the abstraction and tabulation of the results, Coorg was treated as a district of Madras, and the arrangements were identical with those made in that Presidency. They have been fully described in the Madras Census Report, and I need not recapitulate them here. The extracts from the District Magistrate's report printed as an appendix to this chapter, give all the necessary information special to Coorg. There was no difficulty in obtaining enough enumerators, and there was no opposition on the part of the people. The only person prosecuted under the Census Act was a Government official who neglected his duty. The cost of the census was R3,841-7-6 or R22-3-2 per thousand of the population. The charges for abstraction, tabulation and superintendence were arrived at by a *pro rata* distribution of all the charges for the different Provinces and States dealt with by me. Details of the charges are given in the appendix. The expenditure is considerably larger than in 1881, but the cost of printing the tables and report alone is R1,500, and it is this large item which makes the rate on the population so high, for this particular does not vary with the numbers dealt with as it costs as much, or nearly as much, to print tables and a report for a small as for a large population. It is not clear whether the charges for printing the report and tables were included in the expenditure of 1881.

APPENDIX A.

Extract from the Report of B. C. Leggatt, Esq., First Assistant Commissioner and District Magistrate of Coorg.

The lists of villages and hamlets and information regarding the number of houses were furnished by the Nâd Parpatigars. The Taluk Subedars checked these particulars by personal inspection and by comparing them with the information available in the records kept for revenue purposes. The area of every village has been determined.

The maps of the taluks in Coorg, which were specially prepared for census purposes, were utilized for the purpose of determining the blocks and circles in each nâd, although the census divisions were not marked upon them.

Enclosures containing separate huts or houses were marked with a serial number, and the separate huts or houses with separate sub-numbers.

The numbers in each village or block were consecutive.

All unoccupied houses were numbered, ruined houses being omitted.

Buildings other than houses were also numbered. Jails and hospitals were given only one number.

The numbers were marked in English with tar on the doors or on the wall in front of the buildings.

The numbering of houses, etc., was commenced on 10th August 1890 and completed by the end of November. As the numbers were marked with tar, they would have lasted until the census, even if the numbering had been done earlier.

The buildings numbered were entered in a book called the Village List, forms of which were supplied to all Subedars and Parpatigars.

There was no difficulty in obtaining the requisite number of enumerators. There were 11 charge superintendents, 129 supervisors, and 1,312 enumerators. The number of special enumerators appointed to take the census of travellers by road and houseless persons was 30.

Among the supervisors 113 were officials and 16 non-officials (nine schoolmasters, two pleaders, and five agriculturists).

Among the enumerators, 78 were officials and the rest non-officials. The occupation, etc., of non-official enumerators is given below:—

Schoolmasters	44
Vakeels	4
Clerks in private employ	42
Agriculturists	947
Shopkeepers	92
Patails (village headmen)	85
Stamp-vendor	1
Others	19
	1,234

No remuneration was paid to non-official enumerators. It is gratifying to note that the majority of the enumerators worked satisfactorily.

The services of the officials of all the departments in Coorg were utilized for carrying on the census work.

2,657 books containing 42,602 schedule pages, 2,000 loose schedules (vernacular), 1,000 house-holders' schedules for Europeans and Eurasians, and 200 house-holders' schedules for natives of India, were received according to indents sent from my office.

124 books and 320 house-holders' schedules for Europeans were not used. The Native house-holders' schedules were also not issued, as they were received too late. I am of opinion that these schedules should be issued only to those natives who are conversant with English, as those who know only the vernaculars are likely to make mistakes in filling up the columns.

All the enumerators were instructed first by the Parpatigars and subsequently by Subedars. All the supervisors were instructed by me and the officials of my office, who were deputed for that purpose. The majority of the enumerators in every taluk were also instructed by me when I visited the taluk and the nâd head-quarters for the purpose of examining the census work done by the revenue officials. The following method of instruction was adopted :—The rules for the guidance of the enumerators and supervisors were read out and clearly explained. Afterwards people of different ages, castes, and sects were produced, and some of the enumerators were asked to make the necessary entries on manuscript schedules. These entries were read out and the mistakes pointed out to all present. Each enumerator was furnished with a copy of the printed instructions, and the copies of the manual for charge superintendents and supervisors were also distributed to the officers concerned.

* * * * * * *

In rural districts the preliminary record was commenced on 6th January 1891 and completed by the end of the same month. In one nâd the preliminary record was completed on 10th February 1891. In municipalities it was begun on 1st February 1891 and completed by the 10th of the same month.

The preliminary record was checked by the Subedars and the parpatigars generally with reference to the instructions given for filling up the columns. Several books were also examined by me in the course of my tours. The general opinion as to the preliminary record is that it was accurate except in two or three blocks, mistakes of which were rectified afterwards.

The time occupied in taking the final census varied from 2 to 6 hours in different localities. There were trained extra enumerators in every nâd, and there was no difficulty in supplying the places of those who prepared the preliminary record, but were absent at the time of the final census.

There were 30 special enumeration stations (chiefly police stations and toll gates). The work of enumerating travellers, etc., was entrusted to the police. Beat constables were posted at every junction to ensure the enumeration of all travellers.

The census of one estate in Ammathinad was taken by day, as it was, through an oversight, not included by the revenue officials in any of the blocks in that nâd.

The preparation of the enumerators' circle and taluk abstracts was completed by the 3rd March 1891, and the district abstract by the 10th March 1891. The delay in the preparation of the district abstract was due to the fact that *all the abstracts* were checked in my office, as errors were discovered in several abstracts sent from the taluks.

There was no opposition on the part of the people to the taking of the census. This was due to the fact that the people rightly understood the object of Government, and that the experience of the two previous censuses removed all groundless fears in connection with the measure.

A Government official was prosecuted under section 10 of the Census Act for neglect of duty and was fined R 10.

There is no doubt that the census was pretty correctly taken, as all possible endeavours were used to ensure accuracy.

APPENDIX B.—Accounts.

Main Head.		Sub-Head.	1890-91.	1891-92.	1892-93.	1893-94.	Total.
			R a. p.	R a. p.	R a. p.	R a. p.	R a. p.
PART A.—ENUMERATION	I.—District Charges	1. District Office Establishment	148 14 3	......	......	......	148 14 3
		2. Contingent Charges of Establishments and Charges for printing Circle Lists	20 0 0	......	......	......	20 0 0
		3. House-numbering	...	22 3 10	......	......	22 3 10
		4. Lights, Ink, etc.	11 6 0	......	......	......	11 6 0
		5. Remuneration of Census Officers	...	......	......	......	......
		6. Special Travelling Allowances	50 0 0	......	......	......	50 0 0
		7. Freight of Schedules, etc., from stations and landing places	...	61 12 0	......	......	61 12 0
		Total I.—District Charges	230 4 3	83 15 10	......	......	324 4 1
	II.—Enumeration Printing	8. Paper for Schedules, etc., at Press	...	......	......	......	......
		9. Printing and binding	...	......	......	......	......
		10. Despatching from Press	...	......	......	......	......
		Total II.—Paper and Printing	...	......	......	......	......
		Total Enumeration	230 4 3	83 15 10	......	......	324 4 1
PART B.—ABSTRACTION AND COMPILATION.	III.—Tabulation Office	11. Office-rent	2 15 1	31 10 8	6 2 4	0 10 4	41 6 5
		12. Office furniture and repairs, etc.	3 0 0	14 8 1	0 3 10	......	17 11 11
		13 Record Establishment	0 0 5	27 13 9	4 8 0	0 2 1	32 8 3
		14. Correspondence and Accounts Establishment	...	8 13 8	1 5 1	......	10 2 9
		15. Menial Establishment	0 0 8	30 12 3	2 4 1	0 0 9	33 1 9
		16. Working staff, including Superintendence, Officials	1 2 4	177 9 8	29 0 9	0 4 9	208 1 6
		17. Working staff clerks specially entertained	...	1,265 9 7	66 1 5	......	1,331 11 0
		18. Travelling allowance to and from office	...	0 5 8	0 2 8	......	0 8 4
		19. Freight of Schedules, etc., to office	7 7 9	2 7 11	......	......	9 15 8
		20. Petty stationery and contingencies	0 15 2	12 1 8	3 2 4	......	16 3 2
		Total III.—Tabulation	15 9 5	1,571 12 11	112 14 6	1 1 11	1,701 6 9
	IV.—Tabulation Printing	21. Paper for sheets, registers, and tables	45 13 2	35 7 6	......		
		22. Printing of forms, tables, and reports	2 0 7	45 5 6	......	1,500 0 0	1,630 12 4
		23. Freight of sheets, etc., to office	0 6 4	1 11 3	......		
		Total IV.—Tabulation Printing	48 4 1	82 8 3	......	1,500 0 0	1,630 12 4
		Total Abstraction and Compilation	63 13 6	1,654 5 2	112 14 6	1,501 1 11	3,332 3 1
PART C.—SUPERINTENDENCE	V.—Superintendent	24. Provincial Superintendent's deputation allowance	20 2 4	21 15 9	21 15 8	1 10 6	65 12 3
		25. Pay of substitute of Superintendent	16 13 5	14 4 7	15 6 10	1 3 5	47 12 3
		26. Travelling allowance of Superintendent	12 10 9	7 9 2	1 12 8	0 6 7	22 7 2
		Total V.—Superintendent	49 10 6	43 13 6	39 3 2	3 4 6	135 15 8
	VI.—Superintendent's Office	27. Superintendent's Office Establishment	14 7 9	13 1 2	8 1 11	0 12 0	36 6 10
		28. Travelling allowance for establishment	......	1 10 8	0 4 6	0 2 8	2 1 10
		29. Office Contingencies for establishment	12 5 3	2 0 7	1 10 10	......	16 0 8
		30. Rent of Superintendent's Office	......	2 0 1	2 4 2	0 3 1	4 7 4
		Total VI.—Superintendent's Office	26 13 0	18 12 6	12 5 5	1 1 9	59 0 8
		Total Superintendence	76 7 6	62 10 0	51 8 7	4 6 3	195 0 4
		Grand Total	870 9 8	1,800 15 0	164 7 1	1,505 8 2	3,841 7 6

TABLE I.—Area, Houses and Population.

Province.	Area in Square Miles.	Number of Towns.	Number of Villages.	Occupied Houses. Total.	Occupied Houses. In towns.	Occupied Houses. In villages.	Population. Total. Total.	Population. Total. In towns.	Population. Total. In villages.	Population. Males. Total.	Population. Males. In towns.	Population. Males. In villages.	Population. Females. Total.	Population. Females. In towns.	Population. Females. In villages.
1	2	3	4	5	6	7	8	9	10	11	12	13	14	15	16
Coorg	1,583	5	492	26,806	3,174	23,632	173,055	15,511	157,544	95,907	8,630	87,277	77,148	6,881	70,267

TABLE II.—Variation in the Enumerated Population since last Census.

Province.	Total. 1891.	Total. 1881.	Total. Variation.	Males. 1891.	Males. 1881.	Males. Variation.	Females. 1891.	Females. 1881.	Females. Variation.
1	2	3	4	5	6	7	8	9	10
Coorg	173,055	178,302	—5,247	95,907	100,439	—4,532	77,148	77,863	—715

TABLE III.—Towns and Villages classified by Population.

Province.	Total number of Towns and Villages.	Total Population.	1—199. No.	1—199. Population.	200—499. No.	200—499. Population.	500—999. No.	500—999. Population.	1,000—1,999. No.	1,000—1,999. Population.	2,000—2,999. No.	2,000—2,999. Population.
1	2	3	4	5	6	7	8	9	10	11	12	13
Coorg	497*	173,055	226	19,353	162	56,928	87	58,315	18	21,907	2	5,071

Province.	3,000—4,999. No.	3,000—4,999. Population.	5,000—9,999. No.	5,000—9,999. Population.	10,000—14,999. No.	10,000—14,999. Population.	15,000—19,999. No.	15,000—19,999. Population.	20,000—49,999. No.	20,000—49,999. Population.	50,000 and over. No.	50,000 and over. Population.
1	14	15	16	17	18	19	20	21	22	23	24	25
Coorg	1	4,447	1	7,034	...	...	...	...	...	...	...	...

* In addition to these there are 25 uninhabited villages.

TABLE IV.—Towns according to Population, compared with the preceding Census.

TOWN.	PROVINCE.	Municipality, Suburb or Cantonment.	Total. 1891.	Total. 1881.	Total. Variation.	Males. 1891.	Males. 1881.	Males. Variation.	Females. 1891.	Females. 1881.	Females. Variation.
1	2	3	4	5	6	7	8	9	10	11	12
Mercára	Coorg	Municipality and Cantonment	7,034	8,383	− 1,349	3,904	4,800	−896	3,130	3,583	−453
Vírájendrapet	Coorg	Municipality	4,447	4,576	− 129	2,613	2,727	−114	1,834	1,849	− 15
Frazerpet	Coorg	Ditto	1,710	1,310	+ 400	883	631	+252	827	679	+148
Somvárapet	Coorg	Ditto	1,510	1,528	− 18	821	797	+ 24	689	731	− 42
Kodlipet	Coorg	Ditto	810	856	− 46	409	411	− 2	401	445	− 44

TABLE V.—Towns arranged territorially with Population by Religion.

TOWN.	Total Population. Total.	Total Population. Males.	Total Population. Females.	Hindus. Total.	Hindus. Males.	Hindus. Females.	Musalmans. Total.	Musalmans. Males.	Musalmans. Females.	Christians. Total.	Christians. Males.	Christians. Females.	Jains. Total.	Jains. Males.	Jains. Females.	Parsis. Total.	Parsis. Males.	Parsis. Females.
1	2	3	4	5	6	7	8	9	10	11	12	13	14	15	16	17	18	19
Frazerpet	1,710	883	827	1,371	702	669	287	155	132	46	22	24	...	...	...	6	4	2
Kodlipet	810	409	401	671	325	346	137	82	55	2	2	...	...	...	...	...	...	...
Mercára	7,034	3,904	3,130	4,941	2,759	2,182	1,471	835	636	591	292	299	...	...	...	31	18	13
Somvárapet	1,510	821	689	1,371	719	652	129	93	36	10	9	1	...	...	...	...	...	...
Vírájendrapet	4,447	2,613	1,834	2,323	1,378	945	1,593	988	605	468	219	249	62	27	35	1	1	...
Total	15,511	8,630	6,881	10,677	5,888	4,794	3,617	2,153	1,464	1,117	544	573	62	27	35	38	23	15

TABLE VI.—Religions.

PROVINCE.	Total Population. Total.	Total Population. Males.	Total Population. Females.	Hindus. Total.	Hindus. Males.	Hindus. Females.	Musalmans. Total.	Musalmans. Males.	Musalmans. Females.	Christians. Total.	Christians. Males.	Christians. Females.	Jains. Total.	Jains. Males.	Jains. Females.	Parsis. Total.	Parsis. Males.	Parsis. Females.
1	2	3	4	5	6	7	8	9	10	11	12	13	14	15	16	17	18	19
Coorg	173,055	95,907	77,148	156,845	86,057	70,788	12,665	7,903	4,762	3,392	1,868	1,524	114	55	59	39	24	15

TABLE VII.—Ages by Religions.

RELIGIONS.	ALL AGES.			AGE PERIODS.															
				UNDER 1 YEAR.		1 YEAR.		2 YEARS.		3 YEARS.		4 YEARS.		TOTAL 0—4.		5—9.		10—14.	
	TOTAL.	Males.	Females.	Males.	Females.	Males.	Females.	Males.	Females.	Males.	Females.	Males.	Females.	Males.	Females.	Males.	Females.	Males.	Females.
1	2	3	4	5	6	7	8	9	10	11	12	13	14	15	16	17	18	19	20
All Religions	173,055	95,907	77,148	2,112	2,209	1,450	1,520	2,407	2,542	2,523	2,730	2,185	2,225	10,677	11,226	10,986	10,709	9,020	7,619
Hindus	156,845	86,057	70,788	1,962	2,032	1,336	1,394	2,243	2,344	2,337	2,555	2,033	2,046	9,911	10,371	10,104	9,919	8,218	7,050
Musalmans	12,665	7,903	4,762	104	128	79	96	116	147	134	127	111	141	544	639	670	599	677	417
Christians	3,392	1,868	1,524	44	46	32	29	44	51	49	46	38	37	207	209	205	186	122	148
Jains	114	55	59	1	3	1	1	2	...	2	1	1	...	7	5	2	3	3	3
Parsis	39	24	15	1	...	2	...	2	...	1	1	2	1	8	2	5	2	...	1

RELIGIONS.	AGE PERIODS—*contd.*																					
	15—19.		20—24.		25—29.		30—34.		35—39.		40—44.		45—49.		50—54.		55—59.		60 and over.		Not stated.	
	Males.	Females.	Males.	Females.	Males.	Females.	Males.	Females.	Males.	Females.	Males.	Females.	Males.	Females.	Males.	Females.	Males.	Females.	Males.	Females.	Males.	Females.
	21	22	23	24	25	26	27	28	29	30	31	32	33	34	35	36	37	38	39	40	41	42
All Religions	9,471	7,955	10,479	8,642	12,243	8,517	9,892	6,312	7,358	4,161	5,799	4,076	3,487	2,071	3,012	2,524	1,257	889	2,188	2,430	32	17
Hindus	8,451	7,352	9,358	7,908	10,904	7,784	8,676	5,728	6,455	3,785	5,060	3,704	3,094	1,905	2,707	2,275	1,116	817	1,976	2,173	27	17
Musalmans	839	445	918	555	1,103	547	993	453	722	258	588	297	310	113	249	189	111	50	175	200	4	...
Christians	175	150	195	172	236	179	214	126	174	111	146	70	77	47	53	58	27	20	36	48	1	...
Jains	6	7	8	5	5	5	7	3	4	6	3	5	4	5	3	2	2	2	1	8	...	...
Parsis	...	1	...	2	1	2	2	2	3	1	2	...	2	1	...	...	1	...	...	1	..	...

TABLE VIII.—Civil Condition by Religion and Age.

RELIGION.		ALL AGES.			AGE PERIODS.											
					0—4.		5—9.		10—14.		15—19.		20—24.		25—29.	
		TOTAL.	Males.	Females.	Males.	Females.	Males.	Females.	Males.	Females.	Males.	Females.	Males.	Females.	Males.	Females.
1		2	3	4	5	6	7	8	9	10	11	12	13	14	15	16
ALL RELIGIONS	Unmarried	83,598	50,947	32,651	10,614	11,141	10,932	10,600	8,851	6,731	8,424	2,915	6,265	652	3,557	267
	Married	72,809	41,187	31,622	43	55	51	100	162	853	1,012	4,836	4,069	7,366	8,306	7,223
	Widowed	16,559	3,724	12,835	2	7	...	6	4	34	33	202	142	623	385	1,026
	Not stated	89	49	40	18	23	3	3	3	1	2	2	3	1	1	1
HINDUS	Unmarried	76,227	45,948	30,279	9,856	10,291	10,054	9,818	8,058	6,243	7,479	2,764	5,464	606	3,089	242
	Married	65,445	36,596	28,849	37	53	49	94	154	775	938	4,401	3,754	6,721	7,456	6,606
	Widowed	15,098	3,472	11,626	2	7	...	6	4	31	32	185	137	580	358	935
	Not stated	75	41	34	16	20	1	1	2	1	2	2	3	1	1	1
MUSALMANS	Unmarried	5,665	3,945	1,720	539	638	669	594	669	346	778	93	657	24	377	7
	Married	5,931	3,782	2,149	4	1	1	5	8	68	60	340	256	496	709	473
	Widowed	1,066	173	893	...	...	...	...	...	3	1	12	5	35	17	67
	Not stated	3	3	...	1	...	...	...	...	...	...	...	...	...	...	...
CHRISTIANS	Unmarried	1,647	1,010	637	204	205	202	183	121	140	161	57	138	22	88	18
	Married	1,374	777	597	2	1	1	1	...	8	14	89	57	144	139	139
	Widowed	360	76	284	...	...	...	...	...	...	...	4	...	6	9	22
	Not stated	11	5	6	1	3	2	2	1	...	...	...	...	...	...	...
JAINS	Unmarried	39	29	10	7	5	2	3	3	1	6	1	6	...	3	...
	Married	45	25	20	...	...	...	...	...	2	...	5	2	4	2	3
	Widowed	30	1	29	...	...	...	...	...	...	...	1	...	1	...	2
	Not stated	...	...	...	...	...	...	...	...	...	...	...	...	...	...	...
PARSIS	Unmarried	20	15	5	8	2	5	2	...	1	...	...	...	...	...	...
	Married	14	7	7	...	...	...	...	...	...	...	1	...	1	...	2
	Widowed	5	2	3	...	...	...	...	...	...	...	...	...	1	1	...
	Not stated	...	...	...	...	...	...	...	...	...	...	...	...	...	...	...

Table VIII.—Civil Condition by Religion and Age—Coorg.

RELIGION.		AGE PERIODS—*contd.*															
		30—34.		35—39.		40—44.		45—49.		50—54.		55—59.		60 AND OVER.		NOT STATED.	
		Males.	Females.	Males.	Females.	Males.	Females.	Males.	Females.	Males.	Females.	Males.	Females.	Males.	Females.	Males.	Females.
		17	18	19	20	21	22	23	24	25	26	27	28	29	30	31	32
ALL RELIGIONS	Unmarried	1,297	121	497	89	260	68	97	19	69	17	24	6	44	16	16	9
	Married	8,117	4,635	6,397	2,721	4,988	1,917	3,013	858	2,465	618	1,004	198	1,556	237	4	5
	Widowed	475	1,554	460	1,351	551	2,090	377	1,194	477	1,888	229	685	585	2,175	4	...
	Not stated	3	2	4	...	...	1	...	...	1	1	...	...	3	2	8	3
HINDUS	Unmarried	1,093	112	426	79	216	58	83	19	59	17	21	5	35	16	15	9
	Married	7,135	4,186	5,601	2,466	4,335	1,750	2,655	801	2,209	575	878	188	1,393	228	2	5
	Widowed	446	1,428	424	1,240	509	1,895	356	1,085	438	1,682	217	624	545	1,928	4	...
	Not stated	2	2	4	...	...	1	...	...	1	1	...	...	3	1	6	3
MUSALMANS	Unmarried	155	5	47	7	31	5	4	...	8	...	1	1	9	...	1	...
	Married	815	363	652	181	525	134	293	40	214	36	102	5	141	7	2	...
	Widowed	22	85	23	70	32	158	13	73	27	153	8	44	25	193	...	...
	Not stated	1	...	...	...	...	...	...	...	...	...	...	...	...	...	1	...
CHRISTIANS	Unmarried	46	4	23	3	13	5	10	...	2	...	2	...	...	...	...	...
	Married	162	84	138	71	123	32	59	15	39	7	22	5	21	1	...	...
	Widowed	6	38	13	37	10	33	8	32	12	51	3	15	15	46	...	...
	Not stated	...	...	...	...	...	...	...	...	...	...	...	...	...	1	1	...
JAINS	Unmarried	2	...	...	...	...	...	...	...	...	...	...	...	...	...	...	...
	Married	4	...	4	2	3	1	4	2	3	...	2	...	1	1	...	...
	Widowed	1	3	...	4	...	4	...	3	...	2	...	2	...	7	...	...
	Not stated	...	...	...	...	...	...	...	...	...	...	...	...	...	...	...	...
PARSIS	Unmarried	1	...	1	...	...	...	...	...	...	...	...	...	...	...	...	...
	Married	1	2	2	1	2	...	2	...	...	...	...	...	...	—	...	...
	Widowed	...	...	...	...	...	...	...	1	...	...	1	...	...	1	...	...
	Not stated	...	...	...	...	...	...	...	...	...	...	...	...	...	...	...	...

TABLE IX.—Education by Religion and Age.

RELIGIONS.	TOTAL.			TOTAL BY EDUCATION.								AGE PERIODS. 0–9.										AGE PERIODS. 10–14.									
				Learning.		Literate.		Illiterate.		Not stated.		TOTAL.		Learning.		Literate.		Illiterate.		Not stated.		TOTAL.		Learning.		Literate.		Illiterate.		Not stated.	
	TOTAL.	Males.	Females.	Males.	Females.	Males.	Females.	Males.	Females.	Males.	Females.	Males.	Females.	Males.	Females.	Males.	Females.	Males.	Females.	Males.	Females.	Males.	Females.	Males.	Females.	Males.	Females.	Males.	Females.	Males.	Females.
1	2	3	4	5	6	7	8	9	10	11	12	13	14	15	16	17	18	19	20	21	22	23	24	25	26	27	28	29	30	31	32
All Religions . .	173,055	95,907	77,148	4,155	605	10,679	671	80,399	75,297	674	575	21,663	21,935	1,664	361	36	20	19,769	21,347	194	207	9,020	7,619	1,902	222	263	75	6,791	7,269	64	53
Hindus . . .	156,845	86,057	70,788	3,785	497	8,653	444	73,030	69,321	589	526	20,015	20,290	1,470	296	25	11	18,348	19,792	172	191	8,218	7,050	1,769	186	216	64	6,173	6,750	60	50
Musalmans . .	12,665	7,903	4,762	233	31	1,356	45	6,253	4,655	61	31	1,214	1,238	117	19	5	4	1,081	1,208	11	7	677	417	91	10	39	4	544	401	3	2
Christians . .	3,392	1,868	1,524	127	75	636	174	1,081	1,257	24	18	412	395	71	45	6	5	324	336	11	9	122	148	39	25	8	6	74	116	1	1
Jains . . .	114	55	59	5	...	23	2	27	57	...	...	9	8	1	...	...	...	8	8	...	..	3	3	3	...	...	1	...	2	...	...
Parsis . . .	39	24	15	5	2	11	6	8	7	...	...	13	4	5	1	...	...	8	3	...	...	...	1	...	1	...	...	...	...	...	...

AGE PERIODS—*contd.*

RELIGIONS.	15–24.										25 AND OVER.										NOT STATED.									
	TOTAL.		Learning.		Literate.		Illiterate.		Not stated.		TOTAL.		Learning.		Literate.		Illiterate.		Not stated.		TOTAL.		Learning.		Literate.		Illiterate.		Not stated.	
	Males.	Females.	Males.	Females.	Males.	Females.	Males.	Females.	Males.	Females.	Males.	Females.	Males.	Females.	Males.	Females.	Males.	Females.	Males.	Females.	Males.	Females.	Males.	Females.	Males.	Females.	Males.	Females.	Males.	Females.
	33	34	35	36	37	38	39	40	41	42	43	44	45	46	47	48	49	50	51	52	53	54	55	56	57	58	59	60	61	62
All Religions . .	19,950	16,597	575	19	3,109	307	16,124	16,135	142	136	45,242	30,980	14	3	7,268	269	37,695	30,530	265	178	32	17	...	...	3	...	20	16	9	1
Hindus . . .	17,809	15,260	534	13	2,616	232	14,535	14,891	124	124	39,988	28,171	12	2	5,794	137	33,956	27,872	226	160	27	17	...	...	2	...	18	16	7	1
Musalmans . .	1,757	1,000	23	2	357	13	1,362	977	15	8	4,251	2,107	2	...	954	24	3,264	2,069	31	14	4	...	...	...	1	...	2	...	1	...
Christians . .	370	322	17	4	129	60	221	254	3	4	963	659	...	1	493	103	462	551	8	4	1	...	...	...	...	...	...	...	1	...
Jains . . .	14	12	1	...	7	1	6	11	...	...	29	36	...	...	16	...	13	36	...	...	...	...	...	...	...	...	...	...	...	...
Parsis . . .	...	3	...	...	...	1	...	2	...	...	11	7	...	...	11	5	...	2	...	...	...	...	...	...	...	...	...	...	...	...

TABLE X.—Parent tongue.

LANGUAGES.	TOTAL.	Males.	Females.
A.—Coorg Languages—			
Kodagu or Coorgi	35,369	17,993	17,376
Yerava	2,587	1,339	1,248
TOTAL A.—COORG LANGUAGES	37,956	19,332	18,624
B.—Madras Languages—			
Áré	73	58	15
Hindustáni	6,919	3,841	3,078
Kanarese	76,115	40,664	35,451
Konkani	2,129	1,297	832
Koraga	9	4	5
Kurumba	2,791	1,475	1,316
Lambádi	79	60	19
Malayálam	11,299	8,467	2,832
Tamil	16,257	8,591	7,666
Telugu	3,751	2,163	1,588
Tulu	12,090	7,834	4,256
Yerukala	75	33	42
TOTAL B.—MADRAS LANGUAGES	131,587	74,487	57,100
C.—Other Indian Languages—			
Gujaráti	126	90	36
Hindi	23	12	11
Kach'hi	8	8	...
Maráthi	2,621	1,530	1,091
Márvádi	1	1	...
Sindhi	5	5	...
TOTAL C.—OTHER INDIAN LANGUAGES	2,784	1,646	1,138
D.—Non-Indian Asiatic Languages—			
Arabic	4	3	1
Pashtu	10	7	3
Persian	1	1	...
TOTAL D.—NON-INDIAN ASIATIC LANGUAGES	15	11	4
E.—Non-Asiatic Languages—			
Celtic	1	1	...
English	474	288	186
French	8	3	5
German	17	12	5
Portuguese	71	41	30
TOTAL E.—NON-ASIATIC LANGUAGES	571	345	226
Parent tongue—Not returned	142	86	56
GRAND TOTAL	173,055	95,907	77,148

TABLE XI.—Birth-place.

Birth-place.	Total.	Males.	Females.
A.—Districts or States within the Province—			
Coorg	120,110	61,571	58,539
Total, A	120,110	61,571	58,539
B.—Provinces and States in India beyond the Province—			
I.—British Territory.—			
Bengal	16	12	4
Bombay	783	664	119
Burma	6	5	1
Central Provinces	41	20	21
Madras	26,489	18,898	7,591
North-West Provinces	12	11	1
Punjab	16	13	3
Andamans	1	...	1
Total, I	27,364	19,623	7,741
II.—Feudatory States—			
Hyderabad	137	84	53
Mysore	25,139	14,413	10,726
Rájputána States	1	1	...
Bombay States	24	22	2
Madras States	35	21	14
French Settlements — Pondicherry	5	2	3
French Settlements — Mahe	1	1	...
Total	6	3	3
Portuguese Settlements (Goa)	4	4	...
India, Unspecified	20	13	7
Total, II	25,366	14,561	10,805
Total, B	52,730	34,184	18,546
C.—Countries in Asia beyond India—			
I.—Adjacent to India—			
Afghanistan	19	12	7
Turkistan	1	1	...
Ceylon	8	7	1
Total, I	28	20	8

TABLE XI.—Birth-place—*contd.*

BIRTH-PLACE.	TOTAL.	Males.	Females.
C.—Countries in Asia beyond India—*contd.*			
II.—REMOTE FROM INDIA—			
Arabia	2	2	...
Asia Minor	2	2	...
Japan	10	...	10
TOTAL, II	14	4	10
TOTAL, C	42	24	18
D.—Countries in Europe—			
England and Wales	69	50	19
Scotland	30	22	8
Ireland	10	9	1
Channel Islands	1	1	...
France	7	7	...
Switzerland	2	1	1
Germany	5	4	1
Europe, Unspecified	1	1	...
TOTAL, D	125	95	30
E.—Countries in Africa—			
Cape Colony	1	1	...
Egypt	1	1	...
TOTAL, E	2	2	...
F.—Countries in America	...	...	...
G.—Countries in Australasia—			
Australia, Unspecified	1	...	1
TOTAL, G	1	...	1
H.—Born at Sea	...	...	...
I.—Birth-place—Not returned	45	31	14
GRAND TOTAL	173,055	95,907	77,148

TABLES XII—XV.—Infirmities by Ages.

INFIRMITY.	TOTAL AFFLICTED.			DISTRIBUTION BY AGE.											
				0—4.		5—9.		10—14.		15—19.		20—24.		25—29.	
	Total.	Males.	Females.	Males.	Females.	Males.	Females.	Males.	Females.	Males.	Females.	Males.	Females.	Males.	Females.
1	2	3	4	5	6	7	8	9	10	11	12	13	14	15	16
Insane . .	44	25	19	...	...	1	1	4	4	5	1	...	2	2	5
Deaf-mute . .	126	77	49	...	3	9	5	12	8	13	1	14	8	8	4
Blind . .	86	47	39	3	4	5	2	3	5	5	1	1	2	7	1
Leper . .	23	12	11	1	...	...	2	...	...	...	1	2	1	...	1

	DISTRIBUTION BY AGE—*continued.*															
	30—34.		35—39.		40—44.		45—49.		50—54.		55—59.		60 and over.		Not stated.	
	Males.	Females.	Males.	Females.	Males.	Females.	Males.	Females.	Males.	Females.	Males.	Females.	Males.	Females.	Males.	Females.
	17	18	19	20	21	22	23	24	25	26	27	28	29	30	31	32
Insane . .	2	1	1	...	5*	3	1†	1	2	...	1	1	1	...	...	...
Deaf-mute . .	8	5	5	5	4*	1	2	4	2	2	...	2	...	1	...	...
Blind . .	3	...	3	2	7	8	4†	4	4	3	...	2	2	5	...	...
Leper . .	2	2	3	...	3	2	...	...	1	2	...	...	...	...	...	...

* One of them is both insane and deaf-mute.

† One of them is both insane and blind.

TABLE XII (a).—Persons of unsound mind by Caste.

Class.	Group.	Caste.	Religion.	Total.	Males.	Females.
A.—AGRICULTURAL	1.—Military and Dominant.	Kodagu	Hindu	10	7	3
		Náyar	Do.	2	2*	...
		Total, Group A—1		**12**	**9**	**3**
	2(a).—Cultivators	Gauda	Hindu	4	2	2
		Jain	Jain	1	1	...
		Vakkaliga	Hindu	1	...	1
		Total, Group A—2(a)		**6**	**3**	**3**
	(2c).—Field Labourers	Holeya	Hindu	7	3	4
	4.—Forest and Hill Tribes.	Yerava	Do.	1	...	1
		Total, Class A		**26**	**15**	**11**
B.—PROFESSIONAL	5.—Priests	Bráhman Shivalli	Hindu	1	1	...
	10.—Astrologers	Kaniya	Do.	1	1†	...
		Total, Class B		**2**	**2**	...
D.—ARTISAN AND VILLAGE MENIAL.	20.—Carpenters, Masons and Turners.	Badagi	Hindu	1	...	1
	23.—Weavers, Calenderers and Dyers.	Bilimagga	Do.	2	1	1
	26.—Shepherds	Heggade	Do.	1	...	1
		Kuruba	Do.	2	2	...
		Total, Group D—26		**3**	**2**	**1**
	28.—Potters	Koyava	Hindu	1	1	...
		Total, Class D		**7**	**4**	**3**
E.—VAGRANTS, MINOR ARTISANS AND PERFORMERS, ETC.	43.—Mat-makers, cane-splitters, &c.	Méda	Hindu	1	...	1
		Total, Class E		**1**	...	**1**
F.—RACES AND NATIONALITIES.	48.—Non-Indian Asiatic Races.	Saiyad	Musalman	1	1	...
		Sheik	Do.	1	1	...
		Total, Group F—48		**2**	**2**	...
	52.—Christian Converts.	Native Christian	Christian	2	1	1
		Total, Class F		**4**	**3**	**1**
G.—INDEFINITE AND UNKNOWN.	54.—Territorial, Linguistic and Sectarian names.	Lingáyat	Hindu	1	...	1
		Telugu	Do.	1	...	1
		Vírasaiva	Do.	1	...	1
		Total, Class G		**3**	...	**3**
Not stated.	Not stated.	Caste—Not returned	Hindu	1	1	...
		Grand Total		**44**	**25**	**19**

* One of them is also deaf-mute.
† Is also blind.

TABLE XIII (a).—Deaf-mutes by Caste.

Class.	Group.	Caste.	Religion.	Total.	Males.	Females.
A.—AGRICULTURAL	1.—Military and Dominant.	Kodagu	Hindu	21	10	11
		Náyar	Do.	1	1*	...
		Total, Group A—1		22	11	11
	2(a).—Cultivators	Binepatta	Hindu	1	1	...
		Gauda	Do.	6	5	1
		Vakkaliga	Do.	9	4	5
		Total, Group A—2(a)		16	10	6
	2(c).—Field Labourers	Adiyán	Hindu	1	1	...
		Holeya	Do.	23	14	9
		Pále	Do.	4	1	3
		Total, Group A—2(c)		28	16	12
	4.—Forest and Hill Tribes.	Yerava	Hindu	9	7	2
		Total, Class A.		75	44	31
B.—PROFESSIONAL	5.—Priests	Jangam	Hindu	2	1	1
		Total, Class B.		2	1	1
C.—COMMERCIAL	14.—Traders	Máppilla	Musalman	2	2	...
		Total, Class C.		2	2	...
D.—ARTISAN AND VILLAGE MENIAL.	17(a).—Artisans	Pánchála	Hindu	1	...	1
	20.—Carpenters, Masons and Turners.	Áyiri	Do.	2	1	1
		Badagi	Do.	2	1	1
		Total, Group D—20		4	2	2
	23.—Weavers, Calenderers and Dyers.	Bilimagga	Hindu	1	1	...
	24.—Washermen	Agasa	Do.	2	1	1
		Madivála	Do.	1	1	...
		Total, Group D—24		3	2	1
	26.—Shepherds	Golla	Hindu	1	1	...
		Kuruba	Do.	15	10	5
		Total, Group D—26		16	11	5
	27.—Oil-pressers	Gániga	Hindu	1	1	...
	35.—Fishermen, Boatmen, Palki-bearers, Cooks, etc.	Bóyi	Do.	1	1	...
	36.—Distillers and Toddy-drawers.	Tiyyan	Do.	2	1	1
		Total, Class D.		29	19	10
E.—VAGRANTS, MINOR ARTISANS AND PERFORMERS, etc.	41. Earth workers, etc.	Odde	Hindu	1	1	...
	45(a).—Beggars, etc.	Jógi	Do.	1	1	...
		Total, Class E.		2	2	...

* Is also insane.

TABLE XIII(a).—Deaf-mutes by Caste—*contd.*

Class.	Group.	Caste.	Religion.	Total.	Males.	Females.
F.—RACES AND NATIONALITIES.	48.—Non-Indian Asiatic Races	Pathán	Musalman	1	1	...
		Sheik	Do.	2	2	...
		Total, Group F.—48		3	3	...
	52.—Christian Converts	Native Christian	Christian	2	1	1
		Total, Class F.		5	4	1
G.—INDEFINITE AND UNKNOWN.	54.—Territorial, Linguistic and Sectarian names	Lingáyat	Hindu	3	1	2
		Musalman	Musalman	1	1	...
		Pànchàchára	Hindu	2	1	1
		Saiva	Do.	1	1	...
		Virasaiva	Do.	3	1	2
		Total, Class G.		10	5	5
Not stated.	Not stated.	Caste—Not returned	Hindu	1	...	1
		GRAND TOTAL		126	77	49

TABLE XIV (a).—The Blind by Caste.

Class.	Group.	Caste.	Religion.	Total.	Males.	Females.
A.—AGRICULTURAL	1.—Military and Dominant.	Áré	Hindu	1	1	...
		Kodagu	Do.	13	6	7
		Maráthi	Do.	3	2	1
		Total, Group A—1		17	9	8
	2(a).—Cultivators.	Gauda	Hindu	8	3	5
		Vakkaliga	Do.	6	3	3
		Total, Group A—2(a)		14	6	8
	2(c).—Field Labourers.	Adiyán	Hindu	1	...	1
		Holeya	Do.	14	8	6
		Total, Group A—2(c)		15	8	7
	4.—Forest and Hill Tribes.	Yerava	Hindu	12	9	3
		Total, Class A		58	32	26
B.—PROFESSIONAL	5.—Priests.	Bráhman Shivalli	Hindu	2	...	2
	10.—Astrologers.	Kaniya	Do.	1	1*	...
		Total, Class B		3	1	2
C.—COMMERCIAL.	14.—Traders.	Máppilla	Musalman	3	3	...
		Total, Class C		3	3	...
D.—ARTISAN AND VILLAGE MENIAL.	23.—Weavers, Calenderers and Dyers	Dévánga	Hindu	2	1	1
	24.—Washermen.	Agasa	Do.	1	1	...
	26.—Shepherds	Golla	Do.	1	1	...
		Kuruba	Do.	3	2	1
		Total, Group D—26		4	3	1
	27.—Oil-pressers.	Gániga	Hindu	1	1	...
	36.—Distillers and toddy-drawers.	Tiyyan	Do.	1	...	1
		Total, Class D		9	6	3
F.—RACES AND NATIONALITIES.	48.—Non-Indian Asiatic Races.	Sheik	Musalman	4	2	2
	52.—Christian converts	Native Christian	Christian	1	...	1
		Total, Class F		5	2	3
G.—INDEFINITE AND UNKNOWN.	54.—Territorial, Linguistic and Sectarian names.	Musalman	Musalman	1	...	1
		Pancháchára	Hindu	1	...	1
		Vírasaiva	Do.	6	3	3
		Total, Class G		8	3	5
		GRAND TOTAL	......	86	47	39

* is also insane.

TABLE XV (a).—Lepers by Caste.

Class.	Group.	Caste.	Religion.	TOTAL.	Males.	Females.
A.—AGRICULTURAL.	1.—MILITARY AND DOMINANT.	Kodagu	Hindu	2	1	1
	2(a).—CULTIVATORS.	Vakkaliga	Do.	2	...	2
	2(c).—FIELD LABOURERS.	Holeya	Do.	1	1	...
		Pále	Do.	1	1	...
		Total, Group A—2(c).		2	2	...
	4.—FOREST AND HILL TRIBES.	Yerava	Hindu	8	4	4
		Total, Class A.		14	7	7
D.—ARTISAN AND VILLAGE MENIAL.	26.—SHEPHERDS.	Golla	Hindu	1	1	...
		Kuruba	Do.	1	1	...
		Total, Group D—26.		2	2	...
	36.—DISTILLERS AND TODDY-DRAWERS.	Tiyyan	Hindu	1	1	...
		Total, Class D.		3	3	...
E.—VAGRANTS, MINOR ARTISANS AND PERFORMERS, ETC.	43.—MAT-MAKERS, CANE-SPLITTERS, ETC.	Korama	Hindu	1	1	...
		Total, Class E.		1	1	...
F.—RACES AND NATIONALITIES.	52.—CHRISTIAN CONVERTS.	Native Christian	Christian	1	...	1
		Total, Class F.		1	...	1
G.—INDEFINITE AND UNKNOWN.	54.—TERRITORIAL, LINGUISTIC AND SECTARIAN NAMES.	Lingáyat	Hindu	1	...	1
		Pancháchára	Do.	1	...	1
		Sunni	Musalman	1	1	...
		Telugu	Hindu	1	...	1
		Total, Class G.		4	1	3
		GRAND TOTAL		23	12	11

TABLE XVI.—Castes, Tribes and Races.

Classified according to Traditional Occupation or Nationality.

Class.	Group.	Caste, Tribe or Race.	No. of Sub-divisions.	Religion.	Total.	Males.	Females.
A.—AGRICULTURAL.	1.—Military and Dominant.	Agamudaiyan	...	Hindu	8	6	2
		Arasu	4	Do.	30	17	13
		Áré	6	Do.	74	54	20
		Kallan	...	Do.	1	...	1
		Kápála	...	Do.	150	71	79
		Kodagu	8	Do.	32,611	16,527	16,084
		Kshatriya	14	Do.	219	127	92
				Jain	4	2	2
		Maráthi	47	Hindu	2,384	1,388	996
		Náyar	28	Do.	1,097	953	144
		Pindári	1	Musalman	53	31	22
		Ráchevár	...	Hindu	29	13	16
		Rájpinde	...	Do.	3	1	2
		Rájput	13	Do.	337	188	149
		Rávuta	1	Do.	1	1	...
		Sérvégára	6	Do.	101	70	31
		Tírtha Kshatriya	2	Jain	48	21	27
		Total, Group A—1	...	...	37,150	19,470	17,680
	2(a).—Cultivators	Aruchi	...	Hindu	1	...	1
		Ayyambokkalu	...	Do.	4	2	2
		Badaga	...	Do.	1	1	...
		Bálólikára	1	Do.	9	7	2
		Banta	15	Do.	1,117	784	333
		Binepatta	...	Do.	101	55	46
		Gauda	12	Do.	13,323	7,001	6,322
				Christian	2	1	1
		Hallikára	...	Hindu	2	2	...
		Jain	4	Jain	62	32	30
		Kárgóli	...	Hindu	7	3	4
		Kávudi	...	Do.	37	22	15
		Kóvinajáti	...	Do.	8	2	6
		Kunchiga	...	Do.	24	14	10
		Púluvan	...	Do.	4	1	3
		Rájapuri	1	Do.	53	26	27
		Reddi	3	Do.	61	33	28
		Súdra	4	Do.	31	18	13
		Vádári	...	Do.	27	12	15
		Vakkaliga	40	Do.	12,421	7,131	5,290
				Christian	4	2	2
		Vellála	30	Hindu	1,230	655	575
				Christian	9	4	5
		Total, Group A—2(a).	...	...	28,538	15,808	12,730
	2(b).—Cattle-breeders, Graziers, etc.	Gandhári	...	Hindu	3	3	...
		Gauliga	2	Do.	179	94	85
		Total, Group A—2(b).	...	...	182	97	85
	2(c.)—Field Labourers.	Adiyán	2	Hindu	537	303	234
		Agnáni	...	Do.	30	16	14
				Christian	4	2	2
		Ajala	1	Hindu		1	...
		Ánekula	1	Do.	9	4	5
		Bákuda	1	Do.	6	5	1
		Bhaira	2	Do.	58	40	18
		Holeya	43	Do.	24,081	13,724	10,357
				Christian	4	2	2
		Káládi	...	Hindu	5	2	3
		Máyava	...	Do.	1	1	...
		Máyila	6	Do.	130	91	39
		Méra	...	Do.	12	4	8
		Pále	26	Do.	4,045	2,693	1,352
		Pallan	2	Do.	68	30	38
		Paniyan	...	Do.	1	1	...
		Paraiyan	3	Do.	74	35	39
				Christian	3	...	3
		Parava	2	Hindu	11	6	5
		Tigala	2	Do.	23	16	7
				Christian	1	...	1
		Total, Group A—2(c).	...	...	29,104	16,976	12,128

TABLE XVI.—Castes, Tribes and Races—*contd.*

Classified according to Traditional Occupation or Nationality.

Class.	Group.	Caste, Tribe or Race.	No. of Sub-divisions.	Religion.	Total.	Males.	Females.
A.—AGRICULTURAL—*contd.*	4.—Forest and Hill Tribes.	Betta	...	Hindu	3	2	1
		Koraga	1	Do.	8	7	1
				Christian	3	1	2
		Kudiya	4	Hindu	642	321	321
		Malasar	...	Do.	16	6	10
		Yerava	6	Do.	14,209	7,376	6,833
		Total, Group A—4	...		14,881	7,713	7,168
		Total, Class A	...		109,855	60,064	49,791
B.—PROFESSIONAL.	5.—Priests	Bráhman, Advaita	...	Hindu	4	1	3
		,, Aitála	...	Do.	2	2	...
		,, Ándhra	...	Do.	13	10	3
		,, Arádhya	...	Do.	2	...	2
		,, Aravattuvakkalu	...	Do.	14	5	9
		,, Áruvélu	...	Do.	11	6	5
		,, Babbúru Kamme	...	Do.	12	8	4
		,, Badaganádu	...	Do.	75	37	38
		,, Bettadapurada Sankéti	...	Do.	1	1	...
		,, Brahacharanam	...	Do.	1	1	...
		,, Bráhman	...	Do.	47	30	17
		,, Chittapávana	...	Do.	1	1	...
		,, Chólamandala	...	Do.	4	3	1
		,, Désasta	...	Do.	63	31	32
		,, Drávida	...	Do.	14	11	3
		,, Gauda	...	Do.	33	16	17
		,, Golkonda	...	Do.	1	1	...
		,, Hale Kannadiga	...	Do.	6	2	4
		,, Hale Karnátaka	...	Do.	6	5	1
		,, Havig	...	Do.	600	319	281
		,, Hebbára	...	Do.	7	4	3
		,, Hemmige	...	Do.	2	1	1
		,, Hoisala Karnátaka	...	Do.	115	63	52
		,, Hosanádu Karnataka	...	Do.	6	3	3
		,, Kamme	...	Do.	19	13	6
		,, Kanauj	...	Do.	8	4	4
		,, Kandavara	...	Do.	1	1	...
		,, Kannada	...	Do.	4	3	1
		,, Karnátaka	...	Do.	158	94	64
		,, Kóna símaí Drávida	...	Do.	7	4	3
		,, Konkanasta	...	Do.	32	16	16
		,, Kóta	...	Do.	21	11	10
		,, Kudlukára	...	Do.	2	2	...
		,, Mádhva	...	Do.	1	1	...
		,, Maharáshtra	...	Do.	1	1	...
		,, Malanádu Kamme	...	Do.	5	3	2
		,, Malanádu Karnátaka	...	Do.	3	3	...
		,, Márvádi	...	Do.	1	1	...
		,, Pralákaiyanavamsa	...	Do.	4	1	3
		,, Rámánujamatam	...	Do.	1	1	...
		,, Sankéti	...	Do.	67	42	25
		,, Sárašvata	...	Do.	96	55	41
		,, Shivalli	...	Do.	567	302	265
		,, Smárta	...	Do.	107	51	56
		,, Smárta Karnátaka	...	Do.	53	22	31
		,, Srívaishnava	...	Do.	106	61	45
		,, Tengalaí	...	Do.	5	3	2
		,, Tulu	...	Do.	20	9	11
		,, Ulucha Kamme	...	Do.	1	1	...
		,, Uttaráji	...	Do.	4	2	2
		,, Vadagalai	...	Do.	160	73	87
		,, Vadama	...	Do.	18	9	9
		,, Vaidíki	...	Do	6	4	2
		,, Vaishnava	...	Do.	19	10	9
		,, Vélanádu Ándhra	...	Do.	4	3	1
		Total, Bráhmans	55		2,541	1,367	1,174
		Jangam	...	Hindu	981	495	486
		Pandáram	...	Do.	6	4	2
		Total, Group B—5	...		3,528	1,866	1,662

XVI.—Castes, Tribes and Races—*contd.*

Classified according to Traditional Occupation or Nationality.

Class.	Group.	Caste, Tribe or Race.	No. of Sub-divisions.	Religion.	Total.	Males.	Females.
B.—PROFESSIONAL—contd.	6.—Devotees	Gósáyi	1	Hindu	7	4	3
		Sanyási	...	Do.	2	2	...
		Total, Group B—6	...		9	6	3
	7.—Temple—Servants.	Ambalavási	1	Hindu	5	5	...
		Dévadiga	...	Do.	3	1	2
		Moyili	...	Do.	8	8	...
		Mukkáti	2	Do.	23	12	11
		Padárti	2	Do.	205	109	96
		Sátáni	3	Do.	57	30	27
		Siva Bráhman	...	Do.	7	3	4
		Sivadvija	1	Do.	21	14	7
		Stalada Bráhman	1	Do.	177	77	100
		Staladavartaka Bráhman	1	Do.	11	6	5
		Stánika	8	Do.	140	73	67
		Total, Group B—7	...		657	338	319
	10.—Astrologs etc.	Kaniya	1	Hindu	206	124	82
		Panika	1	Do.	157	80	77
		Total, Group B—10	...		363	204	159
	11.—Musicians, etc.	Batta	2	Hindu	18	12	6
		Sappaliga	1	Do.	2	2	...
		Total, Group B—11	...		20	14	6
	12.—Dancers and Singers.	Basavi	...	Hindu	17	9	8
		Total, Group B—12	...		17	9	8
		Total, Class B	...		4,594	2,437	2,157
C.—COMMERCIAL.	14.—Traders	Agravála	...	Hindu	2	2	...
		Banajiga	23	Do.	1,549	830	719
		Baniya	...	Do.	22	14	8
		Chetti	5	Do.	57	34	23
				Christian	30	15	15
		Désiyatvani	...	Hindu	9	9	...
		Kavarai	6	Do.	32	15	17
		Kómati	...	Do.	17	11	6
		Labbai	2	Musalman	513	415	98
		Ládar	1	Hindu	7	3	4
		Máppilla	4	Musalman	5,170	3,466	1,704
		Méman	1	Do.	42	40	2
		Naváyat	2	Do.	325	265	60
		Vaisya	4	Hindu	253	136	117
		Total, Group C—14	...		8,028	5,255	2,773
	16.—Carriers	Lambádi	2	Hindu	156	114	42
		Total, Group C—16	...		156	114	42
		Total, Class C	...		8,184	5,369	2,815
D.—ARTISAN AND VILLAGE MENIAL.	17.—Goldsmiths	Akkasále	28	Hindu	1,191	685	506
				Christian	5	3	2
		Chinnavára	...	Hindu	2	2	...
		Sonégára	1	Do.	63	51	12
		Súrya Bráhman	1	Do.	3	3	...
		Tattán	1	Do.	5	5	...
		Total, Group D—17	...		1,269	749	520

TABLE XVI.—Castes, Tribes and Races—*contd.*

Classified according to Traditional Occupation or Nationality.

Class.	Group.	Caste, Tribe or Race.	No. of Sub-divisions.	Religion.	Total.	Males.	Females.
D.—ARTISAN AND VILLAGE MENIAL—*contd.*	17(*a*).—Artisans	Ásári	8	Hindu	160	131	29
		Kuláchári	1	Do.	2	2	...
		Pánchála	11	Do.	725	395	330
		Visvakarma	7	Do.	235	119	116
		Total, Group D—17(*a*)	...		1,122	647	475
	18.—Barbers	Hajám	12	Hindu	886	451	435
		Kshauraka	...	Do.	2	1	1
		Náyinda	1	Do.	54	26	28
		Total, Group D—18	...		942	478	464
	19.—Blacksmiths	Ayaskári	1	Hindu	3	2	1
		Gejjegára	...	Do.	4	3	1
		Kammara	...	Do.	2	...	2
		Kollan	4	Do.	96	65	31
		Total, Group D—19	...		105	70	35
	20.—Carpenters, Masons and Turners.	Áyiri	13	Hindu	1,007	601	406
		Badagi	17	Do.	581	306	275
		Cháródi	1	Do.	4	4	...
		Cheptégára	2	Do.	54	28	26
		Gudigára	...	Do.	2	2	...
		Kallukutti	1	Do.	78	34	44
		Kóláyiri	5	Do.	392	239	153
		Maniyáni	3	Do.	107	92	15
		Muyáyiri	...	Do.	4	4	...
		Pudála	...	Do.	3	3	...
		Total, Group D—20	...		2,232	1,313	919
	21.—Brass and Copper smiths.	Chembukutti	...	Hindu	23	23	...
		Kanchugára	2	Do.	9	7	2
		Total, Group D—21	...		32	30	2
	22.—Tailors	Darji	2	Hindu	58	34	24
		Námdév	1	Do.	27	17	10
		Total, Group D—22	...		85	51	34
	22(*c*).—Flower Sellers.	Huvvadiga	...	Hindu	2	1	1
		Total, Group D—22(*c*)	...		2	1	1
	23.—Weavers, Calenderers and Dyers.	Bilimagga	4	Hindu	1,103	567	536
		Cháliya	3	Do.	129	98	31
		Dévánga	11	Do.	2,361	1,207	1,154
		Jáda	...	Do.	10	7	3
		Kaikólan	1	Do.	2	2	...
		Maggadava	1	Do.	15	11	4
		Pattusále	1	Do.	3	3	...
		Rangári	1	Do.	41	18	23
		Sále	1	Do.	18	10	8
		Togata	...	Do.	1	1	...
		Total, Group D—23	...		3,683	1,924	1,759
	24.—Washermen	Agasa	11	Hindu	1,367	715	652
		Dhôbi	2	Do.	15	7	8
		Madivála	10	Do.	335	187	148
		Total, Group D—24	...		1,717	909	808
	25.—Cotton-Cleaners.	Pinjári	1	Musalman	3	3	...
		Total, Group D—25	...		3	3	...

TABLE XVI.—Castes, Tribes and Races—*contd.*

Classified according to Traditional Occupation or Nationality.

Class.	Group.	Caste, Tribe or Race.	No. of Sub-divisions.	Religion.	Total.	Males.	Females.
D.—ARTISAN AND VILLAGE MENIÁL—*contd.*	26.—SHEPHERDS, ETC.	Golla	17	Hindu	923	475	448
		Heggade	5	Do.	1,307	696	611
		Kavádi	...	Do.	3	2	1
		Kurikalu	...	Do.	1	1	...
		Kuruba	11	Do.	7,621	4,123	3,498
		Total, Group D—26	...		9,855	5,297	4,558
	27.—OIL-PRESSERS	Gániga	11	Hindu	485	290	195
		Vániya	4	Do.	89	85	4
		Total, Group D—27	...		574	375	199
	28.—POTTERS	Koyava	3	Hindu	323	173	150
		Kumbára	11	Do.	908	495	413
		Total, Group D—28	...	...	1,231	668	563
	29.—GLASS WORKERS	Balegára	1	Hindu	8	2	6
		Total, Group D—29	...	...	8	2	6
	30.—SALT WORKERS	Uppara	20	Hindu	339	210	129
		Total, Group D—30	...	...	339	210	129
	35.—FISHERMEN, BOATMEN, PALKI-BEARERS, COOKS, ETC.	Besta	14	Hindu	627	329	298
		Bóyi	9	Do.	958	482	476
		Kabbéra	...	Do.	3	3	...
		Mogér	...	Do.	1	1	...
		Toreya	12	Do.	428	249	179
		Total, Group D—35	...	...	2,017	1,064	953
	35(*a*).—PERSONAL SERVICE.	Mukkári	...	Hindu	8	8	...
		Total, Group D—35(*a*)	...	...	8	8	...
	36.—DISTILLERS AND TODDY-DRAWERS.	Billava	8	Hindu	1,366	998	368
		Biruva	1	Do.	12	10	2
		Dívar	6	Do.	703	377	326
		Halepaik	...	Do.	28	16	12
		Hummaliga	1	Do.	9	9	...
		Ídiga	...	Do.	23	17	6
		Tiyyan	13	Do.	932	814	118
		Total, Group D—36	...	...	3,073	2,241	832
	37.—BUTCHERS	Kasáyi	1	Hindu	8	5	3
		Total, Group D—37	...	...	8	5	3
	38.—LEATHER WORKERS.	Mádiga	5	Hindu	1,549	920	629
		Muc'chi	...	Do.	14	8	6
		Total, Group D—38	...	...	1,563	928	635
		Total, Class D	...	...	29,868	16,973	12,895
E.—VAGRANTS, MINOR ARTISANS AND PERFORMERS, ETC.	41.—EARTH WORKERS.	Odde	7	Hindu	441	260	181
		Total, Group E—41	...	...	441	260	181
	42.—KNIFE GRINDERS.	Sikligára	...	Hindu	1	1	...
		Total, Group E—42	...	...	1	1	...

TABLE XVI.—Castes, Tribes and Races—*contd.*

Classified according to Traditional Occupation or Nationality.

Class.	Group.	Caste, Tribe or Race.	No. of Subdivisions.	Religion.	Total.	Males.	Females.
E.—Vagrants, minor artisans and performers, etc.—*contd.*	43.—Mat-makers, cane-splitters, etc.	Gauriga	6	Hindu	362	*186*	176
		Korama	16	Do.	324	*154*	170
		Méda	3	Do.	261	*134*	127
		Total, Group E—43	...	...	947	474	473
	44.—Hunters, etc.	Bédar	14	Hindu	223	*129*	94
		Total, Group E—44	...	...	223	129	94
	45.—Miscellaneous and disreputable vagrants.	Mále or Maleya	4	Hindu	195	*107*	88
		Súle	...	Do.	1	*1*	...
		Total, Group E—45	...	...	196	108	88
	45(*a*).—Beggars, etc.	Banna	2	Hindu	147	*81*	66
		Dásari	2	Do.	18	*10*	8
		Helava	1	Do.	1	*1*	...
		Jógi	0	Do.	104	*66*	38
		Kutuma	...	Do.	74	*34*	40
		Paradési	...1	Do.	3	*2*	1
		Siddha		Do.	20	*10*	10
		Total, Group E—45(a)	...	...	367	204	163
	46.—Tumblers and Acrobats.	Domba	2	Hindu	29	*17*	12
		Jetti	...	Do.	3	*1*	2
		Total, Group E—46	...	...	32	18	14
		Total, Class E	...	...	2,207	1,194	1,013
F.—Races and Nationalities.	48.—Non-Indian Asiatic Races.	Armenian	1	Christian	20	*9*	11
		Duráni	1	Musalman	8	*6*	2
		Ehóda	...	Christian	1	*1*	...
		Khurési	...	Musalman	7	*2*	5
		Lódi Pathán	...	Do.	3	*2*	1
		Moghal	3	Do.	101	*58*	43
		Pársi	...	Parsi	39	*24*	15
		Pathán	5	Musalman	873	*465*	408
		Saiyad	5	Do.	725	*411*	314
		Sheik	10	Do.	3,373	*1,889*	1,484
		Total, Group F—48	...	...	5,150	2,867	2,283
	50.—Non-Asiatic Races.	Celtic	...	Christian	1	...	1
		English	...	Do.	4	*3*	1
		European	9	Do.	242	*163*	79
		Portuguese	1	Do.	21	*13*	8
		Scotch	1	Do.	2	*1*	1
		Total, Group F—50	...	...	270	180	90
	51.—Eurasians	Eurasian	3	Christian	212	*114*	98
		Total, Group F—51	...	...	212	114	98
	52.—Christian converts.	Native Christian	14	Christian	2,705	*1,460*	1,245
		Total, Group F—52	...	...	2,705	1,460	1,245
		Total, Class F	...	...	8,337	4,621	3,716

TABLE XVI.—Castes, Tribes and Races—*contd.*

Classified according to Traditional Occupation or Nationality.

Class.	Group.	Caste, Tribe or Race.	No. of Sub-divisions.	Religion.	Total.	Males.	Females.
G.—INDEFINITE AND UNKNOWN.	53.—Titular names.	Mudali	...	Hindu	38	19	19
		Náyaka	6	Do.	80	57	23
		Náyudu	2	Do.	12	9	3
		Pillai	...	Do.	14	6	8
		Total, Group G—53	...	...	144	91	53
	54.—Territorial, Linguistic and Sectarian names.	Ándhra	1	Hindu	5	3	2
		Cháptia Sunni	...	Musalman	3	2	1
		Hanafi	3	Do.	89	39	50
		Islám	...	Do.	13	6	7
		Karnátaka	4	Hindu	37	18	19
		Kongá	3	Do.	86	51	35
		Konkani	22	Do.	612	364	248
				Christian	118	73	45
		Kristnamata	...	Hindu	1	1	...
		Lingáyat	36	Do.	3,539	1,785	1,754
		Malayáli	6	Do.	151	143	8
		Multáni	...	Do.	3	3	...
		Musalman	13	Musalman	1,325	770	555
		Panchácháґa	4	Hindu	503	244	259
		Rámánuja	2	Do.	5	2	3
		Saiva	2	Do.	256	115	141
		Sháfi	3	Musalman	15	14	1
		Sunni	2	Do.	14	12	2
		Tamil	2	Hindu	29	14	15
		Telugu	16	Do.	1,160	597	563
		Tuluva	3	Do.	45	31	14
		Turakaru	1	Musalman	5	5	...
		Vaishnava	8	Hindu	124	75	49
		Vírasaiva	23	Do.	1,580	709	871
		Total, Group G—54	...	...	9,718	5,076	4,642
	55.—Unclassified Castes.	Bánava	...	Hindu	1	1	...
		Bandára	...	Do.	8	4	4
		Chaniya	...	Do.	2	1	1
		Chauriya	...	Do.	1	1	...
		Chipira	...	Musalman	1	...	1
		Davala	...	Hindu	1	...	1
		Gópi	...	Do.	2	1	1
		Kurchi	...	Do.	12	10	2
		Low caste	...	Christian	1	1	...
		Mahale	...	Hindu	3	3	...
		Malkara	1	Do.	1	...	1
		Massadi	...	Musalman	4	2	2
		Native	...	Hindu	1	...	1
		Palinga	...	Do.	5	3	2
		Total, Group G—55	...	...	43	27	16
		Total, Class G.	...	...	9,905	5,194	4,711
Not stated.	Not stated	Caste—Not returned	...	Hindu	105	55	50
		GRAND TOTAL	...	...	173,055	95,907	77,148

TABLE XVII—Part A.—Occupations by Age.

Class.	Order.	Sub-order, Group and Occupation.	PROVINCIAL TOTAL. Total. Total.	0—4.	5—14.	15 and over.	Not stated.	Males. Total.	0—4.	5—14.	15 and over.	Not stated.	Females. Total.	0—4.	5—14.	15 and over.	Not stated.
1	2	3	4	5	6	7	8	9	10	11	12	13	14	15	16	17	18
A.—GOVERNMENT.	I.—ADMINISTRATION.	Sub-order 1.—Service of the Imperial and Provincial Governments.															
		1. Officers	172	27	47	97	1	94	10	19	64	1	78	17	28	33	...
		2. Office superintendents and clerical establishments, etc.	726	100	169	447	...	437	52	96	289	...	279	48	73	158	...
		3. Messengers, constables, etc.	1,058	94	128	835	1	709	46	58	604	1	349	48	70	231	...
		Total, Sub-order 1	1,946	221	344	1,379	2	1,240	108	173	957	2	706	113	171	422	...
		Sub-order 2.—Service of Local and Municipal Bodies.															
		4. Clerical establishments	20	3	4	13	...	8	1	1	6	...	12	2	3	7	...
		5. Menials	42	6	8	27	1	22	4	3	15	...	20	2	5	12	1
		Total, Sub-order 2	62	9	12	40	1	30	5	4	21	...	32	4	8	19	1
		Sub-order 3.—Village Service.															
		6. Headmen, when not agriculturists	1,207	151	282	774	...	673	66	138	469	...	534	85	144	305	...
		7. Accountants	18	2	4	12	...	9	2	...	7	...	9	...	4	5	...
		8. Watchmen and other menials	567	65	141	361	...	343	34	74	235	...	224	31	67	126	...
		Total, Sub-order 3	1,792	218	427	1,147	...	1,025	102	212	711	...	767	116	215	436	...
		Total, Order I	**3,800**	**448**	**783**	**2,566**	**3**	**2,295**	**215**	**389**	**1,689**	**2**	**1,505**	**233**	**394**	**877**	**1**
	II.—DEFENCE.	Sub-order 4.—Army.															
		9. Officers	3	...	...	3	...	2	...	...	2	...	1	...	...	1	...
		10. Non-commissioned officers and privates	7	...	1	6	...	5	...	1	4	...	2	...	...	2	...
		Total, Sub-order 4	10	...	1	9	...	7	...	1	6	...	3	...	...	3	...
		Total, Order II	**10**	...	**1**	**9**	...	**7**	...	**1**	**6**	...	**3**	...	...	**3**	...
	III.—FOREIGN AND FEUDATORY STATE SERVICE.	Sub-order 7.—Army and Marine.															
		11. Privates and seamen, etc.	1	...	...	1	...	1	...	...	1	...	...	...	...	...	...
		Total, Sub-order 7	1	...	...	1	...	1	...	...	1	...	...	...	...	...	...
		Total, Order III	**1**	...	...	**1**	...	**1**	...	...	**1**	...	...	...	...	...	...
		Total, Class A	**3,811**	**448**	**784**	**2,576**	**3**	**2,303**	**215**	**390**	**1,696**	**2**	**1,508**	**233**	**394**	**880**	**1**
B.—PASTURE AND AGRICULTURE.	IV.—PROVISION AND CARE OF CATTLE.	Sub-order 8.—Stock breeding and dealing.															
		Group (a).—Horses and horned cattle.															
		12. Horse breeders and dealers	1	...	...	1	...	1	...	...	1	...	...	...	...	...	...
		13. Cattle breeders and dealers	26	...	3	23	...	22	...	2	20	...	4	...	1	3	...
		14. Herdsmen	1,123	53	495	575	...	979	31	447	501	...	144	22	48	74	...
		15. Buffalo breeders and dealers	2	...	...	2	...	2	...	...	2	...	...	...	...	...	...
		Total, Group (a)	*1,152*	*53*	*498*	*601*	...	*1,004*	*31*	*449*	*524*	...	*148*	*22*	*49*	*77*	...
		Group (c).—Small Stock.															
		16. Sheep and goat breeders and dealers	46	1	6	39	...	38	...	3	35	...	8	1	3	4	...
		17. Shepherds	4	...	1	3	...	2	...	1	1	...	2	...	...	2	...
		Total, Group (c)	*50*	*1*	*7*	*42*	...	*40*	...	*4*	*36*	...	*10*	*1*	*3*	*6*	...
		Total, Sub-order 8	1,202	54	505	643	...	1,044	31	453	560	...	158	23	52	83	...
		Sub-order 9.—Subsidiary Services to Stock.															
		Group (a).—Training and doctoring live-stock.															
		18. Farriers and gelders	43	9	10	24	...	24	3	6	15	...	19	6	4	9	...
		19. Horse, bullock and elephant breakers and trainers, etc.	4	2	...	2	...	2	1	...	1	...	2	1	...	1	...
		Total, Group (a)	*47*	*11*	*10*	*26*	...	*26*	*4*	*6*	*16*	...	*21*	*7*	*4*	*10*	...
		Total, Sub-order 9	47	11	10	26	...	26	4	6	16	...	21	7	4	10	...
		Total, Order IV	**1,249**	**65**	**515**	**669**	...	**1,070**	**35**	**459**	**576**	...	**179**	**30**	**56**	**93**	...

TABLE XVII—Part A.—Occupations by Age—*contd.*

Class.	Order.	Sub-order, Group and Occupation.	TOWN. Total. Total.	0—4.	5—14.	15 and over.	Not stated.	Males. Total.	0—4.	5—14.	15 and over.	Not stated.	Females. Total.	0—4.	5—14.	15 and over.	Not stated.
			19	20	21	22	23	24	25	26	27	28	29	30	31	32	33
A.—GOVERNMENT.	I.—ADMINISTRATION.	SUB-ORDER 1.—SERVICE OF THE IMPERIAL AND PROVINCIAL GOVERNMENTS.															
		1. Officers	63	13	16	34	...	40	7	8	25	...	23	6	8	9	...
		2. Office superintendents and clerical establishments, etc.	409	48	111	250	...	245	23	63	159	...	164	25	48	91	...
		3. Messengers, constables, etc.	532	55	79	398	...	318	23	36	259	...	214	32	46	139	...
		TOTAL, SUB-ORDER 1	1,004	116	206	682	...	603	53	107	443	...	401	63	99	239	...
		SUB-ORDER 2.—SERVICE OF LOCAL AND MUNICIPAL BODIES.															
		4. Clerical establishments	14	2	3	9	...	4	...	...	4	...	10	2	3	5	...
		5. Menials	32	4	8	20	...	16	2	3	11	...	16	2	5	9	...
		TOTAL, SUB-ORDER 2	46	6	11	29	...	20	2	3	15	...	26	4	8	14	...
		SUB-ORDER 3.—VILLAGE SERVICE.															
		6. Headmen, when not agriculturists	40	8	9	23	...	21	5	3	13	...	19	3	6	10	...
		7. Accountants	1	...	...	1	...	...	...	...	...	...	1	...	...	1	...
		8. Watchmen and other menials	9	...	3	6	...	5	...	1	4	...	4	...	2	2	...
		TOTAL, SUB-ORDER 3	50	8	12	30	...	26	5	4	17	...	24	3	8	13	...
		Total, Order I	**1,100**	**130**	**229**	**741**	...	**649**	**60**	**114**	**475**	...	**451**	**70**	**115**	**266**	...
	II.—DEFENCE.	SUB-ORDER 4.—ARMY.															
		9. Officers	3	...	...	3	...	2	...	...	2	...	1	...	...	1	...
		10. Non-commissioned officers and privates	1	...	...	1	...	1	...	...	1	...	...	...	...	...	...
		TOTAL, SUB-ORDER 4	4	...	...	4	...	3	...	...	3	...	1	...	...	1	...
		Total, Order II	**4**	...	...	**4**	...	**3**	...	...	**3**	...	**1**	...	...	**1**	...
	III.—FOREIGN AND FEUDATORY STATE SERVICE.	SUB-ORDER 7.—ARMY AND MARINE.															
		11. Privates and seamen, etc.	...	...	...	...	...	...	...	...	...	...	...	...	...	...	...
		TOTAL, SUB-ORDER 7	...	...	...	...	...	...	...	...	...	...	...	...	...	...	...
		Total, Order III	...	...	...	...	...	...	...	...	...	...	...	...	...	...	...
		Total, Class	**1,104**	**130**	**229**	**745**	...	**652**	**60**	**114**	**478**	...	**452**	**70**	**115**	**267**	...
B.—PASTURE AND AGRICULTURE.	IV.—PROVISION AND CARE OF CATTLE.	SUB-ORDER 8.—STOCK BREEDING AND DEALING.															
		Group (a).—Horses and horned cattle.															
		12. Horse breeders and dealers	1	...	...	1	...	1	...	...	1	...	...	...	...	...	...
		13. Cattle breeders and dealers	1	...	...	1	...	1	...	...	1	...	...	...	...	...	...
		14. Herdsmen	33	5	6	22	...	22	4	6	12	...	11	1	...	10	...
		15. Buffalo breeders and dealers	...	...	...	...	...	...	...	...	...	...	...	...	...	...	...
		Total, Group (a)	*35*	*5*	*6*	*24*	...	*24*	*4*	*6*	*14*	...	*11*	*1*	...	*10*	...
		Group (c).—Small Stock.															
		16. Sheep and goat breeders and dealers	15	1	4	10	...	9	...	1	8	...	6	1	3	2	...
		17. Shepherds	3	...	...	3	...	1	...	...	1	...	2	...	...	2	...
		Total, Group (c)	*18*	*1*	*4*	*13*	...	*10*	...	*1*	*9*	...	*8*	*1*	*3*	*4*	...
		TOTAL, SUB-ORDER 8	53	6	10	37	...	34	4	7	23	...	19	2	3	14	...
		SUB-ORDER 9.—SUBSIDIARY SERVICES TO STOCK.															
		Group (a).—Training and doctoring live-stock.															
		18. Farriers and gelders	40	9	10	21	...	21	3	6	12	...	19	6	4	9	...
		19. Horse, bullock and elephant breakers and trainers, etc.	4	2	...	2	...	2	1	...	1	...	2	1	...	1	...
		Total, Group (a)	*44*	*11*	*10*	*23*	...	*23*	*4*	*6*	*13*	...	*21*	*7*	*4*	*10*	...
		TOTAL, SUB-ORDER 9	44	11	10	23	...	23	4	6	13	...	21	7	4	10	...
		Total, Order IV	**97**	**17**	**20**	**60**	...	**57**	**8**	**13**	**36**	...	**40**	**9**	**7**	**24**	...

TABLE XVII—Part A.—Occupations by Age—*contd.*

Class.	Order.	Sub-order, Group and Occupation.	COUNTRY.														
			Total.					Males.					Females.				
			Total.	0—4.	5—14.	15 and over.	Not stated.	Total.	0—4	5—14	15 and over.	Not stated	Total.	0—4	5—14	15 and over.	Not stated.
			34	35	36	37	38	39	40	41	42	43	44	45	46	47	48
A.—GOVERNMENT.	I.—ADMINISTRATION.	**Sub-order 1.—Service of the Imperial and Provincial Governments.**															
		1. Officers	109	14	31	63	1	54	3	11	39	1	55	11	20	24	...
		2. Office superintendents and clerical establishments, etc.	307	52	58	197	...	192	29	33	130	...	115	23	25	67	...
		3. Messengers, constables, etc.	526	39	49	437	1	391	23	22	345	1	135	16	27	92	...
		Total, Sub-order 1	942	105	138	697	2	637	55	66	514	2	305	50	72	183	...
		Sub-order 2.—Service of Local and Municipal Bodies.															
		4. Clerical establishments	6	1	1	4	...	4	1	1	2	...	2	...	...	2	...
		5. Menials	10	2	...	7	1	6	2	...	4	...	4	...	...	3	1
		Total, Sub-order 2	16	3	1	11	1	10	3	1	6	...	6	...	...	5	1
		Sub-order 3.—Village Service.															
		6. Headmen, when not agriculturists	1,167	143	273	751	...	652	61	135	456	...	515	82	138	295	...
		7. Accountants	17	2	4	11	...	9	2	...	7	...	8	...	4	4	...
		8. Watchmen and other menials	558	65	138	355	...	338	34	73	231	...	220	31	65	124	...
		Total, Sub-order 3	1,742	210	415	1,117	...	999	97	208	694	...	743	113	207	423	...
		Total, Order I	**2,700**	**318**	**554**	**1,825**	**3**	**1,646**	**155**	**275**	**1,214**	**2**	**1,054**	**163**	**279**	**611**	**1**
	II.—DEFENCE.	**Sub-order 4.—Army.**															
		9. Officers	...	...	...	...	...	...	...	...	...	...	...	...	...	...	...
		10. Non-commissioned officers and privates	6	...	1	5	...	4	...	1	3	...	2	...	...	2	...
		Total, Sub-order 4	6	...	1	5	...	4	...	1	3	...	2	...	...	2	...
		Total, Order II	**6**	...	**1**	**5**	...	**4**	...	**1**	**3**	...	**2**	...	...	**2**	...
	III.—FOREIGN AND FEUDATORY STATE SERVICE.	**Sub-order 7.—Army and Marine.**															
		11. Privates and seamen, etc.	1	...	...	1	...	1	...	...	1	...	...	...	...	...	...
		Total, Sub-order 7	1	...	...	1	...	1	...	...	1	...	...	...	...	...	...
		Total, Order III	**1**	...	...	**1**	...	**1**	...	...	**1**	...	...	...	...	...	...
		Total, Class A	**2,707**	**318**	**555**	**1,831**	**3**	**1,651**	**155**	**276**	**1,218**	**2**	**1,056**	**163**	**279**	**613**	**1**
B.—PASTURE AND AGRICULTURE.	IV.—PROVISION AND CARE OF CATTLE.	**Sub-order 8.—Stock breeding and dealing.**															
		Group (a).—Horses and horned cattle.															
		12. Horse breeders and dealers	...	...	...	...	...	...	...	...	...	...	...	...	...	...	...
		13. Cattle breeders and dealers	25	...	3	22	...	21	...	2	19	...	4	...	1	3	...
		14. Herdsmen	1,090	48	489	553	...	957	27	441	489	...	133	21	48	64	...
		15. Buffalo breeders and dealers	2	...	...	2	...	2	...	...	2	...	...	...	...	...	...
		Total, Group (a)	*1,117*	*48*	*492*	*577*	...	*980*	*27*	*443*	*510*	...	*137*	*21*	*49*	*67*	...
		Group (c).—Small Stock.															
		16. Sheep and goat breeders and dealers	31	...	2	29	...	29	...	2	27	...	2	...	...	2	...
		17. Shepherds	1	...	1	...	...	1	...	1	...	...	...	...	...	...	...
		Total, Group (c)	*32*	...	*3*	*29*	...	*30*	...	*3*	*27*	...	*2*	...	...	*2*	...
		Total, Sub-order 8	1,149	48	495	606	...	1,010	27	446	537	...	139	21	49	69	...
		Sub-order 9.—Subsidiary Services to stock.															
		Group (a).—Training and doctoring live-stock.															
		18. Farriers and gelders	3	...	...	3	...	3	...	...	3	...	...	...	...	...	...
		19. Horse, bullock and elephant breakers and trainers, etc.	...	...	...	...	...	...	...	...	...	...	...	...	...	...	...
		Total, Group (a)	*3*	...	...	*3*	...	*3*	...	...	*3*	...	...	...	...	...	...
		Total, Sub-order 9	3	...	...	3	...	3	...	...	3	...	...	...	...	...	...
		Total, Order IV	**1,152**	**48**	**495**	**609**	...	**1,013**	**27**	**446**	**540**	...	**139**	**21**	**49**	**69**	...

TABLE XVII—Part A.—Occupations by Age—*contd.*

Class.	Order.	Sub-order, Group and Occupation.	PROVINCIAL TOTAL. Total. Total.	0—4.	5—14.	15 and over.	Not stated.	Males. Total.	0—4.	5—14.	15 and over.	Not stated.	Females. Total.	0—4.	5—14.	15 and over.	Not stated.
1	2	3	4	5	6	7	8	9	10	11	12	13	14	15	16	17	18
B.—PASTURE AND AGRICULTURE—*contd.*	V.—AGRICULTURE.	**Sub-order 10.—Interest in land.**															
		20. Land occupants, not cultivating	2,688	389	777	1,520	2	1,202	218	393	590	1	1,486	171	384	930	1
		21. Land occupants, cultivating	23,124	3,097	5,619	14,401	7	12,556	1,479	2,840	8,233	4	10,568	1,618	2,779	6,168	3
		22. Tenants, not cultivating	112	19	25	68	...	76	13	15	48	...	36	6	10	20	...
		23. Tenants and sharers, cultivating	48,867	8,014	13,653	27,188	12	23,730	3,899	7,002	12,824	5	25,137	4,115	6,651	14,364	7
		Total, Sub-order 10	74,791	11,519	20,074	43,177	21	37,564	5,609	10,250	21,695	10	37,227	5,910	9,824	21,482	11
		Sub-order 11.—Agricultural labourers.															
		24. Farm-servants	21,756	2,708	4,406	14,641	1	12,226	1,333	2,357	8,535	1	9,530	1,375	2,049	6,106	...
		25. Field labourers and crop-watchers	25,313	2,411	4,330	18,566	6	15,455	1,170	2,248	12,031	6	9,858	1,241	2,082	6,535	...
		Total, Sub-order 11	47,069	5,119	8,736	33,207	7	27,681	2,503	4,605	20,566	7	19,388	2,616	4,131	12,641	...
		Sub-order 12.—Growers of special products and trees.															
		26. Tea, coffee and cinchona planters	2,286	258	400	1,628	...	1,451	138	206	1,107	...	835	120	194	521	...
		27. Betel-vine and areca-nut growers	3	...	...	3	...	3	...	...	3	...	...	...	...	...	...
		28. Market gardeners (vegetable growers)	9	1	1	7	...	9	1	1	7	...	...	...	...	...	...
		29. Gardeners, seedsmen, etc.	4	...	1	3	...	4	...	1	3	...	...	...	...	...	...
		30. Forest rangers, guards, peons	433	46	91	296	...	240	22	44	174	...	193	24	47	122	...
		Total, Sub-order 12	2,735	305	493	1,937	...	1,707	161	252	1,294	...	1,028	144	241	643	...
		Sub-order 13.—Agricultural training and supervision.															
		31. Agents, managers, etc., of landed estates (not planters)	2	1	...	1	...	2	1	...	1	...	...	...	...	...	...
		Total, Sub-order 13	2	1	...	1	...	2	1	...	1	...	...	...	...	...	...
		Total, Order V	**124,597**	**16,944**	**29,303**	**78,322**	**28**	**66,954**	**8,274**	**15,107**	**43,556**	**17**	**57,643**	**8,670**	**14,196**	**34,766**	**11**
		Total, Class B	**125,846**	**17,009**	**29,818**	**78,991**	**28**	**68,024**	**8,309**	**15,566**	**44,132**	**17**	**57,822**	**8,700**	**14,252**	**34,859**	**11**
C.—PERSONAL, SERVICES.	VI.—PERSONAL, HOUSEHOLD AND SANITARY SERVICES.	**Sub-order 14.—Personal and domestic services.**															
		32. Barbers	711	90	174	446	1	391	42	87	261	1	320	48	87	185	...
		33. Washermen	1,390	184	283	923	...	694	84	142	468	...	696	100	141	455	...
		34. Water-carriers	54	6	8	40	...	24	1	3	20	...	30	5	5	20	...
		35. Cooks	706	45	94	564	3	373	17	47	308	1	333	28	47	256	2
		36. Indoor servants	813	82	145	586	...	370	46	64	260	...	443	36	81	326	...
		37. Grooms, coachmen and dog boys, etc.	267	19	33	215	...	212	8	24	180	...	55	11	9	35	...
		38. Door-keepers, etc.	35	2	2	31	...	28	...	2	26	...	17	2	...	15	...
		Total, Sub-order 14	3,976	428	739	2,805	4	2,082	198	369	1,513	2	1,894	230	370	1,292	2
		Sub-order 15.—Non-domestic Establishment.															
		39. Hotel, boarding-house, etc., keepers	2	...	...	2	...	1	...	...	1	...	1	...	...	1	...
		40. Club secretaries, managers, stewards, etc.	10	1	2	7	...	3	1	1	1	...	7	...	1	6	...
		Total, Sub-order 15	12	1	2	9	...	4	1	1	2	...	8	...	1	7	...
		Sub-order 16.—Sanitation.															
		41. Sanitary Inspectors, etc., local and municipal	5	2	1	2	...	3	1	1	1	...	2	1	...	1	...
		42. Sweepers and scavengers	146	28	26	92	...	68	14	12	42	...	78	14	14	50	...
		Total, Sub-order 16	151	30	27	94	...	71	15	13	43	...	80	15	14	51	...
		Total, Order VI	**4,139**	**459**	**768**	**2,908**	**4**	**2,157**	**214**	**383**	**1,558**	**2**	**1,982**	**245**	**385**	**1,350**	**2**
		Total, Class C	**4,139**	**459**	**768**	**2,908**	**4**	**2,157**	**214**	**383**	**1,558**	**2**	**1,982**	**245**	**385**	**1,350**	**2**

TABLE XVII—Part A.—Occupations by Age—*contd.*

Class.	Order.	Sub-order, Group and Occupation.	Town. Total. Total.	Total. 0—4.	Total. 5—14.	Total. 15 and over.	Total. Not stated.	Males. Total.	Males. 0—4.	Males. 5—14.	Males. 15 and over.	Males. Not stated.	Females. Total.	Females. 0—4.	Females. 5—14.	Females. 15 and over.	Females. Not stated.
			19	20	21	22	23	24	25	26	27	28	29	30	31	32	33
B.—Pasture and Agriculture—*contd.*	V.—Agriculture.	Sub-order 10.—Interest in land.															
		20. Land occupants, not cultivating	576	76	138	362	...	269	41	69	159	...	307	35	69	203	...
		21. Land occupants, cultivating	280	31	58	190	1	174	19	31	123	1	106	12	27	67	...
		22. Tenants, not cultivating	16	1	2	13	...	11	...	1	10	...	5	1	1	3	...
		23. Tenants and sharers, cultivating	522	53	141	328	...	321	23	91	207	...	201	30	50	121	...
		Total, Sub-order 10	1394	161	339	893	1	775	83	192	499	1	619	78	147	394	...
		Sub-order 11.—Agricutural labourers.															
		24. Farm-servants	306	22	58	226	...	187	7	31	149	...	119	15	27	77	...
		25. Field labourers and crop-watchers	553	56	84	413	...	290	30	42	218	...	263	26	42	195	...
		Total, Sub-order 11	859	78	142	639	...	477	37	73	367	...	382	41	69	272	...
		Sub-order 12.—Growers of special products and trees.															
		26. Tea, coffee and cinchona planters, etc.	806	102	218	486	...	412	51	118	243	...	394	51	100	243	...
		27. Betel-vine and areca-nut growers	...	...	...	...	...	...	...	...	...	...	...	...	...	...	...
		28. Market gardeners (vegetable growers)	3	1	1	1	...	3	1	1	1	...	...	...	...	...	...
		29. Gardeners, seedsmen, etc.	1	...	1	...	...	1	...	1	...	...	...	...	...	...	...
		30. Forest rangers, guards, peons	16	2	6	8	...	9	1	4	4	...	7	1	2	4	...
		Total, Sub-order 12	826	105	226	495	...	425	53	124	248	...	401	52	102	247	...
		Sub-order 13.—Agricultural training and supervision.															
		31. Agents, managers, etc., of landed estates	...	...	...	...	...	...	...	...	...	...	...	...	...	...	...
		Total, Sub-order 13	...	...	...	...	...	...	...	...	...	...	...	...	...	...	...
		Total, Order V	**3,079**	**344**	**707**	**2,027**	**1**	**1,677**	**173**	**389**	**1,114**	**1**	**1,402**	**171**	**318**	**913**	...
		Total, Class B	**3,176**	**361**	**727**	**2,087**	**1**	**1,734**	**181**	**402**	**1,150**	**1**	**1,442**	**180**	**325**	**937**	...
C.—Personal Services.	VI.—Personal, Household, and Sanitary Services.	Sub-order 14.—Personal and domestic services.															
		32. Barbers	136	17	31	87	1	70	9	17	43	1	66	8	14	44	...
		33. Washermen	170	25	36	109	...	73	10	12	51	...	97	15	24	58	...
		34. Water-carriers	33	5	5	23	...	12	1	2	9	...	21	4	3	14	...
		35. Cooks	208	15	41	152	...	144	7	24	113	...	64	8	17	39	...
		36. Indoor servants	239	38	42	159	...	113	18	17	78	...	126	20	25	81	...
		37. Grooms, coachmen and dog-boys, etc.	116	15	18	83	...	84	6	14	64	...	32	9	4	19	...
		38. Door-keepers	19	2	1	16	...	10	...	1	9	...	9	2	...	7	...
		Total, Sub-order 14	921	127	174	619	1	506	51	87	367	1	415	66	87	262	...
		Sub-order 15.—Non-Domestic Establishment.															
		39. Hotel, boarding-house, etc., keepers.	1	...	...	1	...	...	...	...	...	...	1	...	...	1	...
		40. Club secretaries, managers, stewards, etc.	10	1	2	7	...	3	1	1	1	...	7	...	1	6	...
		Total, Sub-order 15	11	1	2	8	...	3	1	1	1	...	8	...	1	7	...
		Sub-Order 16.—Sanitation.															
		41. Sanitary inspectors, etc., local and municipal.	5	2	1	2	...	3	1	1	1	...	2	1	...	1	...
		42. Sweepers and scavengers	105	23	21	61	...	54	12	11	31	...	51	11	10	30	...
		Total, Sub-order 16	110	25	22	63	...	57	13	12	32	...	53	12	10	31	...
		Total, Order VI	**1,042**	**148**	**198**	**700**	**1**	**566**	**65**	**100**	**400**	**1**	**476**	**78**	**98**	**300**	...
		Total, Class C	**1,042**	**148**	**198**	**700**	**1**	**566**	**65**	**100**	**400**	**1**	**476**	**78**	**98**	**300**	...

TABLE XVII—Part A.—Occupations by Age—*contd.*

Class.	Order.	Sub-order, Group and Occupation.	COUNTRY. Total. Total.	0—4.	5—14.	15 and over.	Not stated.	Males. Total.	0—4.	5—14.	15 and over.	Not stated.	Females. Total.	0—4.	5—14.	15 and over.	Not stated.
			34	35	36	37	38	39	40	41	42	43	44	45	46	47	48
B.—Pasture and Agriculture—*contd.*	V.—Agriculture.	Sub-order 10.—Interest in land.															
		20. Land occupants, not cultivating	2,112	313	639	1,158	2	933	177	324	431	1	1,179	136	315	727	1
		21. Land occupants, cultivating	22,844	3,066	5,561	14,211	6	12,382	1,460	2,809	8,110	3	10,462	1,606	2,752	6,101	3
		22. Tenants, not cultivating	96	18	23	55	...	65	13	14	38	...	31	5	9	17	...
		23. Tenants and sharers, cultivating	48,345	7,961	13,512	26,860	12	23,409	3,876	6,911	12,617	5	24,936	4,085	6,601	14,243	7
		Total, Sub-order 10	73,397	11,358	19,735	42,284	20	36,789	5,526	10,058	21,196	9	36,608	5,832	9,677	21,088	11
		Sub-order 11.—Agricultural labourers.															
		24. Farm-servants	21,450	2,686	4,348	14,415	1	12,039	1,326	2,326	8,386	1	9,411	1,360	2,022	6,029	...
		25. Field labourers and crop-watchers	24,760	2,355	4,246	18,153	6	15,165	1,140	2,206	11,813	6	9,595	1,215	2,040	6,340	...
		Total, Sub-order 11	46,210	5,041	8,594	32,568	7	27,204	2,466	4,532	20,199	7	19,006	2,575	4,062	12,369	...
		Sub-order 12.—Growers of special products and trees.															
		26. Tea, coffee and cinchona planters, etc.	1,480	156	182	1,142	...	1,039	87	88	864	...	441	69	94	278	...
		27. Betel-vine and areca-nut growers	3	...	...	3	...	3	...	...	3	...	...	...	...	...	...
		28. Market gardeners (vegetable growers)	6	...	...	6	...	6	...	...	6	...	...	...	...	...	...
		29. Gardeners, seedsmen, etc.	3	...	...	3	...	3	...	...	3	...	...	...	...	...	...
		30. Forest rangers, guards, peons	417	44	85	288	...	231	21	40	170	...	186	23	45	118	...
		Total, Sub-order 12	1,909	200	267	1,442	...	1,282	108	128	1,046	...	627	92	139	396	...
		Sub-order 13.—Agricultural training and supervision.															
		31. Agents, managers, etc., of landed estates	2	1	...	1	...	2	1	...	1	...	...	...	...	...	...
		Total, Sub-order 13	2	1	...	1	...	2	1	...	1	...	...	...	...	...	...
		Total, Order V	**121,518**	**16,600**	**28,596**	**76,295**	**27**	**65,277**	**8,101**	**14,718**	**42,442**	**16**	**56,241**	**8,499**	**13,878**	**33,853**	**11**
		Total, Class B	**122,670**	**16,648**	**29,091**	**76,904**	**27**	**66,290**	**8,128**	**15,164**	**42,982**	**16**	**56,380**	**8,520**	**13,927**	**33,922**	**11**
C.—Personal Services.	VI.—Personal, Household and Sanitary Services.	Sub-order 14.—Personal and domestic services.															
		32. Barbers	475	73	143	359	...	221	33	70	118	...	254	40	73	141	...
		33. Washermen	1,220	159	247	814	...	621	74	130	417	...	599	85	117	397	...
		34. Water-carriers	21	1	3	17	...	12	...	1	11	...	9	1	2	6	...
		35. Cooks	498	30	53	412	3	229	10	23	195	1	269	20	30	217	2
		36. Indoor servants	574	44	103	427	...	257	28	47	182	...	317	16	56	245	...
		37. Grooms, coachmen and dog-boys, etc.	151	4	15	132	...	128	2	10	116	...	23	2	5	16	...
		38. Door-keepers	16	...	1	15	...	8	...	1	7	...	8	...	...	8	...
		Total, Sub-order 14	3,055	311	565	2,176	3	1,576	147	282	1,146	1	1,479	164	283	1,030	2
		Sub-order 15.—Non-domestic Establishment.															
		39. Hotel, boarding-house, etc., keepers	1	...	...	1	...	1	...	...	1	...	...	...	...	...	...
		40. Club secretaries, managers, stewards, etc.	...	...	...	...	...	...	...	...	...	...	...	...	...	...	...
		Total, Sub-order 15	1	...	...	1	...	1	...	...	1	...	...	...	...	...	...
		Sub-order 16.—Sanitation.															
		41. Sanitary inspectors, etc., local and municipal	...	...	...	...	...	...	...	...	...	...	...	...	...	...	...
		42. Sweepers and scavengers	41	5	5	31	...	14	2	1	11	...	27	3	4	20	...
		Total, Sub-order 16	41	5	5	31	...	14	2	1	11	...	27	3	4	20	...
		Total, Order VI	**3,097**	**316**	**570**	**12,208**	**3**	**1,591**	**149**	**283**	**1,158**	**1**	**1,506**	**167**	**287**	**1,050**	**2**
		Total, Class C	**3,097**	**316**	**570**	**2,208**	**3**	**1,591**	**149**	**283**	**1,158**	**1**	**1,506**	**167**	**287**	**1,050**	**2**

TABLE XVII—Part A.—Occupations by Age—*contd.*

Class.	Order.	Sub-order, Group and Occupation.	PROVINCIAL TOTAL.														
			Total.					Males.					Females.				
			Total.	0—4.	5—14.	15 and over.	Not stated.	Total.	0—4.	5—14.	15 and over.	Not stated.	Total.	0—4.	5—14.	15 and over.	Not stated.
1	2	3	4	5	6	7	8	9	10	11	12	13	14	15	16	17	18
D.—Preparation and supply of material substances.	VII.—Food and drink.	**Sub-order 17.—Animal food.**															
		43. Cow and buffalo keepers and milk, etc., sellers	274	26	60	188	...	125	15	29	81	...	149	11	31	107	...
		44. Cheese makers and sellers	9	1	1	7	...	5	1	1	3	...	4	...	...	4	...
		45. Butchers	193	22	31	140	...	103	8	22	73	...	90	14	9	67	...
		46. Fowl and egg dealers	4	...	...	4	...	4	...	...	4	...	...	...	...	...	...
		47. Fishermen and fish curers	74	11	13	50	...	52	6	12	34	...	22	5	1	16	...
		48. Fish dealers	443	45	52	346	...	310	20	27	263	...	133	25	25	83	...
		Total, Sub-order 17	997	105	157	735	...	599	50	91	458	...	398	55	66	277	...
		Sub-order 18.—Vegetable food.															
		49. Grain dealers	2,274	262	457	1,555	...	1,208	111	219	878	...	1,066	151	238	677	...
		50. Grain parchers	29	3	9	17	...	14	1	6	7	...	15	2	3	10	...
		51. Pulse and flour preparers and sellers	20	3	3	14	...	8	3	1	4	...	12	...	2	10	...
		52. Bakers	37	4	8	25	...	18	2	4	12	...	19	2	4	13	...
		53. Vegetable sellers	127	12	24	91	...	50	5	13	32	...	77	7	11	59	...
		54. Fruit sellers	86	10	20	56	...	51	4	12	35	...	35	6	8	21	...
		55. Cocoanut dealers	87	3	16	68	...	64	2	12	50	...	23	1	4	18	...
		56. Confectioners and sweetmeat makers and sellers	426	47	86	293	...	219	25	43	151	...	207	22	43	142	...
		57. Sweetmeat pedlars	258	19	49	190	...	71	4	21	46	...	187	15	28	144	...
		Total, Sub-order 18	3,344	363	672	2,309	...	1,703	157	331	1,215	...	1,641	206	341	1,094	...
		Sub-order 19.—Drink, condiments and narcotics.															
		58. Sharbat preparers and sellers	11	1	...	10	...	8	1	...	7	...	3	...	...	3	...
		59. Country spirits distillers and sellers	237	31	52	154	...	132	15	31	86	...	105	16	21	68	...
		60. Toddy drawers and sellers	1,646	192	252	1,202	...	1,092	95	128	869	...	554	97	124	333	...
		61. Foreign wine and spirit dealers	45	10	16	19	...	20	4	10	6	...	25	6	6	13	...
		62. Tea sellers and tasters	5	1	1	3	...	3	...	1	2	...	2	1	...	1	...
		63. Coffee preparers and sellers (not planters)	772	78	185	509	...	495	39	105	351	...	277	39	80	158	...
		64. Molasses makers and sellers	31	1	8	22	...	14	1	4	9	...	17	...	4	13	...
		65. Salt preparers and sellers	84	7	16	61	...	53	4	11	38	...	31	3	5	23	...
		66. Grocers and general condiment dealers	1,305	154	234	916	1	747	88	141	517	1	558	66	93	399	...
		67. Cardamom preparers and dealers	1	...	...	1	...	1	...	...	1	...	...	...	...	...	...
		68. Betel-leaf and areca-nut sellers	870	90	161	619	...	457	37	81	339	...	413	53	80	280	...
		69. Tobacco and snuff manufacturers and sellers	376	42	71	263	...	206	23	37	147	...	170	20	34	116	...
		70. Opium, etc., manufacturers and sellers	1	...	...	1	...	1	...	...	1	...	...	...	...	...	...
		71. Bhang, ganja, etc., preparers and sellers	8	2	...	6	...	2	...	...	2	...	6	2	...	4	...
		Total, Sub-order 19	5,392	609	996	3,786	1	3,231	306	549	2,375	1	2,161	303	447	1,411	...
		Total, Order VII	**9,733**	**1,077**	**1,825**	**6,830**	**1**	**5,533**	**513**	**971**	**4,048**	**1**	**4,200**	**564**	**854**	**2,782**	...
	VIII.—Light, firing and forage.	**Sub-order 20.—Lighting.**															
		72. Oil pressers and sellers	386	38	71	277	...	215	18	34	163	...	171	20	37	114	...
		73. Oil-cake dealers	1	...	...	1	...	1	...	...	1	...	...	...	...	...	...
		74. Kerosine oil dealers	1	...	...	1	...	1	...	...	1	...	...	...	...	...	...
		Total, Sub-order 20	388	38	71	279	...	217	18	34	165	...	171	20	37	114	...
		Sub-order 21.—Fuel and forage.															
		75. Firewood and grass gatherers and sellers	106	14	13	79	...	48	7	5	36	...	58	7	8	43	...
		76. Firewood contractors and dealers	12	1	3	8	...	5	1	1	3	...	7	...	2	5	...
		77. Coal dealers	1	...	...	1	...	1	...	...	1	...	...	...	...	...	...
		78. Cowdung-fuel preparers and sellers	3	1	...	2	...	...	...	...	...	...	3	1	...	2	...
		79. Hay, etc., contractors and dealers	4	1	...	3	...	2	...	...	2	...	2	1	...	1	...
		Total, Sub-order 21	126	17	16	93	...	56	8	6	42	...	70	9	10	51	...
		Total, Order VIII	**514**	**55**	**87**	**372**	...	**273**	**26**	**40**	**207**	...	**241**	**29**	**47**	**165**	...
	IX.—Buildings.	**Sub-order 22.—Building materials.**															
		80. Brick and tile burners and sellers	44	1	5	38	...	36	...	3	33	...	8	1	2	5	...
		81. Lime, chunam and shell burners and sellers	100	12	20	68	...	43	5	5	33	...	57	7	15	35	...
		82. Stone-quarry owners, contractors, etc.	4	...	...	4	...	4	...	...	4	...	...	...	...	...	...
		Total, Sub-order 22	148	13	25	110	...	83	5	8	70	...	65	8	17	40	...
		Sub-order 23.—Artificers in building.															
		83. Stone and marble workers	119	5	11	103	...	93	...	2	91	...	26	5	9	12	...
		84. Masons	43	12	8	23	...	24	7	5	12	...	19	5	3	11	...
		85. Builders and joiners	3	...	...	3	...	3	...	...	3	...	...	...	...	...	...
		86. Plasterers and house painters	180	20	21	139	...	104	6	10	88	...	76	14	11	51	...
		87. Mud wall and roof builders	170	...	5	165	...	163	...	3	160	...	7	...	2	5	...
		Total, Sub-order 23	515	37	45	433	...	387	13	20	354	...	128	24	25	79	...
		Total, Order IX	**663**	**50**	**70**	**543**	...	**470**	**18**	**28**	**424**	...	**193**	**32**	**42**	**119**	...

TABLE XVII—Part A.—Occupations by Age—*contd.*

Class.	Order.	Sub-order, Group and Occupation.	TOWN. Total. Total.	0—4.	5—14.	15 and over.	Not stated.	Males. Total.	0—4.	5—14.	15 and over.	Not stated.	Females. Total.	0—4.	5—14.	15 and over.	Not stated.
			19	20	21	22	23	24	25	26	27	28	29	30	31	32	33
D.—Preparation and supply of material substances.	VII.—Food and drink.	**Sub-order 17.—Animal food.**															
		43. Cow and buffalo keepers and milk, etc., sellers	266	19	35	212	...	75	12	15	48	...	91	7	20	64	...
		44. Cheese makers and sellers	9	1	1	7	...	5	1	1	3	...	4	...	...	4	...
		45. Butchers	106	16	20	70	...	53	4	14	35	...	53	12	6	35	...
		46. Fowl and egg dealers	...	...	...	...	...	...	...	...	...	...	...	...	...	...	...
		47. Fishermen and fish curers	...	...	...	...	...	...	...	...	...	...	...	...	...	...	...
		48. Fish dealers	97	6	4	87	...	82	3	3	76	...	15	3	1	11	...
		Total, Sub-order 17	378	42	60	276	...	215	20	33	162	...	163	22	27	114	...
		Sub-order 18.—Vegetable food.															
		49. Grain dealers	1,117	147	251	719	...	542	64	106	372	...	575	83	145	347	...
		50. Grain parchers	6	1	1	4	...	...	...	...	...	...	6	1	1	4	...
		51. Pulse and flour preparers and sellers	18	2	3	13	...	7	2	1	4	...	11	...	2	9	...
		52. Bakers	16	3	2	11	...	6	1	...	5	...	10	2	2	6	...
		53. Vegetable sellers	87	11	21	55	...	34	4	12	18	...	53	7	9	37	...
		54. Fruit sellers	10	2	3	5	...	3	...	1	2	...	7	2	2	3	...
		55. Cocoanut dealers	56	1	10	45	...	45	...	8	37	...	11	1	2	8	...
		56. Confectioners and sweetmeat makers and sellers	163	22	35	106	...	87	16	17	54	...	76	6	18	52	...
		57. Sweetmeat pedlars	94	7	16	71	...	17	2	6	9	...	77	5	10	62	...
		Total, Sub-order 18	1,567	196	342	1,029	...	741	89	151	501	...	826	107	191	528	...
		Sub-order 19.—Drink, condiments and narcotics.															
		58. Sharbat preparers and sellers	3	...	...	3	...	3	...	...	3	...	...	...	...	...	...
		59. Country spirits distillers and sellers	124	20	35	69	...	69	10	22	37	...	55	10	13	32	...
		60. Toddy drawers and sellers	10	...	...	10	...	10	...	...	10	...	...	...	...	...	...
		61. Foreign wine and spirit dealers	41	10	14	17	...	17	4	8	5	...	24	6	6	12	...
		62. Tea sellers and tasters	5	1	1	3	...	3	...	1	2	...	2	1	...	1	...
		63. Coffee preparers and sellers (not planters)	312	38	88	186	...	163	23	36	104	...	149	15	52	82	...
		64. Molasses makers and sellers	25	1	6	18	...	11	1	3	7	...	14	...	3	11	...
		65. Salt preparers and sellers	55	6	10	39	...	31	4	7	20	...	24	2	3	19	...
		66. Grocers and general condiment dealers	497	69	102	326	...	250	35	56	159	...	247	34	46	167	...
		67. Cardamom preparers and dealers	1	...	...	1	...	1	...	...	1	...	...	...	...	...	...
		68. Betel-leaf and areca-nut sellers	352	52	90	210	...	175	23	43	109	...	177	29	47	101	...
		69. Tobacco and snuff manufacturers and sellers	251	29	50	172	...	133	16	25	92	...	118	13	25	80	...
		70. Opium, etc., manufacturers and sellers	1	...	...	1	...	1	...	...	1	...	...	...	...	...	...
		71. Bhang, ganja, etc., preparers and sellers	8	2	...	6	...	2	...	...	2	...	6	2	...	4	...
		Total, Sub-order 19	1,685	228	396	1,061	...	869	116	201	552	...	816	112	195	509	...
		Total, Order VII	**3,630**	**466**	**798**	**2,366**	...	**1,825**	**225**	**385**	**1,215**	...	**1,805**	**241**	**418**	**1,151**	...
	VIII.—Light, firing and forage.	**Sub-order 20.—Lighting.**															
		72. Oil pressers and sellers	175	21	42	112	...	77	10	19	48	...	98	11	23	64	...
		73. Oil-cake dealers	...	...	...	...	...	...	...	...	...	...	...	...	...	...	...
		74. Kerosine oil dealers	...	...	...	...	...	...	...	...	...	...	...	...	...	...	...
		Total, Sub-order 20	175	21	42	112	...	77	10	19	48	...	98	11	23	64	...
		Sub-order 21.—Fuel and Forage.															
		75. Firewood and grass gatherers and sellers	11	2	1	8	...	6	2	1	3	...	5	...	...	5	...
		76. Firewood contractors and dealers	10	1	3	6	...	5	1	1	3	...	5	...	2	3	...
		77. Coal dealers	1	...	...	1	...	1	...	...	1	...	...	...	...	...	...
		78. Cowdung-fuel preparers and sellers	3	1	...	2	...	...	...	...	...	...	3	1	...	2	...
		79. Hay, etc., contractors and dealers	4	1	...	3	...	2	...	...	2	...	2	1	...	1	...
		Total, Sub-order 21	29	5	4	20	...	14	3	2	9	...	15	2	2	11	...
		Total, Order VIII	**204**	**26**	**46**	**132**	...	**91**	**13**	**21**	**57**	...	**113**	**13**	**25**	**75**	...
	IX.—Buildings.	**Sub-order 22.—Building Materials.**															
		80. Brick and tile burners and sellers	5	1	...	4	...	3	...	...	3	...	2	1	...	1	...
		81. Lime, chunam and shell burners and sellers	5	...	1	4	...	2	...	...	2	...	3	...	1	2	...
		82. Stone-quarry owners, contractors, etc.	...	...	...	...	...	...	...	...	...	...	...	...	...	...	...
		Total, Sub-order 22	10	1	1	8	...	5	...	...	5	...	5	1	1	3	...
		Sub-order 23.—Artificers in Building.															
		83. Stone and marble workers	25	...	...	25	...	25	...	...	25	...	...	...	...	...	...
		84. Masons	21	4	5	12	...	15	4	4	7	...	6	...	1	5	...
		85. Builders and joiners	...	...	...	...	...	...	...	...	...	...	...	...	...	...	...
		86. Plasterers and house painters	114	18	13	83	...	62	6	6	50	...	52	12	7	33	...
		87. Mud wall and roof builders	3	...	1	2	...	2	...	...	2	...	1	...	1	...	...
		Total, Sub-order 23	163	22	19	122	...	104	10	10	84	...	59	12	9	38	...
		Total, Order IX	**173**	**23**	**20**	**130**	...	**109**	**10**	**10**	**89**	...	**64**	**13**	**10**	**41**	...

TABLE XVII—Part A—Occupations by Age—*contd.*

Class.	Order.	Sub-order, Group and Occupation.	COUNTRY.														
			Total.					Males.					Females.				
			Total.	0—4.	5—14.	15 and over.	Not stated.	Total.	0—4.	5—14.	15 and over.	Not stated.	Total.	0—4.	5—14.	15 and over.	Not stated.
			34	35	36	37	38	39	40	41	42	43	44	45	46	47	48
D.—PREPARATION AND SUPPLY OF MATERIAL SUBSTANCES.	VII.—FOOD AND DRINK.	**Sub-order 17.—Animal food.**															
		43. Cow and buffalo keepers and milk, etc., sellers	108	7	25	76	...	50	3	14	33	...	58	4	11	43	...
		44. Cheese makers and sellers	...	...	...	...	...	...	...	...	...	...	...	...	...	...	...
		45. Butchers	87	6	11	70	...	50	4	8	38	...	37	2	3	32	...
		46. Fowl and egg dealers	4	...	...	4	...	4	...	...	4	...	...	...	...	...	...
		47. Fishermen and fish curers	74	11	13	50	...	52	6	12	34	...	22	5	1	16	...
		48. Fish dealers	346	39	48	259	...	228	17	24	187	...	118	22	24	72	...
		Total, Sub-order 17	619	63	97	459	...	384	30	58	296	...	235	33	39	163	...
		Sub-order 18.—Vegetable food.															
		49. Grain dealers	1,157	115	205	836	...	666	47	113	506	...	491	68	92	330	...
		50. Grain parchers	23	2	8	13	...	14	1	6	7	...	9	1	2	6	...
		51. Pulse and flour preparers and sellers	2	1	...	1	...	1	1	...	...	...	1	...	...	1	...
		52. Bakers	21	1	6	14	...	12	1	4	7	...	9	...	2	7	...
		53. Vegetable sellers	40	1	3	36	...	16	1	1	14	...	24	...	2	22	...
		54. Fruit sellers	76	8	17	51	...	48	4	11	33	...	28	4	6	18	...
		55. Cocoanut dealers	31	2	6	23	...	19	2	4	13	...	12	...	2	10	...
		56. Confectioners and sweetmeat makers and sellers	263	25	51	187	...	132	9	26	97	...	131	16	25	90	...
		57. Sweetmeat pedlars	164	12	33	119	...	54	2	15	37	...	110	10	18	82	...
		Total, Sub-order 18	1,777	167	330	1,280	...	962	68	180	714	...	815	99	150	566	...
		Sub-order 19.—Drink, condiments and narcotics.															
		58. Sharbat preparers and sellers	8	1	...	7	...	5	1	...	4	...	3	...	...	3	...
		59. Country spirits distillers and sellers	113	11	17	85	...	63	5	9	49	...	50	6	8	36	...
		60. Toddy drawers and sellers	1,636	192	251	1,192	...	1,082	95	128	859	...	554	97	124	333	...
		61. Foreign wine and spirit dealers	4	...	2	2	...	3	...	2	1	...	1	...	...	1	...
		62. Tea sellers and tasters	...	...	...	...	...	...	...	...	...	...	...	...	...	...	...
		63. Coffee preparers and sellers (not planters)	460	40	97	323	...	332	16	69	247	...	128	24	28	76	...
		64. Molasses makers and sellers	6	...	2	4	...	3	...	1	2	...	3	...	1	2	...
		65. Salt preparers and sellers	29	1	6	22	...	22	...	4	18	...	7	1	2	4	...
		66. Grocers and general condiment dealers	808	85	132	590	1	497	53	85	358	1	311	32	47	232	...
		67. Cardamom preparers and dealers	...	...	...	...	...	...	...	...	...	...	...	...	...	...	...
		68. Betel-leaf and areca-nut sellers	518	38	71	409	...	282	14	38	230	...	236	24	33	179	...
		69. Tobacco and snuff manufacturers and sellers	125	13	21	91	...	73	6	12	55	...	52	7	9	36	...
		70. Opium, etc., manufacturers and sellers	...	...	...	...	...	...	...	...	...	...	...	...	...	...	...
		71. Bhang, ganja, etc., preparers and sellers	...	...	...	...	...	...	...	...	...	...	...	...	...	...	...
		Total, Sub-order 19	3,707	381	600	2,725	1	2,362	190	348	1,823	1	1,345	191	252	902	...
		Total, Order VII	**6,103**	**611**	**1,027**	**4,464**	**1**	**3,708**	**288**	**586**	**2,833**	**1**	**2,395**	**323**	**441**	**1,631**	...
	VIII.—LIGHT, FIRING AND FORAGE.	**Sub-order 20.—Lighting.**															
		72. Oil pressers and sellers	211	17	29	165	...	138	8	15	115	...	73	9	14	50	...
		73. Oil-cake dealers	1	...	...	1	...	1	...	...	1	...	...	...	...	...	...
		74. Kerosine oil dealers	1	...	...	1	...	1	...	...	1	...	...	...	...	...	...
		Total, Sub-order 20	213	17	29	167	...	140	8	15	117	...	73	9	14	50	...
		Sub-order 21.—Fuel and forage.															
		75. Firewood and grass gatherers and sellers	95	12	12	71	...	42	5	4	33	...	53	7	8	38	...
		76. Firewood contractors and dealers	2	...	...	2	...	...	...	...	...	...	2	...	...	2	...
		77. Coal dealers	...	...	...	...	...	...	...	...	...	...	...	...	...	...	...
		78. Cowdung-fuel preparers and sellers	...	...	...	...	...	...	...	...	...	...	...	...	...	...	...
		79. Hay, etc., contractors and dealers	...	...	...	...	...	...	...	...	...	...	...	...	...	...	...
		Total, Sub-order 21	97	12	12	73	...	42	5	4	33	...	55	7	8	40	...
		Total, Order VIII	**310**	**29**	**41**	**240**	...	**182**	**13**	**19**	**150**	...	**128**	**16**	**22**	**90**	...
	IX.—BUILDINGS.	**Sub-order 22.—Building materials.**															
		80. Brick and tile burners and sellers	39	...	5	34	...	33	...	3	30	...	6	...	2	4	...
		81. Lime, chunam and shell burners and sellers	95	12	19	64	...	41	5	5	31	...	54	7	14	33	...
		82. Stone-quarry owners, contractors, etc.	4	...	...	4	...	4	...	...	4	...	...	...	...	...	...
		Total, Sub-order 22	138	12	24	102	...	78	5	8	65	...	60	7	16	37	...
		Sub-order 23.—Artificers in building.															
		83. Stone and marble workers	94	5	11	78	...	68	...	2	66	...	26	5	9	12	...
		84. Masons	22	8	3	11	...	9	3	1	5	...	13	5	2	6	...
		85. Builders and joiners	3	...	...	3	...	3	...	...	3	...	...	...	...	...	...
		86. Plasterers and house painters	66	2	8	56	...	42	...	4	38	...	24	2	4	18	...
		87. Mud wall and roof builders	167	...	4	163	...	161	...	3	158	...	6	...	1	5	...
		Total, Sub-order 23	352	15	26	311	...	283	3	10	270	...	69	12	16	41	...
		Total, Order IX	**490**	**27**	**50**	**413**	...	**361**	**8**	**18**	**335**	...	**129**	**19**	**32**	**78**	...

TABLE XVII—Part A.—Occupations by Age—*contd.*

Class.	Order.	Sub-order, Group and Occupation.	Provincial Total. Total. Total.	0—4.	5—14.	15 and over.	Not stated.	Males. Total.	0—4.	5—14.	15 and over.	Not stated.	Females. Total.	0—4.	5—14.	15 and over.	Not stated.
1	2	3	4	5	6	7	8	9	10	11	12	13	14	15	16	17	18
D.—Preparation and supply of material substances—*contd.*	X.—Vehicles and vessels.	Sub-order 24.—Railway plant.															
		88. Railway permanent-way foremen, platelayers, inspectors, etc.	2	1	...	1	...	1	1	...	...	...	1	...	...	1	...
		Total, Sub-order 24	2	1	...	1	...	1	1	...	...	...	1	...	...	1	...
		Sub-order 25.—Carts, carriages, etc.															
		89. Cart and carriage makers and sellers	28	3	7	18	...	17	2	3	12	...	11	1	4	6	...
		Total, Sub-order 25	28	3	7	18	...	17	2	3	12	...	11	1	4	6	...
		Total, Order X	**30**	**4**	**7**	**19**	...	**18**	**3**	**3**	**12**	...	**12**	**1**	**4**	**7**	...
	XI.—Supplementary requirements.	Sub-order 28.—Books and prints.															
		90. Book-binders	23	1	5	17	...	14	...	3	11	...	9	1	2	6	...
		91. Book-sellers and publishers	4	1	1	2	...	2	1	...	1	...	2	...	1	1	...
		Total, Sub-order 28	27	2	6	19	...	16	1	3	12	...	11	1	3	7	...
		Sub-order 29.—Watches, clocks, etc.															
		92. Watch and clock makers and sellers	2	...	...	2	...	2	...	...	2	...	...	...	...	...	...
		Total, Sub-order 29	2	...	...	2	...	2	...	...	2	...	...	...	...	...	...
		Sub-order 30.—Carving, engraving, etc.															
		93. Wood and ebony carvers	2	...	...	2	...	1	...	...	1	...	1	...	...	1	...
		94. Turners and lacquerers	7	...	...	7	...	5	...	...	5	...	2	...	...	2	...
		Total, Sub-order 30	9	...	...	9	...	6	...	...	6	...	3	...	...	3	...
		Sub-order 32.—Music and musical instruments.															
		95. Music and musical instrument dealers	2	...	...	2	...	2	...	...	2	...	...	...	...	...	...
		Total, Sub-order 32	2	...	...	2	...	2	...	...	2	...	...	...	...	...	...
		Sub-order 33.—Necklaces, bracelets, beads, etc.															
		96. Bangle makers and sellers in glass	198		43	138	...	100	9	26	65	...	98	8	17	73	...
		97. Bangle fitters	4	...	...	4	...	1	...	...	1	...	3	...	...	3	...
		98. Bead makers and sellers	45	7	8	30	...	32	6	5	21	...	13	1	3	9	...
		99. Flower garland makers and sellers	4	1	...	3	...	2	1	...	1	...	2	...	...	2	...
		Total, Sub-order 33	251	25	51	175	...	125	16	31	88	...	126	9	20	87	...
		Sub-order 34.—Furniture.															
		100. Furniture makers	2	...	...	2	...	2	...	...	2	...	...	...	...	...	...
		Total, Sub-order 34	2	...	...	2	...	2	...	...	2	...	...	...	...	...	...
		Sub-order 36.—Tools and machinery.															
		101. Knife and tool makers and sellers	8	2	2	4	...	4	...	1	3	...	4	2	1	1	...
		102. Knife and tool grinders	13	2	2	9	...	5	1	1	3	...	8	1	1	6	...
		103. Mechanics (not Railway)	5	...	1	4	...	3	...	...	3	...	2	...	1	1	...
		104. Machinery dealers, etc.	1	...	...	1	...	1	...	...	1	...	...	...	...	...	...
		Total, Sub-order 36	27	4	5	18	...	13	1	2	10	...	14	3	3	8	...
		Sub-order 37.—Arms and Ammunition.															
		105. Gun-powder makers and sellers	5	...	...	5	...	5	...	...	5	...	...	...	...	...	...
		106. Fire-work makers and sellers	9	3	2	4	...	7	2	2	3	...	2	1	...	1	...
		107. Sword and scabbard makers and sellers	1	...	...	1	...	1	...	...	1	...	...	...	...	...	...
		Total, Sub-order 37	15	3	2	10	...	13	2	2	9	...	2	1	...	1	...
		Total, Order XI	**335**	**34**	**64**	**237**	...	**189**	**20**	**38**	**131**	...	**146**	**14**	**26**	**106**	...

TABLE XVII—Part A.—Occupations by Age—*contd.*

Class.	Order.	Sub-order, Group and Occupation.	TOWN.														
			Total.					Males.					Females.				
			Total.	0—4.	5—14.	15 and over.	Not stated.	Total.	0—4.	5—14.	15 and over.	Not stated.	Total.	0—4.	5—14.	15 and over.	Not stated.
			19	20	21	22	23	24	25	26	27	28	29	30	31	32	33
D.—Preparation and supply of material substances—*continued.*	X.—Vehicles and vessels.	Sub-order 24.—Railway Plant.															
		88. Railway permanent-way foremen, platelayers, inspectors, etc.															
		Total, Sub-order 24															
		Sub-order 25.—Carts, carriages, etc.															
		89. Cart and carriage makers and sellers.	28	3	7	18	...	17	2	3	12	...	11	1	4	6	...
		Total, Sub-order 25	28	3	7	18	...	17	2	3	12	...	11	1	4	6	...
		Total, Order X	**28**	**3**	**7**	**18**	...	**17**	**2**	**3**	**12**	...	**11**	**1**	**4**	**6**	...
	XI.—Supplementary requirements.	Sub-order 28.—Books and prints.															
		90. Book-binders 91. Book-sellers and publishers	22	1	5	16	...	13	...	3	10	...	9	1	2	6	...
		Total, Sub-order 28	22	1	5	16	...	13	...	3	10	...	9	1	2	6	...
		Sub-order 29.—Watches, clocks, etc.															
		92. Watch and clock makers and sellers.															
		Total, Sub-order 29															
		Sub-order 30.—Carving, engraving, etc.															
		93. Wood and ebony carvers	2	...	...	2	...	1	...	...	1	...	1	...	...	1	...
		94. Turners and lacquerers	3	...	...	3	...	1	...	...	1	...	2	...	...	2	...
		Total, Sub-order 30	5	...	...	5	...	2	...	...	2	...	3	...	...	3	...
		Sub-order 32.—Music and musical instruments.															
		95. Music and musical instrument dealers.	2	...	...	2	...	2	...	...	2	...	...	...	...	...	...
		Total, Sub-order 32	2	...	...	2	...	2	...	...	2	...	...	...	...	...	...
		Sub-order 33.—Necklaces, bracelets, beads, etc.															
		96. Bangle makers and sellers in glass	31	3	6	22	...	7	...	...	7	...	24	3	6	15	...
		97. Bangle fitters	...	...	...	...	...	...	...	...	...	...	...	...	...	...	...
		98. Bead makers and sellers	25	5	6	14	...	13	4	3	6	...	12	1	3	8	...
		99. Flower garland makers and sellers.	1	...	...	1	...	...	...	...	...	...	1	...	...	1	...
		Total, Sub-order 33	57	8	12	37	...	20	4	3	13	...	37	4	9	24	...
		Sub-order 34.—Furniture.															
		100. Furniture makers	...	...	...	...	...	...	...	...	...	...	...	...	...	...	...
		Total, Sub-order 34	...	...	...	...	...	...	...	...	...	...	...	...	...	...	...
		Sub-order 36.—Tools and machinery.															
		101. Knife and tool makers and sellers	1	...	...	1	...	1	...	...	1	...	...	...	...	...	...
		102. Knife and tool grinders	13	2	2	9	...	5	1	1	3	...	8	1	1	6	...
		103. Mechanics (not Railway)	3	...	1	2	...	2	...	...	2	...	1	...	1	...	...
		104. Machinery-dealers, etc.	1	...	...	1	...	1	...	...	1	...	...	...	...	...	...
		Total, Sub-order 36	18	2	3	13	...	9	1	1	7	...	9	1	2	6	...
		Sub-order 37.—Arms and ammunition.															
		105. Gun-powder makers and sellers	5	...	...	5	...	5	...	...	5	...	...	...	...	...	...
		106. Fire-work makers and sellers	5	2	1	2	...	3	1	1	1	...	2	1	...	1	...
		107. Sword and scabbard makers and sellers.	1	...	...	1	...	1	...	...	1	...	...	...	...	...	...
		Total, Sub-order 37	11	2	1	8	...	9	1	1	7	...	2	1	...	1	...
		Total, Order XI	**115**	**13**	**21**	**81**	...	**55**	**6**	**8**	**41**	...	**60**	**7**	**13**	**40**	...

TABLE XVII—Part A.—Occupations by Age—*contd.*

Class.	Order.	Sub-order, Group and Occupation.	COUNTRY.														
			Total.					Males.					Females.				
			Total.	0—4.	5—14.	15 and over.	Not stated.	Total.	0—4.	5—14.	15 and over.	Not stated.	Total.	0—4.	5—14.	15 and over.	Not stated.
			34	35	36	37	38	39	40	41	42	43	44	45	46	47	48
D.—Preparation and Supply of Material Substances—*continued.*	X.—Vehicles and Vessels.	Sub-order 24.—Railway plant.															
		88. Railway permanent-way foremen, platelayers, inspectors, etc.	2	1	...	1	...	1	1	...	...	...	1	...	...	1	...
		Total, Sub-order 24	2	1	...	1	...	1	1	...	...	...	1	...	...	1	...
		Sub-order 25.—Carts, carriages, etc.															
		89. Cart and Carriage makers and sellers	...	...	...	...	...	...	...	...	...	...	...	...	...	...	...
		Total, Sub-order 25	...	...	...	...	...	...	...	...	...	...	...	...	...	...	...
		Total, Order X	2	1	...	1	...	1	1	...	...	...	1	...	...	1	...
	XI.—Supplementary Requirements.	Sub-order 28.—Books and prints.															
		90. Book-binders	1	...	...	1	...	1	...	...	1	...	...	...	...	...	...
		91. Book-sellers and publishers	4	1	1	2	...	2	1	...	1	...	2	...	1	1	...
		Total, Sub-order 28	5	1	1	3	...	3	1	...	2	...	2	...	1	1	...
		Sub-order 29.—Watches, clocks, etc.															
		92. Watch and clock makers and sellers	2	...	...	2	...	2	...	...	2	...	...	...	...	...	...
		Total, Sub-order 29	2	...	...	2	...	2	...	...	2	...	...	...	...	...	...
		Sub-order 30.—Carving, engraving, etc.															
		93. Wood and ebony carvers	...	...	...	...	...	...	...	...	...	...	...	...	...	...	...
		94. Turners and lacquerers	4	...	...	4	...	4	...	...	4	...	...	...	...	...	...
		Total, Sub-order 30	4	...	...	4	...	4	...	...	4	...	...	...	...	...	...
		Sub-order 32.—Music and musical instruments.															
		95. Music and musical instrument dealers	...	...	...	...	...	...	...	...	...	...	...	...	...	...	...
		Total, Sub-order 32	...	...	...	...	...	...	...	...	...	...	...	...	...	...	...
		Sub-order 33.—Necklaces, bracelets, beads, etc.															
		96. Bangle makers and sellers in glass	167	14	37	116	...	93	9	26	58	...	74	5	11	58	...
		97. Bangle fitters	4	...	...	4	...	1	...	...	1	...	3	...	...	3	...
		98. Bead makers and sellers	20	2	2	16	...	19	2	2	15	...	1	...	...	1	...
		99. Flower garland makers and sellers	3	1	...	2	...	2	1	...	1	...	1	...	...	1	...
		Total, Sub-order 33	194	17	39	138	...	115	12	28	75	...	79	5	11	63	...
		Sub-order 34.—Furniture.															
		100. Furniture makers	2	...	...	2	...	2	...	...	2	...	...	...	...	...	...
		Total, Sub-order 34	2	...	...	2	...	2	...	...	2	...	...	...	...	...	...
		Sub-order 36.—Tools and machinery.															
		101. Knife and tool makers and sellers	7	2	2	3	...	3	...	1	2	...	4	2	1	1	...
		102. Knife and tool grinders	...	...	...	...	...	...	...	...	...	...	...	...	...	...	...
		103. Mechanics (not Railway)	2	...	...	2	...	1	...	...	1	...	1	...	...	1	...
		104. Machinery dealers, etc.	...	...	...	...	...	...	...	...	...	...	...	...	...	...	...
		Total, Sub-order 36	9	2	2	5	...	4	...	1	3	...	5	2	1	2	...
		Sub-order 37.—Arms and Ammunition.															
		105. Gun-powder makers and sellers	...	...	...	...	...	...	...	...	...	...	...	...	...	...	...
		106. Fire-work makers and sellers	4	1	1	2	...	4	1	1	2	...	...	...	...	...	...
		107. Sword and scabbard makers and sellers	...	...	...	...	...	...	...	...	...	...	...	...	...	...	...
		Total, Sub-order 37	4	1	1	2	...	4	1	1	2	...	...	...	...	...	...
		Total, Order XI	220	21	43	156	...	134	14	30	90	...	86	7	13	66	...

TABLE XVII—Part A.—Occupations by Age—*contd.*

Class.	Order.	Sub-order, Group and Occupation.	PROVINCIAL TOTAL.														
			Total.					Males.					Females.				
			Total.	0—4.	5—14.	15 and over.	Not stated.	Total.	0—4.	5—14.	15 and over.	Not stated.	Total.	0—4.	5—14.	15 and over.	Not stated.
1	2	3	4	5	6	7	8	9	10	11	12	13	14	15	16	17	18
D.—Preparation and supply of material substances—contd.	XII.—Textile fabrics and dress.	Sub-order 38.—Wool and fur.															
		108. Blanket weavers and sellers.	29	5	5	19	...	15	1	3	11	...	14	4	2	8	...
		Total, Sub-order 38	29	5	5	19	...	15	1	3	11	...	14	4	2	8	...
		Sub-order 39.—Silk.															
		109. Silk weavers and dealers	2	...	...	2	...	2	...	...	2	...	...	...	...	...	...
		Total, Sub-order 39	2	...	...	2	...	2	...	...	2	...	...	...	...	...	...
		Sub-order 40.—Cotton.															
		110. Cotton cleaners, pressers and ginners	4	...	...	4	...	4	...	...	4	...	...	...	...	...	...
		111. Cotton spinners, sizers and yarn beaters	3	...	...	3	...	2	...	...	2	...	1	...	...	1	...
		112. Cotton weavers, mill owners and Managers	491	57	104	330	...	285	31	55	199	...	206	26	49	131	...
		113. Cotton dyers	3	...	1	2	...	1	...	...	1	...	2	...	1	1	...
		Total, Sub-order 40	501	57	105	339	...	292	31	55	206	...	209	26	50	133	...
		Sub-order 42.—Dress.															
		114. Tailors and darners	485	56	118	311	...	263	31	61	171	...	222	25	57	140	...
		115. Outfitters and clothes and quilt dealers	758	56	142	560	...	553	23	89	441	...	205	33	53	119	...
		116. Hosiers and haberdashers	185	23	47	115	...	91	9	22	60	...	94	14	25	55	...
		117. Umbrella makers and sellers	10	2	3	5	...	7	1	3	3	...	3	1	...	2	...
		118. Piece-goods dealers	21	2	2	17	...	13	..	2	11	...	8	2	...	6	...
		Total, Sub-order 42	1,459	139	312	1,008	...	927	64	177	686	...	532	75	135	322	...
		Total, Order XII	**1,991**	**201**	**422**	**1,368**	...	**1,236**	**96**	**235**	**905**	...	**755**	**105**	**187**	**468**	...
	XIII.—Metals and precious stones.	Sub-order 43.—Gold, silver and precious stones.															
		119. Gold and silver dealers	6	...	...	6	...	4	...	...	4	...	2	...	...	2	...
		120. Gold and silver workers	1,606	163	307	1,135	1	985	90	155	739	1	621	73	152	396	...
		121. Pearl and other precious stone dealers	2	...	...	2	...	2	...	...	2	...	...	...	...	...	...
		122. Coral dealers	24	...	...	24	...	24	...	...	24	...	...	...	...	...	...
		Total, Sub-order 43	1,638	163	307	1,167	1	1,015	90	155	769	1	623	73	152	398	...
		Sub-order 44.—Brass, Copper and bell-metal.															
		123. Brass pot makers and sellers	8	...	...	8	...	8	...	...	8	...	...	...	...	...	...
		124. Copper workers and sellers	152	1	17	134	...	144	1	13	130	...	8	...	4	4	...
		125. Bell-metal workers and sellers	44	5	10	29	...	37	4	8	25	...	7	1	2	4	...
		126. General workers in brass, copper, etc.	21	3	3	15	...	13	1	2	10	...	8	2	1	5	...
		127. Brass and copper dealers	14	...	1	13	...	9	...	...	9	...	5	...	1	4	...
		Total, Sub-order 44	239	9	31	199	...	211	6	23	182	...	28	3	8	27	...
		Sub-order 45.—Tin, zinc, mercury and lead.															
		128. Tin workers and sellers	40	2	10	28	...	28	...	7	21	...	12	2	3	7	...
		Total, Sub-order 45	40	2	10	28	...	28	...	7	21	...	12	2	3	7	...
		Sub-order 46.—Iron and Steel.															
		129. Iron and steel founders, etc.	1	...	...	1	...	1	...	...	1	...	...	...	...	...	...
		130. Blacksmiths	822	100	179	543	...	487	47	87	353	...	335	53	92	190	...
		131. Iron and hardware dealers	5	1	1	3	...	3	1	1	1	...	2	...	...	2	...
		Total, Sub-order 46	828	101	180	547	...	492	48	88	355	...	337	53	92	192	...
		Total, Order XIII	**2,745**	**275**	**528**	**1,941**	**1**	**1,745**	**144**	**273**	**1,327**	**1**	**1,000**	**131**	**255**	**614**	...
	XIV.—Glass, pottery and stone ware.	Sub-order 47.—Glass and China ware.															
		132. Glass and Chinaware dealers	23	2	3	18	...	20	1	3	16	...	3	1	...	2	...
		Total, Sub-order 47	23	2	3	18	...	20	1	3	16	...	3	1	...	2	...
		Sub-order 48.—Earthen and stone ware.															
		133. Potters and pot and pipe-bowl makers, etc.	817	103	173	540	1	414	48	80	285	1	403	55	93	255	...
		134. Grindstone and millstone makers, etc.	1	...	...	1	...	1	...	...	1	...	...	...	...	...	...
		135. Pestle and mortar makers, etc.	11	2	1	8	...	5	...	...	5	...	6	2	1	3	...
		Total, Sub-order 48	829	105	174	549	1	420	48	80	291	1	409	57	94	258	...
		Total, Order XIV	**852**	**107**	**177**	**567**	**1**	**440**	**49**	**83**	**307**	**1**	**412**	**58**	**94**	**260**	...

TABLE XVII—Part A.—Occupations by Age—*contd.*

Class.	Order.	Sub-order, Group and Occupation.	TOWN. Total. Total.	0—4.	5—14.	15 and over.	Not stated.	Males. Total.	0—4.	5—14.	15 and over.	Not stated.	Females. Total.	0—4.	5—14.	15 and over.	Not stated.
			19	20	21	22	23	24	25	26	27	28	29	30	31	32	33
D.—PREPARATION AND SUPPLY OF MATERIAL SUBSTANCES—*contd.*	XII.—TEXTILE FABRICS AND DRESS.	SUB-ORDER 38.—WOOL AND FUR.															
		108. Blanket weavers and sellers	19	4	4	11	...	10	1	2	7	...	9	3	2	4	...
		TOTAL, SUB-ORDER 38	19	4	4	11	...	10	1	2	7	...	9	3	2	4	...
		SUB-ORDER 39.—SILK.															
		109. Silk weavers and dealers	1	...	...	1	...	1	...	...	1	...	...	...	...	...	...
		TOTAL, SUB-ORDER 39	1	...	...	1	...	1	...	...	1	...	...	...	...	...	...
		SUB-ORDER 40.—COTTON.															
		110. Cotton cleaners, pressers and ginners	4	...	...	4	...	4	...	...	4	...	...	...	...	...	...
		111. Cotton spinners, sizers, and yarn beaters	...	...	...	...	...	...	...	...	...	...	...	...	...	...	...
		112. Cotton weavers, mill owners and managers	18	1	1	16	...	12	1	...	11	...	6	...	1	5	...
		113. Cotton dyers	3	...	1	2	...	1	...	...	1	...	2	...	1	1	...
		TOTAL, SUB-ORDER 40	25	1	2	22	...	17	1	...	16	...	8	...	2	6	...
		SUB-ORDER 42.—DRESS.															
		114. Tailors and darners	348	42	95	211	...	180	23	49	108	...	168	19	46	103	...
		115. Out-fitters and clothes and quilt dealers	436	35	90	311	...	301	10	55	236	...	135	25	35	75	...
		116. Hosiers and haberdashers	181	22	47	112	...	90	9	22	59	...	91	13	25	53	...
		117. Umbrella makers and sellers	...	...	...	...	...	...	...	...	...	...	...	...	...	...	...
		118. Piece-goods dealers	18	2	2	14	...	11	...	2	9	...	7	2	...	5	...
		TOTAL, SUB-ORDER 42	983	101	234	648	...	582	42	128	412	...	401	59	106	236	...
		Total, Order XII	**1,028**	**106**	**240**	**682**	...	**610**	**44**	**130**	**436**	...	**418**	**62**	**110**	**246**	...
	XIII.—METALS AND PRECIOUS STONES.	SUB-ORDER 43.—GOLD, SILVER AND PRECIOUS STONES.															
		119. Gold and silver dealers	2	...	...	2	...	2	...	...	2	...	...	...	...	...	...
		120. Gold and silver workers	289	35	64	190	...	156	22	34	100	...	133	13	30	90	...
		121. Pearl and other precious stone dealers	...	...	...	...	...	...	...	...	...	...	...	...	...	...	...
		122. Coral dealers	...	...	...	...	...	...	...	...	...	...	...	...	...	...	...
		TOTAL, SUB-ORDER 43	291	35	64	192	...	158	22	34	102	...	133	13	30	90	...
		SUB-ORDER 44.—BRASS, COPPER AND BELL-METAL.															
		123. Brass pot makers and sellers	5	...	...	5	...	5	...	...	5	...	...	...	...	...	...
		124. Copper workers and sellers	15	...	3	12	...	15	...	3	12	...	...	...	...	...	...
		125. Bell-metal workers and sellers	9	2	2	5	...	4	1	1	2	...	5	1	1	3	...
		126. General workers in brass, copper, etc.	6	...	2	4	...	3	...	1	2	...	3	...	1	2	...
		127. Brass and copper dealers	9	...	1	8	...	4	...	...	4	...	5	...	1	4	...
		TOTAL, SUB-ORDER 44	44	2	8	34	...	31	1	5	25	...	13	1	3	9	...
		SUB-ORDER 45.—TIN, ZINC, MERCURY AND LEAD.															
		128. Tin workers and sellers	20	1	6	13	...	16	...	6	10	...	4	1	...	3	...
		TOTAL, SUB-ORDER 45	20	1	6	13	...	16	...	6	10	...	4	1	...	3	...
		SUB-ORDER 46.—IRON AND STEEL.															
		129. Iron and steel founders, etc.	...	...	...	...	...	...	...	...	...	...	...	...	...	...	...
		130. Blacksmiths	68	6	12	50	...	42	3	8	31	...	26	3	4	19	...
		131. Iron and hardware dealers	5	1	1	3	...	3	1	1	1	...	2	...	...	2	...
		TOTAL, SUB-ORDER 46	73	7	13	53	...	45	4	9	32	...	28	3	4	21	...
		Total, Order XIII	**428**	**45**	**91**	**292**	...	**250**	**27**	**54**	**169**	...	**178**	**18**	**37**	**123**	...
	XIV.—GLASS, POTTERY AND STONE WARE.	SUB-ORDER 47.—GLASS AND CHINA WARE.															
		132. Glass and China ware dealers	16	1	3	12	...	16	1	3	12	...	...	...	...	...	...
		TOTAL, SUB-ORDER 47	16	1	3	12	...	16	1	3	12	...	...	...	...	...	...
		SUB-ORDER 48.—EARTHEN AND STONE WARE.															
		133. Potters and pot and pipe bowl makers, etc.	55	6	15	34	...	31	3	9	19	...	24	3	6	15	...
		134. Grindstone and millstone makers, etc.	...	...	...	...	...	...	...	...	...	...	...	...	...	...	...
		135. Pestle and mortar makers, etc.	...	...	...	...	...	...	...	...	...	...	...	...	...	...	...
		TOTAL, SUB-ORDER 48	55	6	15	34	...	31	3	9	19	...	24	3	6	15	...
		Total, Order XIV	**71**	**7**	**18**	**46**	...	**47**	**4**	**12**	**31**	...	**24**	**3**	**6**	**15**	...

TABLE XVII—Part A.—Occupations by Age—*contd.*

Class.	Order.	Sub-order, Group and Occupation.	COUNTRY. Total. Total.	Total. 0—4.	Total. 5—14.	Total. 15 and over.	Total. Not stated.	Males. Total.	Males. 0—4.	Males. 5—14.	Males. 15 and over.	Males. Not stated.	Females. Total.	Females. 0—4.	Females. 5—14.	Females. 15 and over.	Females. Not stated.
			34	35	36	37	38	39	40	41	42	43	44	45	46	47	48
D.—Preparation and supply of material substances—contd.	XII.—Textile fabrics and dress.	Sub-order 38.—Wool and fur.															
		108. Blanket weavers and sellers	10	1	1	8	...	5	...	1	4	...	5	1	...	4	...
		Total, Sub-order 38	10	1	1	8	...	5	...	1	4	...	5	1	...	4	...
		Sub-order 39.—Silk.															
		109. Silk weavers and dealers	1	...	...	1	...	1	...	...	1	...	...	...	...	...	...
		Total, Sub-order 39	1	...	...	1	...	1	...	...	1	...	...	...	...	...	...
		Sub-order 40.—Cotton.															
		110. Cotton cleaners, pressers and ginners	...	...	...	...	...	...	...	...	...	...	...	...	...	...	...
		111. Cotton spinners, sizers and yarn beaters	3	...	...	3	...	2	...	...	2	...	1	...	...	1	...
		112. Cotton weavers, mill owners, and managers	473	56	103	314	...	273	30	55	188	...	200	26	48	126	...
		113. Cotton dyers	...	...	...	...	...	...	...	...	...	...	...	...	...	...	...
		Total, Sub-order 40	476	56	103	317	...	275	30	55	190	...	201	26	48	127	...
		Sub-order 42.—Dress.															
		114. Tailors and darners	137	14	23	100	...	83	8	12	63	...	54	6	11	37	...
		115. Outfitters and clothes and quilt dealers	322	21	52	249	...	252	13	34	205	...	70	8	18	44	...
		116. Hosiers and haberdashers	4	1	...	3	...	1	...	...	1	...	3	1	...	2	...
		117. Umbrella makers and sellers	10	2	3	5	...	7	1	3	3	...	3	1	...	2	...
		118. Piece-goods dealers	3	...	...	3	...	2	...	...	2	...	1	...	...	1	...
		Total Sub-order 42	476	38	78	360	...	345	22	49	274	...	131	16	29	86	...
		Total, Order XII	**963**	**95**	**182**	**686**	...	**626**	**52**	**105**	**469**	...	**337**	**43**	**77**	**217**	...
	XIII.—Metals and precious stones.	Sub-order 43.—Gold, silver and precious stones.															
		119. Gold and silver dealers	4	...	...	4	...	2	...	...	2	...	2	...	...	2	...
		120. Gold and silver workers	1,317	128	243	945	1	829	68	121	639	1	488	60	122	306	...
		121. Pearl and other precious stone dealers	2	...	...	2	...	2	...	...	2	...	...	...	...	...	...
		122. Coral dealers	24	...	...	24	...	24	...	...	24	...	...	...	...	...	...
		Total, Sub-order 43	1,347	128	243	975	1	857	68	121	667	1	490	60	122	308	...
		Sub-order 44.—Brass, copper and bell-metal.															
		123. Brass pot makers and sellers	3	...	...	3	...	3	...	...	3	...	...	...	...	...	...
		124. Copper workers and sellers	137	1	14	122	...	129	1	10	118	...	8	...	4	4	...
		125. Bell-metal workers and sellers	35	3	8	24	...	33	3	7	23	...	2	...	1	1	...
		126. General workers in brass, copper, etc.	15	3	1	11	...	10	1	1	8	...	5	2	...	3	...
		127. Brass and copper dealers	5	...	...	5	...	5	...	...	5	...	...	...	...	...	...
		Total, Sub-order 44	195	7	23	165	...	180	5	18	157	...	15	2	5	8	...
		Sub-order 45.—Tin, zinc, mercury and lead.															
		128. Tin workers and sellers	20	1	4	15	...	12	...	1	11	...	8	1	3	4	...
		Total, Sub-order 45	20	1	4	15	...	12	...	1	11	...	8	1	3	4	...
		Sub-order 46.—Iron and steel.															
		129. Iron and steel founders, etc.	1	...	...	1	...	1	...	...	1	...	...	...	...	...	...
		130. Blacksmiths	754	94	167	493	...	445	44	79	322	...	309	50	88	171	...
		131. Iron and hardware dealers	...	...	...	...	...	...	...	...	...	...	...	...	...	...	...
		Total, Sub-order 46	755	94	167	494	...	446	44	79	323	...	309	50	88	171	...
		Total, Order XIII	**2,317**	**230**	**437**	**1,649**	**1**	**1,495**	**117**	**219**	**1,158**	**1**	**822**	**113**	**218**	**491**	...
	XIV.—Glass, pottery and stoneware.	Sub-order 47.—Glass and china ware.															
		132. Glass and china ware dealers	7	1	...	6	...	4	..	...	4	...	3	1	...	2	...
		Total, Sub-order 47	7	1	...	6	...	4	...	...	4	...	3	1	...	2	...
		Sub-order 48.—Earthen and stone ware.															
		133. Potters and pot and pipe-bowl makers, etc.	762	97	158	505	1	383	45	71	266	1	379	52	87	240	...
		134. Grindstone and millstone makers	1	...	...	1	...	1	...	...	1	...	...	...	—	...	...
		135. Pestle and mortar makers, etc.	11	2	1	8	...	5	...	...	5	...	6	2	1	3	...
		Total, Sub-order 48	774	99	159	515	1	389	45	71	272	1	385	54	88	243	...
		Total, Order XIV	**781**	**100**	**159**	**521**	**1**	**393**	**45**	**71**	**276**	**1**	**388**	**55**	**88**	**245**	...

TABLE XVII—Part A.—Occupations by Age—*contd.*

Class.	Order.	Sub-order, Group and Occupation.	PROVINCIAL TOTAL.														
			Total.					Males.					Females.				
			Total.	0—4.	5—14.	15 and over.	Not stated.	Total.	0—4.	5—14.	15 and over.	Not stated.	Total.	0—4.	5—14.	15 and over.	Not stated.
1	2	3	4	5	6	7	8	9	10	11	12	13	14	15	16	17	18
D.—PREPARATION AND SUPPLY OF MATERIAL SUBSTANCES—*continued.*	XV.—WOOD, CANE AND LEAVES, ETC.	SUB-ORDER 49.—TIMBER AND WOOD.															
		136. Timber and bamboo agents and dealers	9	...	1	8	...	5	...	...	5	...	4	...	1	3	—
		137. Wood cutters and sawyers	233	1	8	224	...	225	1	4	220	...	8	...	4	4	—
		138. Carpenters	908	72	111	723	2	672	30	54	587	1	236	42	57	136	1
		TOTAL, SUB-ORDER 49	1,250	73	120	1,055	2	1,002	31	58	912	1	248	42	62	143	1
		SUB-ORDER 50.—CANE-WORK, MATTING AND LEAVES, ETC.															
		139. Bamboo and rattan splitters, etc.	37	7	8	22	...	20	2	3	15	...	17	5	5	7	—
		140. Basket weavers, winnowing-pan makers, etc.	1,602	188	383	1,031	...	856	95	207	554	...	746	93	176	477	—
		141. Mat makers and sellers	74	8	12	54	...	36	3	4	29	...	38	5	8	25	—
		142. Brush and comb makers and sellers	10	...	1	9	...	5	...	1	4	...	5	...	...	5	—
		143. Broom makers and sellers	12	...	2	10	...	...	...	...	...	...	12	...	2	10	—
		TOTAL, SUB-ORDER 50	1,735	203	406	1,126	...	917	100	215	602	...	818	103	191	524	—
		Total, Order XV	**2,985**	**276**	**526**	**2,181**	**2**	**1,919**	**131**	**273**	**1,514**	**1**	**1,066**	**145**	**253**	**667**	**1**
	XVI.—DRUGS, GUMS, DYES, ETC.	SUB-ORDER 52.—DRUGS, DYES, ETC.															
		144. Chemists and druggists	1	...	...	1	...	1	...	...	1	...	...	...	...	—	—
		145. Antimony preparers and sellers	3	...	...	3	...	...	...	...	...	...	3	...	...	3	—
		146. Kanku preparers and sellers	16	3	2	11	...	7	1	2	4	...	9	2	...	7	—
		TOTAL, SUB-ORDER 52	20	3	2	15	...	8	1	2	5	...	12	2	...	10	—
		Total, Order XVI	**20**	**3**	**2**	**15**	...	**8**	**1**	**2**	**5**	...	**12**	**2**	...	**10**	—
	XVII.—LEATHER, HORNS, BONES AND GREASE.	SUB-ORDER 53.—LEATHER, ETC.															
		147. Tanners, curriers and hide sellers	29	2	9	18	...	18	1	6	11	...	11	1	3	7	—
		148. Shoe, sandal, boot, etc., makers and sellers	348	48	72	227	1	216	21	41	154	...	132	27	31	73	1
		TOTAL, SUB-ORDER 53	377	50	81	245	1	234	22	47	165	...	143	28	34	80	1
		Total, Order XVII	**377**	**50**	**81**	**245**	**1**	**234**	**22**	**47**	**165**	...	**143**	**28**	**34**	**80**	**1**
		Total, Class D	**20,245**	**2,132**	**3,789**	**14,318**	**6**	**12,065**	**1,023**	**1,993**	**9,045**	**4**	**8,180**	**1,109**	**1,796**	**5,273**	**2**
E.—COMMERCE, TRANSPORT AND STORAGE.	XVIII.—COMMERCE.	SUB-ORDER 54.—DEALERS IN MONEY AND SECURITIES.															
		149. Money lenders and pawn brokers, etc.	8	...	...	8	...	1	...	...	1	...	7	...	...	7	—
		150. Money changers and testers	24	2	2	20	...	17	1	...	16	...	7	1	2	4	—
		151. Bank clerks, cashiers, accountants, etc.	4	...	3	1	...	2	...	2	...	...	2	...	1	1	—
		TOTAL, SUB-ORDER 54	36	2	5	29	...	20	1	2	17	...	16	1	3	12	—
		SUB-ORDER 55.—GENERAL MERCHANDISE.															
		152. General merchants	39	2	8	29	...	25	1	4	20	...	14	1	4	9	—
		153. Merchants' managers, clerks, etc.	60	6	7	47	...	41	4	4	33	...	19	2	3	14	—
		TOTAL, SUB-ORDER 55	99	8	15	76	...	66	5	8	53	...	33	3	7	23	—
		SUB-ORDER 56.—DEALING UNSPECIFIED.															
		154. Shopkeepers' clerks, salesmen, etc.	35	2	9	24	...	26	1	6	19	...	9	1	3	5	—
		155. Shopkeepers' and money lenders' servants	94	1	16	77	...	89	...	15	74	...	5	1	1	3	—
		156. Shopkeepers' otherwise unspecified	228	16	40	172	...	144	7	22	115	...	84	9	18	57	—
		157. Pedlars, hawkers, etc.	2	...	...	2	...	2	...	...	2	...	...	...	...	...	—
		TOTAL, SUB-ORDER 56	359	19	65	275	...	261	8	43	210	...	98	11	22	65	—
		SUB-ORDER 57.—MIDDLEMEN, ETC.															
		Group (a) Brokers, etc.															
		158. Brokers, agents, dubash	15	2	3	10	...	5	...	...	5	...	10	2	3	5	—
		159. Auctioneers, auditors, etc.	3	1	1	1	...	...	...	...	...	...	3	1	1	1	—
		Total, Group (a)	*18*	*3*	*4*	*11*	...	*5*	...	...	*5*	...	*13*	*3*	*4*	*6*	...
		Group (b) Contractors and Farmers.															
		160. Farmers of tolls, ferries, etc.	7	...	2	5	...	6	...	2	4	...	1	...	...	1	—
		161. Farmers of liquor, opium, etc.	8	1	1	6	...	7	1	1	5	...	1	...	...	1	—
		162. Contractors, otherwise unspecified	108	7	16	85	...	68	1	11	56	...	40	6	5	29	—
		163. Contractors for labour, emigration agents, etc.	3	...	...	3	...	2	...	...	2	...	1	...	...	1	—
		Total, Group (b)	*126*	*8*	*19*	*99*	...	*83*	*2*	*14*	*67*	...	*43*	*6*	*5*	*32*	...
		TOTAL, SUB-ORDER 57	144	11	23	110	...	88	2	14	72	...	56	9	9	38	...
		Total, Order XVIII	**638**	**40**	**108**	**490**	...	**485**	**16**	**67**	**352**	...	**203**	**24**	**41**	**138**	—

TABLE XVII—Part A.—Occupations by Age—*contd.*

Class.	Order.	Sub-order, Group and Occupation.	TOWN. Total. Total.	0—4.	5—14.	15 and over.	Not stated.	Males. Total.	0—4.	5—14.	15 and over.	Not stated.	Females. Total.	0—4.	5—14.	15 and over.	Not stated.
			19	20	21	22	23	24	25	26	27	28	29	30	31	32	33
D.—Preparation and supply of material substances—*continued.*	XV.—Wood, cane and leaves, etc.	**Sub-order 49.—Timber and wood.**															
		136. Timber and bamboo agents and dealers	3	...	...	3	...	1	...	...	1	...	2	...	...	2	...
		137. Wood cutters and sawyers	25	...	2	23	...	22	...	...	22	...	3	...	2	1	...
		138. Carpenters	258	26	39	191	2	178	10	18	149	1	80	16	21	42	1
		Total, Sub-order 49	286	26	41	217	2	201	10	18	172	1	85	16	23	45	1
		Sub-order 50.—Cane-work, matting and leaves, etc.															
		139. Bamboo and rattan splitters, etc.	...	...	...	...	...	...	...	...	...	...	...	...	...	...	...
		140. Basket weavers, winnowing-pan makers, etc.	9	1	5	3	...	4	1	3	...	...	5	...	2	3	...
		141. Mat makers and sellers	...	...	...	...	...	...	...	...	...	...	...	...	...	...	...
		142. Brush and comb makers and sellers	...	...	...	...	...	...	...	...	...	...	...	...	...	...	...
		143. Broom makers and sellers	...	...	...	...	...	...	...	...	...	...	...	...	...	...	...
		Total, Sub-order 50	9	1	5	3	...	4	1	3	...	...	5	...	2	3	...
		Total, Order XV	**295**	**27**	**46**	**220**	**2**	**205**	**11**	**21**	**172**	**1**	**90**	**16**	**25**	**48**	**1**
	XVI.—Drugs, gums, dyes, etc.	**Sub-order 52.—Drugs, dyes, etc.**															
		144. Chemists and druggists	1	...	...	1	...	1	...	...	1	...	...	...	...	...	...
		145. Antimony preparers and sellers	3	...	...	3	...	...	...	...	...	...	3	...	...	3	...
		146. Kanku preparers and sellers	3	...	...	3	...	2	...	...	2	...	1	...	...	1	...
		Total, Sub-order 52	7	...	...	7	...	3	...	...	3	...	4	...	...	4	...
		Total, Order XVI	**7**	...	...	**7**	...	**3**	...	...	**3**	...	**4**	...	...	**4**	...
	XVII.—Leather, horns, bones and grease.	**Sub-order 53.—Leather, etc.**															
		147. Tanners, curriers and hide sellers	9	1	2	6	...	1	...	...	1	...	8	1	2	5	...
		148. Shoe, sandal, boot, etc., makers and sellers	103	9	21	73	...	63	4	12	47	...	40	5	9	26	...
		Total, Sub-order 53	112	10	23	79	...	64	4	12	48	...	48	6	11	31	...
		Total, Order XVII	**112**	**10**	**23**	**79**	...	**64**	**4**	**12**	**48**	...	**48**	**6**	**11**	**31**	...
		Total, Class D	**6,091**	**726**	**1,310**	**4,053**	**2**	**3,276**	**346**	**656**	**2,273**	**1**	**2,815**	**380**	**654**	**1,780**	**1**
E.—Commerce, transport and storage.	XVIII.—Commerce.	**Sub-order 54.—Dealers in money and securities.**															
		149. Money lenders and pawn brokers	5	...	...	5	...	1	...	...	1	...	4	...	...	4	...
		150. Money changers and testers	24	2	2	20	...	17	1	...	16	...	7	1	2	4	...
		151. Bank clerks, cashiers, accountants, etc.	4	...	3	1	...	2	...	2	...	...	2	...	1	1	...
		Total, Sub-order 54	33	2	5	26	...	20	1	2	17	...	13	1	3	9	...
		Sub-order 55.—General merchandise.															
		152. General merchants	23	1	4	18	...	12	...	2	10	...	11	1	2	8	...
		153. Merchants' managers, clerks, etc.	44	6	7	31	...	25	4	4	17	...	19	2	3	14	...
		Total, Sub-order 55	67	7	11	49	...	37	4	6	27	...	30	3	5	22	...
		Sub-order 56.—Dealing unspecified.															
		154. Shopkeepers' clerks, salesmen, etc.	26	2	8	16	...	17	1	5	11	...	9	1	3	5	...
		155. Shopkeepers' and money lenders' servants	27	...	4	23	...	25	...	3	22	...	2	...	1	1	...
		156. Shopkeepers, otherwise unspecified	38	1	9	28	...	24	...	5	19	...	14	1	4	9	...
		157. Pedlars, hawkers, etc.	2	...	...	2	...	2	...	...	2	...	...	...	...	...	...
		Total, Sub-order 56	93	3	21	69	...	68	1	13	54	...	25	2	8	15	...
		Sub-order 57.—Middlemen, etc.															
		Group (a). Brokers, etc.															
		158. Brokers, agents, dubash	15	2	3	10	...	5	...	...	5	...	10	2	3	5	...
		159. Auctioneers, auditors, etc.	3	1	1	1	...	...	...	...	...	...	3	1	1	1	...
		Total, Group (a)	*18*	*3*	*4*	*11*	...	*5*	...	...	*5*	...	*13*	*3*	*4*	*6*	...
		Group (b). Contractors and farmers.															
		160. Farmers of tolls, ferries, etc.	...	...	...	...	...	...	...	...	...	...	...	...	...	...	...
		161. Farmers of liquor, opium, etc.	4	...	1	3	..	4	...	1	3	...	...	...	...	...	...
		162. Contractors, otherwise unspecified	60	6	12	42	...	38	1	9	28	...	22	5	3	14	...
		163. Contractors for labour, emigration agents, etc.	...	...	...	...	...	...	...	...	...	...	...	...	...	...	...
		Total, Group (b)	*64*	*6*	*13*	*45*	...	*42*	*1*	*10*	*31*	...	*22*	*5*	*3*	*14*	...
		Total, Sub-order 57	82	9	17	56	...	47	1	10	36	...	35	8	7	20	...
		Total, Order XVIII	**275**	**21**	**54**	**200**	...	**172**	**7**	**31**	**134**	...	**103**	**14**	**23**	**66**	...

TABLE XVII—Part A.—Occupations by Age—*contd.*

Class.	Order.	Sub-order, Group and Occupation.	COUNTRY.														
			Total.					Males.					Females.				
			Total.	0—4.	5—14.	15 and over.	Not stated.	Total.	0—4.	5—14.	15 and over.	Not stated.	Total.	0—4.	5—14.	15 and over.	Not stated.
			34	35	36	37	38	39	40	41	42	43	44	45	46	47	48
D.—PREPARATION AND SUPPLY OF MATERIAL SUBSTANCES—*contd.*	XV.—WOOD, CANE AND LEAVES, ETC.	**Sub-order 49.—Timber and wood.**															
		136. Timber and bamboo agents and dealers	6	...	1	5	...	4	...	...	4	...	2	...	1	1	...
		137. Wood cutters and sawyers	308	1	6	301	...	303	1	4	298	...	5	...	2	3	...
		138. Carpenters	650	46	72	532	...	494	20	36	438	...	156	26	36	94	...
		Total, Sub-order 49	964	47	79	838	...	801	21	40	740	...	163	26	39	98	...
		Sub-order 50.—Cane work, matting and leaves, etc.															
		139. Bamboo and rattan splitters, etc.	37	7	8	22	...	20	2	3	15	...	17	5	5	7	...
		140. Basket weavers, winnowing-pan makers, etc.	1,593	187	378	1,028	...	852	94	204	554	...	741	93	174	474	...
		141. Mat makers and sellers	74	8	12	54	...	36	3	4	29	...	38	5	8	25	...
		142. Brush and comb makers and sellers	10	...	1	9	...	5	...	1	4	...	5	...	...	5	...
		143. Broom makers and sellers	12	...	2	10	...	...	...	...	...	...	12	...	2	10	...
		Total, Sub-order 50	1,726	202	401	1,123	...	913	99	212	602	...	813	103	189	522	...
		Total, Order XV	**2,690**	**249**	**480**	**1,961**	...	**1,714**	**120**	**252**	**1,342**	...	**976**	**129**	**228**	**619**	...
	XVI.—DRUGS, GUMS, DYES, ETC.	**Sub-order 52.—Drugs, dyes, etc.**															
		144. Chemists and druggists	...	...	...	...	...	...	...	...	...	...	...	...	...	...	...
		145. Antimony preparers and sellers	...	...	...	...	...	...	...	...	...	...	...	...	...	...	...
		146. Kanku preparers and sellers	13	3	2	8	...	5	1	2	2	...	8	2	...	6	...
		Total, Sub-order 52	13	3	2	8	...	5	1	2	2	...	8	2	...	6	...
		Total, Order XVI	**13**	**3**	**2**	**8**	...	**5**	**1**	**2**	**2**	...	**8**	**2**	...	**6**	...
	XVII.—LEATHER, HORNS, BONES AND GREASE.	**Sub-order 53.—Leather, etc.**															
		147. Tanners, curriers and hide sellers	20	1	7	12	...	17	1	6	10	...	3	...	1	2	...
		148. Shoe, sandal, boot, etc., makers and sellers	245	39	51	154	1	153	17	29	107	...	92	22	22	47	1
		Total, Sub-order 53	265	40	58	166	1	170	18	35	117	...	95	22	23	49	1
		Total, Order XVII	**265**	**40**	**58**	**166**	**1**	**170**	**18**	**35**	**117**	...	**95**	**22**	**23**	**49**	**1**
		Total, Class D.	**14,154**	**1,406**	**2,479**	**10,265**	**4**	**8,789**	**677**	**1,337**	**6,772**	**3**	**5,365**	**729**	**1,142**	**3,493**	**1**
E.—COMMERCE, TRANSPORT AND STORAGE.	XVIII.—COMMERCE.	**Sub-order 54.—Dealers in money and securities.**															
		149. Money lenders and pawn brokers	3	...	...	3	...	...	...	...	...	...	3	...	...	3	...
		150. Money changers and testers	...	...	...	...	...	...	...	...	...	...	...	...	...	...	...
		151. Bank clerks, cashiers, accountants, etc.	...	...	...	...	...	...	...	...	...	...	...	...	...	...	...
		Total, Sub-order 54	3	...	...	3	...	...	...	...	...	...	3	...	...	3	...
		Sub-order 55.—General merchandise.															
		152. General merchants	15	1	4	11	...	13	1	2	10	...	3	...	2	1	...
		153. Merchants' managers, clerks, etc.	16	...	...	16	...	16	...	...	16	...	...	...	...	...	...
		Total, Sub-order 55	32	1	4	27	...	29	1	2	26	...	3	...	2	1	...
		Sub-order 56.—Dealing unspecified.															
		154. Shopkeepers' clerks, salesmen, etc.	9	...	1	8	...	9	...	1	8	...	...	...	...	...	...
		155. Shopkeepers' and money lenders' servants	67	1	12	54	...	64	...	12	52	...	3	1	...	2	...
		156. Shopkeepers, otherwise unspecified	190	15	31	144	...	120	7	17	96	...	70	8	14	48	...
		157. Pedlars, hawkers, etc.	...	...	...	...	...	...	...	...	...	...	...	...	...	...	...
		Total, Sub-order 56	266	16	44	206	...	193	7	30	156	...	73	9	14	50	...
		Sub-order 57.—Middlemen, etc.															
		Group (a) Brokers, etc.															
		158. Brokers, agents, dubash	...	...	...	...	...	...	...	...	...	...	...	...	...	...	...
		159. Auctioneers, auditors, etc.	...	...	...	...	...	...	...	...	...	...	...	...	...	...	...
		Total, Group (a)	...	...	...	...	...	...	...	...	...	...	...	...	...	...	...
		Group (b) Contractors and Farmers.															
		160. Farmers of tolls, ferries, etc.	7	...	2	5	...	6	...	2	4	...	1	...	...	1	...
		161. Farmers of liquor, opium, etc.	4	1	...	3	...	3	1	...	2	...	1	...	...	1	...
		162. Contractors, otherwise unspecified	48	1	4	43	...	30	...	2	28	...	18	1	2	15	...
		163. Contractors for labour, emigration agents, etc.	3	...	...	3	...	2	...	...	2	...	1	...	...	1	...
		Total, Group (b)	*62*	*2*	*6*	*54*	...	*41*	*1*	*4*	*36*	...	*21*	*1*	*2*	*18*	...
		Total, Sub-order 57	62	2	6	54	...	41	1	4	36	...	21	1	2	18	...
		Total, Order XVIII	**363**	**19**	**54**	**290**	...	**263**	**9**	**36**	**218**	...	**100**	**10**	**18**	**72**	...

TABLE XVII—Part A.—Occupations by Age—*contd.*

Class.	Order.	Sub-order, Group and Occupation.	PROVINCIAL TOTAL.														
			Total.					Males.					Females.				
			Total.	0—4.	5—14.	15 and over.	Not stated.	Total.	0—4.	5—14.	15 and over.	Not stated.	Total.	0—4.	5—14.	15 and over.	Not stated.
1	2	3	4	5	6	7	8	9	10	11	12	13	14	15	16	17	18
E.—COMMERCE, TRANSPORT AND STORAGE—*contd.*	XIX.—TRANSPORT AND STORAGE.	**Sub-order 58.—Railway.**															
		Group (b)—Working Staff.															
		164. Guards, drivers, firemen, etc.	1	...	1	...	...	1	...	1	...	...	...	...	...	...	...
		Total, Group (b)	*1*	...	*1*	...	...	*1*	...	*1*	...	...	...	...	...	...	...
		Total, Sub-order 58	1	...	1	...	...	1	...	1	...	...	...	...	...	...	...
		Sub-order 59.—Road.															
		Group (a)—Cart, etc., owners and drivers.															
		165. Cart owners and drivers, carting agents, etc.	1,832	76	160	1,596	...	1,578	40	112	1,426	...	254	36	48	170	...
		166. Livery stable keepers, etc.	18	1	4	13	...	12	...	3	9	...	6	1	1	4	...
		167. Drivers, stable-boys, etc.	49	1	2	46	...	45	...	2	43	...	4	1	...	3	...
		168. Palki, etc., owners, bearers, etc.	2	...	...	2	...	2	...	...	2	...	...	...	...	...	...
		Total, Group (a)	*1,901*	*78*	*166*	*1,657*	...	*1,637*	*40*	*117*	*1,480*	...	*264*	*38*	*49*	*177*	...
		Group (b).—Carriers by pack animals.															
		169. Pack bullock owners, drivers, etc.	65	2	6	57	...	47	...	5	42	...	18	2	1	15	...
		170. Pack camel, elephant, mule, etc. owners and drivers	10	...	8	2	...	10	...	8	2	...	...	...	...	...	...
		Total, Group (b)	*75*	*2*	*14*	*59*	...	*57*	...	*13*	*44*	...	*18*	*2*	*1*	*15*	...
		Total, Sub-order 59	1,976	80	180	1,716	...	1,694	40	130	1,524	...	282	40	50	192	...
		Sub-order 60.—Water.															
		Group (b)—Working staff of vessels.															
		171. Boat and barge men	5	2	...	3	...	2	1	...	1	...	3	1	...	2	...
		Total, Group (b)	*5*	*2*	...	*3*	...	*2*	*1*	...	*1*	...	*3*	*1*	...	*2*	...
		Total, Sub-order 60	5	2	...	3	...	2	1	...	1	...	3	1	...	2	...
		Sub-order 61.—Messages.															
		Group (a).—Post, etc.															
		172. Postal directors, postmasters and clerks	87	11	11	65	...	62	9	7	46	...	25	2	4	19	...
		173. Postal messengers, runners, etc.	98	6	9	83	...	73	3	5	65	...	25	3	4	18	...
		174. Messengers (unspecified)	42	3	14	25	...	19	...	4	15	...	23	3	10	10	...
		Total, Group (a)	*227*	*20*	*34*	*173*	...	*154*	*12*	*16*	*126*	...	*73*	*8*	*18*	*47*	...
		Group (b)—Telegraph and Telephone.															
		175. Telegraph officers, etc.	9	...	1	8	...	7	...	1	6	...	2	...	...	2	...
		176. Signallers and messengers	20	3	5	12	...	8	1	2	5	...	12	2	3	7	...
		Total, Group (b)	*29*	*3*	*6*	*20*	...	*15*	*1*	*3*	*11*	...	*14*	*2*	*3*	*9*	...
		Total, Sub-order 61	256	23	40	193	...	169	13	19	137	...	87	10	21	56	...
		Sub-order 62.—Storage and weighing.															
		177. Porters (general)	26	...	3	23	...	23	...	3	20	...	3	...	...	3	...
		178. Weighmen and measurers	21	...	...	21	...	13	...	...	13	...	8	...	...	8	...
		179. Watchmen (not village)	1	...	...	1	...	...	...	...	...	...	1	...	...	1	...
		Total, Sub-order 62	48	...	3	45	...	36	...	3	33	...	12	...	...	12	...
		Total, Order XIX	**2,286**	**105**	**224**	**1,957**	...	**1,902**	**54**	**153**	**1,695**	...	**384**	**51**	**71**	**262**	...
		Total, Class E	**2,924**	**146**	**331**	**2,447**	...	**2,337**	**70**	**220**	**2,047**	...	**587**	**75**	**112**	**400**	...
F.—PROFESSIONS.	XX.—LEARNED AND ARTISTIC PROFESSIONS.	**Sub-order 63.—Religion.**															
		Group (a).—Priests, ministers, etc.															
		180. Priests, ministers, preachers, etc.	649	66	129	454	...	387	28	69	290	...	262	38	60	164	...
		181. Catechists, readers, etc.	25	6	7	12	...	10	2	1	7	...	15	4	6	5	...
		182. Exorcists, hail-averters, etc.	110	13	17	80	...	51	2	7	42	...	59	11	10	38	...
		Total, Group (a)	*784*	*85*	*153*	*546*	...	*448*	*32*	*77*	*339*	...	*336*	*53*	*76*	*207*	...
		Group (b).—Subsidiary religious services.															
		183. Religious mendicants, etc.	245	20	35	190	...	161	9	18	134	...	84	11	17	56	...
		184. Church, temple, masjid, etc., service	74	7	8	59	...	48	4	3	41	...	26	3	5	18	...
		Total, Group (b)	*319*	*27*	*43*	*249*	...	*209*	*13*	*21*	*175*	...	*110*	*14*	*22*	*74*	...
		Total, Sub-order 63	1,103	112	196	795	...	657	45	98	514	...	446	67	98	281	...

TABLE XVII—Part A.—Occupations by Age—*contd.*

Class.	Order.	Sub-order, Group and Occupation.	TOWN. Total. Total.	0–4.	5–14.	15 and over.	Not stated.	Males. Total.	0–4.	5–14.	15 and over.	Not stated.	Females. Total.	0–4.	5–14.	15 and over.	Not stated.
			19	20	21	22	23	24	25	26	27	28	29	30	31	32	33
E.—COMMERCE, TRANSPORT AND STORAGE—*contd.*	XIX.—TRANSPORT AND STORAGE.	**Sub-order 58.—Railway.**															
		Group (b).—Working staff.															
		164. Guards, drivers, firemen, etc.	1	...	1	...	...	1	...	1	...	...	...	...	...	...	...
		Total, Group (b)	*1*	...	*1*	...	...	*1*	...	*1*	...	...	...	...	...	...	...
		TOTAL, SUB-ORDER 58	1	...	1	...	...	1	...	1	...	...	...	...	...	...	...
		Sub-order 59.—Road.															
		Group (a).—Cart, etc., owners and drivers.															
		165. Cart owners and drivers, carting agents, etc.	518	37	53	428	...	399	23	31	345	...	119	14	22	83	...
		166. Livery stable-keepers, etc.	17	1	3	13	...	11	...	2	9	...	6	1	1	4	...
		167. Drivers, stable-boys, etc.	...	...	...	...	...	...	...	...	...	...	...	...	...	...	...
		168. Palki, etc., owners, drivers, etc.	...	...	...	...	...	...	...	...	...	...	...	...	...	...	...
		Total, Group (a)	*535*	*38*	*56*	*441*	...	*410*	*23*	*33*	*354*	...	*125*	*15*	*23*	*87*	...
		Group (b)—Carriers by pack, animals.															
		169. Pack bullock owners, drivers, etc.	...	...	...	...	...	...	...	...	...	...	...	...	...	...	...
		170. Pack camel, elephant, mule, etc., owners and drivers	8	...	8	...	...	8	...	8	...	...	...	...	...	...	...
		Total, Group (b)	*8*	...	*8*	...	...	*8*	...	*8*	...	...	...	...	...	...	...
		TOTAL, SUB-ORDER 59	543	38	64	441	...	418	23	41	354	...	125	15	23	87	...
		Sub-order 60.—Water.															
		Group (b).—Working-staff of vessels															
		171. Boat and barge men	...	...	...	...	...	...	...	...	...	...	...	...	...	...	...
		Total, Group (b)	...	...	...	...	...	...	...	...	...	...	...	...	...	...	...
		TOTAL, SUB-ORDER 60	...	...	...	...	...	...	...	...	...	...	...	...	...	...	...
		Sub-order 61.—Messages.															
		Group (a).—Post, etc.															
		172. Postal directors, postmasters and clerks	42	5	5	32	...	28	4	4	20	...	14	1	1	12	...
		173. Postal messengers, runners, etc.	26	2	1	23	...	22	1	1	20	...	4	1	...	3	...
		174. Messengers (unspecified.)	34	3	14	17	...	11	...	4	7	...	23	3	10	10	...
		Total, Group (a)	*102*	*10*	*20*	*72*	...	*61*	*5*	*9*	*47*	...	*41*	*5*	*11*	*25*	...
		Group (b).—Telegraph and Telephone.															
		175. Telegraph officers, etc.	...	...	...	...	...	...	...	...	...	...	...	...	...	...	...
		176. Signallers and messengers	16	2	5	9	...	6	...	2	4	...	10	2	3	5	...
		Total, Group (b)	*16*	*2*	*5*	*9*	...	*6*	...	*2*	*4*	...	*10*	*2*	*3*	*5*	...
		TOTAL, SUB-ORDER 61	118	12	25	81	...	67	5	11	51	...	51	7	14	30	...
		Sub-order 62.—Storage and Weighing.															
		177. Porters (general)	...	...	...	...	...	...	...	...	...	...	...	...	...	...	...
		178. Weighmen and measurers	...	...	...	...	...	...	...	...	...	...	...	...	...	...	...
		179. Watchmen (not village)	1	...	...	1	...	...	...	...	...	...	1	...	...	1	...
		TOTAL, SUB-ORDER 62	1	...	...	1	...	...	...	...	...	...	1	...	...	1	...
		Total, Order XIX	**663**	**50**	**90**	**523**	...	**486**	**28**	**53**	**405**	...	**177**	**22**	**37**	**118**	...
		Total, Class E	**938**	**71**	**144**	**723**	...	**658**	**35**	**84**	**539**	...	**280**	**36**	**60**	**184**	...
F.—PROFESSIONS.	XX.—LEARNED AND ARTISTIC PROFESSIONS.	**Sub-order 63.—Religion.**															
		Group (a).—Priests, Ministers, etc.															
		180. Priests, ministers, preachers, etc.	84	12	17	55	...	57	6	11	40	...	27	6	6	15	...
		181. Catechists, readers, etc.	15	3	6	6	...	5	1	1	3	...	10	2	5	3	...
		182. Exorcists, hail-averters, etc.	...	...	...	...	...	...	...	...	...	...	...	...	...	...	...
		Total, Group (a)	*99*	*15*	*23*	*61*	...	*62*	*7*	*12*	*43*	...	*37*	*8*	*11*	*18*	...
		Group (b).—Subsidiary religious services.															
		183. Religious mendicants, etc.	60	5	6	49	...	40	2	3	35	...	20	3	3	14	...
		184. Church, temple, masjid, etc. service	30	3	8	19	...	16	1	3	12	...	14	2	5	7	...
		Total, Group (b)	*90*	*8*	*14*	*68*	...	*56*	*3*	*6*	*47*	...	*34*	*5*	*8*	*21*	...
		TOTAL, SUB-ORDER 63	189	23	37	129	...	118	10	18	90	...	71	13	19	39	...

TABLE XVII—Part A.—Occupations by Age—*contd.*

Class	Order	Sub-order, Group and Occupation.	COUNTRY. Total. Total.	Total. 0—4.	Total. 5—14.	Total. 15 and over.	Total. Not stated.	Males. Total.	Males. 0—4.	Males. 5—14.	Males. 15 and over.	Males. Not stated.	Females. Total.	Females. 0—4.	Females. 5—14.	Females. 15 and over.	Females. Not stated.
			34	35	36	37	38	39	40	41	42	43	44	45	46	47	48
E.—Commerce, Transport and Storage—*contd.*	XIX.—Transport and Storage.	Sub-order 58.—Railway. *Group (b).—Working staff.*															
		164. Guards, drivers, firemen, etc.	...	...	...	...	...	...	...	...	...	...	...	...	...	...	...
		Total, Group (b)	...	...	...	...	...	...	...	...	...	...	...	...	...	...	...
		Total, Sub-order 58	...	...	...	...	...	...	...	...	...	...	...	...	...	...	...
		Sub-order 59.—Road. *Group (a).—Cart, etc., owners and drivers.*															
		165. Cart owners and drivers, carting agents, etc.	1,314	39	107	1,168	...	1,179	17	81	1,081	...	135	22	26	87	...
		166. Livery stable-keepers, etc.	1	...	1	...	...	1	...	1	...	...	...	...	...	...	...
		167. Drivers, stable-boys, etc.	49	1	2	46	...	45	...	2	43	...	4	1	...	3	...
		168. Palki, etc., owners, bearers, etc.	2	...	...	2	...	2	...	...	2	...	...	...	...	...	...
		Total, Group (a)	*1,366*	*40*	*110*	*1,216*	...	*1,227*	*17*	*84*	*1,126*	...	*139*	*23*	*26*	*90*	...
		Group (b).—Carriers by pack animals.															
		169. Pack bullock owners, drivers etc.	65	2	6	57	...	47	...	5	42	...	18	2	1	15	...
		170. Pack camel, elephant, mule, etc., owners and drivers	2	...	...	2	...	2	...	...	2	...	...	...	...	...	...
		Total, Group (b)	*67*	*2*	*6*	*59*	...	*49*	...	*5*	*44*	...	*18*	*2*	*1*	*15*	...
		Total, Sub-order 59	1,433	42	116	1,275	...	1,276	17	89	1,170	...	157	25	27	105	...
		Sub-order 60.—Water. *Group (b).—Working staff of vessels.*															
		171. Boat and barge men	5	2	...	3	...	2	1	...	1	...	3	1	...	2	...
		Total, Group (b)	*5*	*2*	...	*3*	...	*2*	*1*	...	*1*	...	*3*	*1*	...	*2*	...
		Total, Sub-order 60	5	2	...	3	...	2	1	...	1	...	3	2	...	2	...
		Sub-order 61.—Messages. *Group (a).—Post, etc.*															
		172. Postal directors, postmasters and clerks	45	6	6	33	...	34	5	3	26	...	11	1	3	7	...
		173. Postal messengers, runners, etc.	72	4	8	60	...	51	2	4	45	...	21	2	4	15	...
		174. Messengers (unspecified)	8	...	...	8	...	8	...	...	8	...	...	...	...	...	...
		Total, Group (a)	*125*	*10*	*14*	*101*	...	*93*	*7*	*7*	*79*	...	*32*	*3*	*7*	*22*	...
		Group (b).—Telegraph and Telephone.															
		175. Telegraph officers, etc.	9	...	1	8	...	7	...	1	6	...	2	...	...	2	...
		176. Signallers and messengers	4	1	...	3	...	2	1	...	1	...	2	...	...	2	...
		Total, Group (b)	*13*	*1*	*1*	*11*	...	*9*	*1*	*1*	*7*	...	*4*	...	...	*4*	...
		Total, Sub-order 61	138	11	15	112	...	102	8	8	86	...	36	3	7	26	...
		Sub-order 62.—Storage and weighing.															
		177. Porters (general)	26	...	3	23	...	23	...	3	20	...	3	...	...	3	...
		178. Weighmen and measurers	21	...	...	21	...	13	...	...	13	...	8	...	...	8	...
		179. Watchmen (not village)	...	...	...	...	...	...	...	...	...	...	...	...	...	...	...
		Total, Sub-order 62	47	...	3	44	...	36	...	3	33	...	11	...	...	11	...
		Total, Order XIX	**1,623**	**55**	**134**	**1,434**	...	**1,416**	**26**	**100**	**1,290**	...	**207**	**29**	**34**	**144**	...
		Total, Class E.	**1,986**	**74**	**188**	**1,724**	...	**1,679**	**35**	**136**	**1,508**	...	**307**	**39**	**52**	**216**	...
F.—Professions.	XX.—Learned and Artistic Professions.	Sub-order 63.—Religion. *Group (a).—Priests, Ministers, etc.*															
		180. Priests, ministers, preachers, etc.	565	54	112	399	...	330	22	58	250	...	235	32	54	149	...
		181. Catechists, readers, etc.	10	3	1	6	...	5	1	...	4	...	5	2	1	2	...
		182. Exorcists, hail-averters, etc.	110	13	17	80	...	51	2	7	42	...	59	11	10	38	...
		Total, Group (a)	*685*	*70*	*130*	*485*	...	*386*	*25*	*65*	*296*	...	*299*	*45*	*65*	*189*	...
		Group (b).—Subsidiary religious services.															
		183. Religious mendicants, etc.	185	15	29	141	...	121	7	15	99	...	64	8	14	42	...
		184. Church, temple, masjid, etc. service	44	4	...	40	...	32	3	...	29	...	12	1	...	11	...
		Total, Group (b)	*229*	*19*	*29*	*181*	...	*153*	*10*	*15*	*128*	...	*76*	*9*	*14*	*53*	...
		Total, Sub-order 63	914	89	159	666	...	539	35	80	424	...	375	54	79	242	...

TABLE XVII—Part A.—Occupations by Age—*contd.*

Class.	Order.	Sub-order, Group and Occupation.	PROVINCIAL TOTAL. Total. Total.	0—4.	5—14.	15 and over.	Not stated.	Males. Total.	0—4.	5—14.	15 and over.	Not stated.	Females. Total.	0—4.	5—14.	15 and over.	Not stated.
1	2	3	4	5	6	7	8	9	10	11	12	13	14	15	16	17	18
F.—PROFESSIONS—*continued.*	XX.—LEARNED AND ARTISTIC PROFESSIONS—*contd.*	**Sub-order 64.—Education.**															
		185. Administrative and inspecting officials	2	...	...	2	...	2	...	...	2	...	...	...	...	...	...
		186. Principals, professors, etc., in colleges, etc.	466	49	77	340	...	327	35	46	246	...	139	14	31	94	...
		Total, Sub-order 64	468	49	77	342	...	329	35	46	248	...	139	14	32	94	...
		Sub-order 65.—Literature.															
		187. Reporters, short-hand writers, etc.	1	...	...	1	...	1	...	...	1	...	...	...	...	...	...
		188. Private secretaries and clerks	548	68	82	398	...	350	41	43	266	...	198	27	39	132	...
		189. Public scribes and copyists	51	7	11	33	...	30	3	8	19	...	21	4	3	14	...
		190. Service in libraries and literary institutions	15	1	7	7	...	7	...	4	3	...	8	1	3	4	...
		Total, Sub-order 65	615	76	100	439	...	388	44	55	289	...	227	32	45	150	...
		Sub-order 66.—Law.															
		191. Barristers, advocates and pleaders	128	19	19	90	...	66	8	12	46	...	62	11	7	44	...
		192. Solicitors and attorneys	1	...	...	1	...	1	...	...	1	...	...	...	...	...	...
		193. Law agents, mukhtiārs, etc.	1	...	1	...	...	1	...	1	...	...	...	...	...	...	...
		194. Articled clerks and other lawyers' clerks	12	1	2	9	...	7	...	1	6	...	5	1	1	3	...
		195. Stamp-vendors	22	3	4	15	...	12	1	3	8	...	10	2	1	7	...
		196. Petition-writers	11	1	1	9	...	4	...	...	4	...	7	1	1	5	...
		Total, Sub-order 66	175	24	27	124	...	91	9	17	65	...	84	15	10	59	...
		Sub-order 67.—Medicine.															
		Group (a).—Practitioners.															
		197. Administrative and inspecting staff	8	2	2	4	...	4	2	...	2	...	4	...	2	2	...
		198. Practitioners by diploma	5	1	1	3	...	2	...	...	2	...	3	1	1	1	...
		199. Practitioners without diploma	159	12	18	129	...	103	7	8	88	...	56	5	10	41	...
		200. Vaccinators	31	5	8	18	...	19	4	7	8	...	12	1	1	10	...
		201. Midwifery	10	1	1	8	...	1	...	1	...	...	9	1	...	8	...
		Total, Group (a)	*213*	*21*	*30*	*162*	...	*129*	*13*	*16*	*100*	...	*84*	*8*	*14*	*62*	...
		Group (b).—Subsidiary Medical Services.															
		202. Hospital and asylum services	10	...	4	6	...	9	...	4	5	...	1	...	...	1	...
		203. Compounders, nurses, etc.	20	4	1	15	...	12	3	...	9	...	8	2	1	6	...
		Total, Group (b)	*30*	*4*	*5*	*21*	...	*21*	*3*	*4*	*14*	...	*9*	*1*	*1*	*7*	...
		Total, Sub-order 67	243	25	35	183	...	150	16	20	114	...	93	9	15	69	...
		Sub-order 68.—Engineering and Surveying.															
		Group (a).—Engineers, Architects and Surveyors.															
		204. Administrative and inspecting staff	2	...	...	1	...	2	...	...	1	...	...	...	...	...	...
		205. Civil Engineers and architects	13	2	5	6	...	9	1	4	4	...	4	1	1	2	...
		206. Topographical, etc., surveyors	51	4	3	44	...	45	3	3	39	...	6	1	...	5	...
		Total, Group (a)	*65*	*6*	*8*	*51*	...	*55*	*4*	*7*	*44*	...	*10*	*2*	*1*	*7*	...
		Group (b).—Subsidiary Staff.															
		207. Draughtsmen and operators in survey offices	83	6	20	57	...	46	5	4	37	...	37	1	16	20	...
		208. Clerks, etc., in offices of the above	49	3	2	44	...	42	2	2	38	...	7	1	...	6	...
		Total, Group (b)	*132*	*9*	*22*	*101*	...	*88*	*7*	*6*	*75*	...	*44*	*2*	*16*	*26*	...
		Total, Sub-order 68	197	15	30	152	...	143	11	13	119	...	54	4	17	33	...
		Sub-order 69.—Other Sciences.															
		Group (a).—Astronomy.															
		209. Botanists, naturalists, etc.	3	...	1	2	...	2	...	1	1	...	1	...	...	1	...
		Total, Group (a)	*3*	...	*1*	*2*	...	*2*	...	*1*	*1*	...	*1*	...	...	*1*	...
		Group (b).—Minor Sciences.															
		210. Astrologers, genealogists, etc.	47	2	6	39	...	35	...	2	33	...	12	2	4	6	...
		Total, Group (b)	*47*	*2*	*6*	*39*	...	*35*	...	*2*	*33*	...	*12*	*2*	*4*	*6*	...
		Total, Sub-order 69	50	2	7	41	...	37	...	3	34	...	13	2	4	7	...
		Sub-order 70.—Pictorial Art and Sculpture.															
		211. Sculptors	3	...	...	3	...	3	...	...	3	...	...	...	...	...	...
		Total, Sub-order 70	3	...	...	3	...	3	...	...	3	...	...	...	...	...	...
		Sub-order 71.—Music, Acting, Dancing.															
		212. Bandmasters and players (not military)	97	14	21	62	...	55	5	11	39	...	42	9	10	23	...
		213. Actors, singers and dancers	49	...	5	44	...	47	...	5	42	...	2	...	...	2	...
		Total, Sub-order 71	146	14	26	106	...	102	5	16	81	...	44	9	10	25	...
		Total, Order XX	**3,000**	**317**	**498**	**2,185**	...	**1,900**	**165**	**268**	**1,467**	...	**1,100**	**152**	**230**	**718**	...

TABLE XVII—Part A.—Occupations by Age—*contd.*

Class.	Order.	Sub-order, Group and Occupation.	TOWN. Total. Total.	Total. 0—4.	Total. 5—14.	Total. 15 and over.	Total. Not stated.	Males. Total.	Males. 0—4.	Males. 5—14.	Males. 15 and over.	Males. Not stated.	Females. Total.	Females. 0—4.	Females. 5—14.	Females. 15 and over.	Females. Not stated.
			19	20	21	22	23	24	25	26	27	28	29	30	31	32	33
P.—PROFESSIONS—*contd.*	XX.—LEARNED AND ARTISTIC PROFESSIONS—*contd.*	**Sub-order 64.—Education.**															
		185. Administrative and inspecting officials	2	...	...	2	...	2	...	...	2	...	...	...	...	...	...
		186. Principals, professors, etc., in colleges, etc.	134	17	26	91	...	82	10	16	56	...	52	7	10	35	...
		Total, Sub-order 64	136	17	26	93	...	84	10	16	58	...	52	7	10	35	...
		Sub-order 65.—Literature.															
		187. Reporters, short-hand writers, etc.	1	...	...	1	...	1	...	...	1	...	...	...	...	...	...
		188. Private secretaries and clerks	65	9	14	42	...	38	5	10	23	...	27	4	4	19	...
		189. Public scribes and copyists	15	2	5	8	...	12	1	5	6	...	3	1	...	2	...
		190. Service in libraries and literary institutions	15	1	7	7	...	7	...	4	3	...	8	1	3	4	...
		Total, Sub-order 65	96	12	26	58	...	58	6	19	33	...	38	6	7	25	...
		Sub-order 66.—Law.															
		191. Barristers, advocates and pleaders	95	13	16	66	...	50	6	11	33	...	45	7	5	33	...
		192. Solicitors and attorneys	1	...	...	1	...	1	...	...	1	...	...	...	...	...	...
		193. Law agents, mukhtiārs, etc.	...	...	...	...	...	...	...	...	...	...	...	...	...	...	...
		194. Articled clerks and other lawyers' clerks	12	1	2	9	...	7	...	1	6	...	5	1	1	3	...
		195. Stamp-vendors	8	...	...	8	...	3	...	...	3	...	5	...	...	5	...
		196. Petition-writers	9	1	1	7	...	2	...	...	2	...	7	1	1	5	...
		Total, Sub-order 66	125	15	19	91	...	63	6	12	45	...	62	9	7	46	...
		Sub-order 67.—Medicine.															
		Group (a).—Practitioners.															
		197. Administrative and inspecting staff	8	2	2	4	...	4	2	...	2	...	4	...	2	2	...
		198. Practitioners by diploma	5	1	1	3	...	2	...	...	2	...	3	1	1	1	...
		199. Practitioners without diploma	54	6	7	41	...	32	6	3	23	...	22	...	4	18	...
		200. Vaccinators	31	5	8	18	...	19	4	7	8	...	12	1	1	10	...
		201. Midwifery	10	1	1	8	...	1	...	1	...	...	9	1	...	8	...
		Total, Group (a)	*108*	*15*	*19*	*74*	...	*58*	*12*	*11*	*35*	...	*50*	*3*	*8*	*39*	...
		Group (b).—Subsidiary Medical Services.															
		202. Hospital and asylum services	4	...	2	2	...	4	...	2	2	...	...	...	...	...	...
		203. Compounders, nurses, etc.	17	4	1	12	...	9	3	...	6	...	8	1	1	6	...
		Total, Group (b)	*21*	*4*	*3*	*14*	...	*13*	*3*	*2*	*8*	...	*8*	*1*	*1*	*6*	...
		Total, Sub-order 67	129	19	22	88	...	71	15	13	43	...	58	4	9	45	...
		Sub-order 68.—Engineering and Surveying.															
		Group (a).—Engineers, Architects and Surveyors.															
		204. Administrative and inspecting staff	1	...	...	1	...	1	...	...	1	...	...	...	...	...	...
		205. Civil Engineers and architects	9	...	5	4	...	7	...	4	3	...	2	...	1	1	...
		206. Topographical, etc., surveyors	23	4	3	16	...	18	3	3	12	...	5	1	...	4	...
		Total, Group (a)	*33*	*4*	*8*	*21*	...	*26*	*3*	*7*	*16*	...	*7*	*1*	*1*	*5*	...
		Group (b).—Subsidiary Staff.															
		207. Draughtsmen and operators in survey offices	42	4	14	24	...	21	3	4	14	...	21	1	10	10	...
		208. Clerks, etc., in offices of the above	17	3	2	12	...	10	2	2	6	...	7	1	...	6	...
		Total, Group (b)	*59*	*7*	*16*	*36*	...	*31*	*5*	*6*	*20*	...	*28*	*2*	*10*	*16*	...
		Total, Sub-order 68	92	11	24	57	...	57	8	13	36	...	35	3	11	21	...
		Sub-order 69.—Other Sciences.															
		Group (a).—Astronomy.															
		209. Botanists, naturalists, etc.	...	...	...	...	...	...	...	...	...	...	...	...	...	...	...
		Total, Group (a)	...	...	...	...	...	...	...	...	...	...	...	...	...	...	...
		Group (b).—Minor Sciences.															
		210. Astrologers, genealogists, etc.	5	...	1	4	...	5	...	1	4	...	...	...	...	...	...
		Total, Group (b)	*5*	...	*1*	*4*	...	*5*	...	*1*	*4*	...	...	...	...	...	...
		Total, Sub-order 69	5	...	1	4	...	5	...	1	4	...	...	...	...	...	...
		Sub-order 70.—Pictorial Art and Sculpture.															
		211. Sculptors	3	...	...	3	...	3	...	...	3	...	...	...	...	...	...
		Total, Sub-order 70	3	...	...	3	...	3	...	...	3	...	...	...	...	...	...
		Sub-order 71.—Music, Acting, Dancing.															
		212. Bandmasters and players (not military)	13	2	5	6	...	7	1	3	3	...	6	1	2	3	...
		213. Actors, singers and dancers	17	...	1	16	...	16	...	1	15	...	1	...	...	1	...
		Total, Sub-order 71	30	2	6	22	...	23	1	4	18	...	7	1	2	4	...
		Total, Order XX.	**805**	**99**	**161**	**545**	...	**482**	**56**	**96**	**330**	...	**323**	**43**	**65**	**215**	...

TABLE XVII—Part A.—Occupations by Age—*contd.*

Class.	Order.	Sub-order, Group and Occupation.	COUNTRY.														
			Total.					Males.					Females.				
			Total.	0—4.	5—14.	15 and over.	Not stated.	Total.	0—4.	5—14.	15 and over.	Not stated.	Total.	0—4.	5—14.	15 and over.	Not stated.
			34	35	36	37	38	39	40	41	42	43	44	45	46	47	48
F.—PROFESSIONS—*continued.*	XX.—LEARNED AND ARTISTIC PROFESSIONS—*contd.*	**Sub-order 64.—Education.**															
		185. Administrative and inspecting officials	...	...	...	...	...	...	...	...	...	...	...	...	...	...	...
		186. Principals, professors, etc., in colleges, etc.	332	32	51	249	...	245	25	30	190	...	87	7	21	59	...
		Total, Sub-order 64	332	32	51	249	...	245	25	30	190	...	87	7	21	59	...
		Sub-order 65.—Literature.															
		187. Reporters, short hand writers, etc.	...	...	...	...	...	...	...	...	...	...	...	...	...	...	...
		188. Private secretaries and clerks	483	59	68	355	...	212	36	33	243	...	271	23	35	113	...
		189. Public scribes and copyists	36	5	6	25	...	18	2	3	13	...	18	3	3	12	...
		190. Service in libraries and literary institutions	...	...	...	...	...	...	...	...	...	...	...	...	...	...	...
		Total, Sub-order 65	519	64	74	381	...	330	38	36	256	...	189	26	38	125	...
		Sub-order 66.—Law.															
		191. Barristers, advocates and pleaders	33	6	3	24	...	16	2	1	13	...	17	4	2	11	...
		192. Solicitors and attorneys	...	...	...	...	...	...	...	...	...	...	...	...	...	...	...
		193. Law agents, mukhtiárs, etc.	1	...	1	...	...	1	...	1	...	...	...	...	...	...	...
		194. Articled clerks and other lawyers' clerks	...	...	...	...	...	...	...	...	...	...	...	...	...	...	...
		195. Stamp-vendors	14	3	4	7	...	9	1	3	5	...	5	2	1	2	...
		196. Petition-writers	2	...	...	2	...	2	...	...	2	...	...	...	...	...	...
		Total, Sub-order 66	50	9	8	33	...	28	3	5	20	...	22	6	3	13	...
		Sub-order 67.—Medicine.															
		Group (a).—Practitioners.															
		197. Administrative and inspecting staff	...	...	...	...	...	...	...	...	...	...	...	...	...	...	...
		198. Practitioners by diploma	...	...	...	...	...	...	...	...	...	...	...	...	...	...	...
		199. Practitioners without diploma	105	6	11	88	...	71	1	5	65	...	34	5	6	23	...
		200. Vaccinators	...	...	...	...	...	...	...	...	...	...	...	...	...	...	...
		201. Midwifery	...	...	...	...	...	...	...	...	...	...	...	...	...	...	...
		Total, Group (a)	*105*	*6*	*11*	*88*	...	*71*	*1*	*5*	*65*	...	*34*	*5*	*6*	*23*	...
		Group (b).—Subsidiary Medical Services.															
		202. Hospital and asylum services	6	...	2	4	...	5	...	2	3	...	1	...	...	1	...
		203. Compounders, nurses, etc.	3	...	...	3	...	3	...	...	3	...	...	...	...	...	...
		Total, Group (b)	*9*	...	*2*	*7*	...	*8*	...	*2*	*6*	...	*1*	...	...	1	...
		Total Sub-order 67	114	6	13	95	...	79	1	7	71	...	35	5	6	24	...
		Sub-order 68.—Engineering and Surveying.															
		Group (a).—Engineers, Architects and Surveyors.															
		204. Administrative and inspecting staff	...	...	...	...	...	...	...	...	...	...	...	...	...	...	...
		205. Civil Engineers and architects	4	2	...	2	...	2	1	...	1	...	2	1	...	1	...
		206. Topographical, etc., surveyors	28	...	...	28	...	27	...	...	27	...	1	...	...	1	...
		Total, Group (a)	*32*	*2*	...	*30*	...	*29*	*1*	...	*28*	...	*3*	*1*	...	*2*	...
		Group (b).—Subsidiary Staff.															
		207. Draughtsmen and operators in survey offices	41	2	6	33	...	25	2	...	23	...	16	...	6	10	...
		208. Clerks, etc., in offices of the above	32	...	...	32	...	32	...	...	32	...	...	...	...	...	...
		Total, Group (b)	*73*	*2*	*6*	*65*	...	*57*	*2*	...	*55*	...	*16*	...	*6*	*10*	...
		Total, Sub-order 68	105	4	6	95	...	86	3	...	83	...	19	1	6	12	...
		Sub-order 69.—Other Sciences.															
		Group (a).—Astronomy.															
		209. Botanists, naturalists, etc.	3	...	1	2	...	2	...	1	1	...	1	...	...	1	...
		Total, Group (a)	*3*	...	1	*2*	...	*2*	...	*1*	*1*	...	*1*	...	...		...
		Group (b).—Minor Sciences.															
		210. Astrologers, genealogists, etc.	42	2	5	35	...	30	...	1	29	...	12	2	4	6	...
		Total, Group (b)	*42*	2	*5*	*35*	...	*30*	...	*1*	*29*	...	*12*	*2*	*4*	6	...
		Total, Sub-order 69	45	2	6	37	...	32	...	2	30	...	13	2	4	7	...
		Sub-order 70.—Pictorial Art and Sculpture.															
		211. Sculptors	...	...	...	...	...	...	...	...	...	...	...	...	...	...	...
		Total, Sub-order 70	...	...	...	...	...	...	...	...	...	...	...	...	...	...	...
		Sub-order 71.—Music, Acting, Dancing.															
		212. Bandmasters and players (not military)	84	12	16	56	...	48	4	8	36	...	36	8	8	20	...
		213. Actors, singers and dancers	32	...	4	28	...	31	...	4	27	...	1	...	...	1	...
		Total, Sub-order 71	116	12	20	84	...	79	4	12	63	...	37	8	8	21	...
		Total, Order XX	**2,195**	**218**	**337**	**1,640**	...	**1,418**	**109**	**172**	**1,137**	...	**777**	**109**	**165**	**503**	...

TABLE XVII—Part A.—Occupations by Age.—*contd.*

Class.	Order.	Sub-order, Group and Occupation.	PROVINCIAL TOTAL. Total. Total.	0—4.	5—14.	15 and over.	Not stated	Males. Total.	0—4.	5—14.	15 and over.	Not stated	Females. Total.	0—4.	5—14.	15 and over.	Not stated
1	2	3	4	5	6	7	8	9	10	11	12	13	14	15	16	17	18
F.—PROFESSIONS—*contd.*	XXI.—SPORT AND AMUSEMENTS.	SUB-ORDER 72.—SPORT.															
		214. Shikaris, falconers, bird-catchers	33	13	3	17	...	19	8	1	10	...	14	5	2	7	...
		TOTAL, SUB-ORDER 72	33	13	3	17	...	19	8	1	10	...	14	5	2	7	...
		SUB-ORDER 73.—EXHIBITION AND GAMES.															
		Group (a).—Catching, training and exhibiting animals.															
		215. Exhibitors of trained animals	88	8	16	64	...	59	7	12	40	...	29	1	4	24	...
		Total, Group (a)	*88*	*8*	*16*	*64*	...	*59*	*7*	*12*	*40*	...	*29*	*1*	*4*	*24*	...
		Group (b).—Conjuring, fortune-telling and other exhibitions.															
		216. Story and ballad reciters	15	4	2	9	...	6	2	...	4	...	9	2	2	5	...
		217. Exhibitors of puppets	15	3	4	8	...	5	1	2	2	...	10	2	2	6	...
		218. Conjurors and fortune-tellers	2	...	...	2	...	2	...	...	2	...	...	...	...	...	...
		Total, Group (b)	*32*	*7*	*6*	*19*	...	*13*	*3*	*2*	*8*	...	*19*	*4*	*4*	*11*	...
		Group (c).—Acrobatics and Athletics.															
		219. Tumblers, acrobats, wrestlers, etc.	7	1	3	3	...	4	...	2	2	...	3	1	1	1	...
		Total, Group (c)	*7*	*1*	*3*	*3*	...	*4*	...	*2*	*2*	...	*3*	*1*	*1*	*1*	...
		Group (d).—Service of places of entertainment.															
		220. Tennis and racquet court service	4	...	1	3	...	1	...	...	1	...	3	...	1	2	...
		Total, Group (d)	*4*	...	*1*	*3*	...	*1*	...	...	*1*	...	*3*	...	*1*	*2*	...
		TOTAL, SUB-ORDER 73	131	16	26	89	...	77	10	16	51	...	54	6	10	38	...
		Total, Order XXI	**164**	**29**	**29**	**106**	...	**96**	**18**	**17**	**61**	...	**68**	**11**	**12**	**45**	...
		Total, Class F.	**3,164**	**346**	**527**	**2,291**	...	**1,996**	**183**	**285**	**1,528**	...	**1,168**	**163**	**242**	**763**	...
G.—INDEFINITE AND INDEPENDENT.	XXIII.—INDEFINITE.	SUB-ORDER 74.—UNSKILLED LABOUR.															
		Group (a).—Special Branches.															
		221. Well sinkers	33	7	4	22	...	26	5	3	18	...	7	2	1	4	...
		222. Road, canal, etc., labourers	277	13	39	225	...	197	5	16	176	...	80	8	23	49	...
		223. Quarrymen	22	...	...	22	...	20	...	...	20	...	2	...	...	2	...
		224. Rice-pounders and huskers	955	112	194	649	...	180	46	68	66	...	775	66	126	583	...
		Total, Group (a)	*1,287*	*132*	*237*	*918*	...	*423*	*56*	*87*	*280*	...	*864*	*76*	*150*	*638*	...
		Group (b).—General.															
		225. General labour	10,414	1,097	1,854	7,456	7	5,933	534	971	4,421	7	4,481	563	883	3,035	...
		Total, Group (b)	*10,414*	*1,097*	*1,854*	*7,456*	*7*	*5,933*	*534*	*971*	*4,421*	*7*	*4,481*	*563*	*883*	*3,035*	...
		TOTAL, SUB-ORDER 74	11,701	1,229	2,091	8,374	7	6,356	590	1,058	4,701	7	5,345	639	1,033	3,673	...
		SUB-ORDER 75.—UNDEFINED, ETC.															
		226. Disreputable means of livelihood	80	15	12	53	...	12	7	1	4	...	68	8	11	49	...
		227. Undefined means of livelihood	182	44	53	84	1	108	28	32	48	...	74	16	21	36	1
		TOTAL, SUB-ORDER 75	262	59	65	137	1	120	35	33	52	...	142	24	32	85	1
		Total, Order XXIII	**11,963**	**1,288**	**2,156**	**8,511**	**8**	**6,476**	**625**	**1,091**	**4,753**	**7**	**5,487**	**663**	**1,065**	**3,758**	**1**

TABLE XVII—Part A.—Occupations by Age—*contd.*

Class.	Order.	Sub-order, Group and Occupation.	TOWN. Total. Total.	Total. 0—4.	Total. 5—14.	Total. 15 and over	Total. Not stated	Males. Total.	Males. 0—4.	Males. 5—14.	Males. 15 and over.	Males. Not stated	Females. Total.	Females. 0—4.	Females. 5—14.	Females. 15 and over.	Females. Not stated
			19	20	21	22	23	24	25	26	27	28	29	30	31	32	33
F.—PROFESSIONS—*contd.*	XXI.—SPORT AND AMUSEMENTS.	SUB-ORDER 72.—SPORT.															
		214. Shikaris, falconers, bird-catchers	16	9	1	6	...	8	6	...	2	...	8	3	1	4	...
		TOTAL, SUB-ORDER 72	16	9	1	6	...	8	6	...	2	...	8	3	1	4	...
		SUB-ORDER 73.—EXHIBITION AND GAMES.															
		Group (a).—Catching, training and exhibiting animals.															
		215. Exhibitors of trained animals	13	1	2	10	...	9	1	2	6	...	4	...	...	4	...
		Total, Group (a)	*13*	*1*	*2*	*10*	...	*9*	*1*	*2*	*6*	...	*4*	...	...	*4*	...
		Group (b).—Conjuring, fortune-telling and other exhibitions.															
		216. Story and ballad reciters	...	...	...	...	...	...	...	...	...	...	...	...	...	...	...
		217. Exhibitors of puppets	...	...	...	...	...	...	...	...	...	...	...	...	...	...	...
		218. Conjurors and fortune-tellers	...	...	...	...	...	...	...	...	...	...	...	...	...	...	...
		Total, Group (b)	...	...	...	...	...	...	...	...	...	...	...	...	...	...	...
		Group (c).—Acrobatics and Athletics.															
		219. Tumblers, acrobats, wrestlers, etc.	7	1	3	3	...	4	...	2	2	...	3	1	1	1	...
		Total, Group (c)	*7*	*1*	*3*	*3*	...	*4*	...	*2*	*2*	...	*3*	*1*	*1*	*1*	...
		Group (d).—Service of places of entertainment.															
		220. Tennis and racquet court service	2	...	...	2	...	1	...	...	1	...	1	...	...	1	...
		Total, Group (d)	*2*	...	...	*2*	...	*1*	...	...	*1*	...	*1*	...	...	*1*	...
		TOTAL, SUB-ORDER 73	22	2	5	15	...	14	1	4	9	...	8	1	1	6	...
		Total, Order XXI.	**38**	**11**	**6**	**21**	...	**22**	**7**	**4**	**11**	...	**16**	**4**	**2**	**10**	...
		Total, Class F	**843**	**110**	**167**	**566**	...	**504**	**63**	**100**	**341**	...	**339**	**47**	**67**	**225**	...
G.—INDEFINITE AND INDEPENDENT.	XXIII.—INDEFINITE.	SUB-ORDER 74.—UNSKILLED LABOUR.															
		Group (a).—Special Branches.															
		221. Well sinkers	3	...	...	3	...	3	...	...	3	...	...	...	...	...	...
		222. Road, canal, etc., labourers	...	...	...	...	...	...	...	...	...	...	...	...	...	...	...
		223. Quarry men	...	...	...	...	...	...	...	...	...	...	...	...	...	...	...
		224. Rice-pounders and huskers	198	24	55	119	...	54	11	33	10	...	144	13	22	109	...
		Total, Group (a)	*201*	*24*	*55*	*122*	...	*57*	*11*	*33*	*13*	...	*144*	*13*	*22*	*109*	...
		Group (b).—General.															
		225. General labour	1,634	155	273	1,206	...	904	71	138	695	...	730	84	135	511	...
		Total, Group (b)	*1,634*	*155*	*273*	*1,206*	...	*904*	*71*	*138*	*695*	...	*730*	*84*	*135*	*511*	...
		TOTAL, SUB-ORDER 74	1,835	179	328	1,328	...	961	82	171	708	...	874	97	157	620	...
		SUB-ORDER 75.—UNDEFINED, ETC.															
		226. Disreputable means of livelihood	56	10	7	39	...	8	4	...	4	...	48	6	7	35	...
		227. Undefined means of livelihood	9	2	3	4	...	4	2	1	1	...	5	...	2	3	...
		TOTAL, SUB-ORDER 75	65	12	10	43	...	12	6	1	5	...	53	6	9	38	...
		Total, Order XXIII	**1,900**	**191**	**338**	**1,371**	...	**973**	**88**	**172**	**713**	...	**927**	**103**	**166**	**658**	...

TABLE XVII—Part A.—Occupations by Age—*contd.*

Class.	Order.	Sub-order, Group and Occupation.	COUNTRY.														
			Total.					Males.					Females.				
			Total.	0—4.	5—14.	15 and over.	Not stated	Total.	0—4.	5—14.	15 and over.	Not stated	Total.	0—4.	5—14.	15 and over.	Not stated
			34	35	36	37	38	39	40	41	42	43	44	45	46	47	48
F.—PROFESSIONS—contd.	XXI.—SPORT AND AMUSEMENTS.	**Sub-order 72.—Sport.**															
		224. Shikaris, falconers, bird-catchers	17	4	2	11	...	11	2	1	8	...	6	2	1	3	...
		Total, Sub-order 72	17	4	2	11	...	11	2	1	8	...	6	2	1	3	...
		Sub-order 73.—Exhibition and Games.															
		Group (a).—Catching, training and exhibiting animals.															
		215. Exhibitors of trained animals	75	7	14	54	...	50	6	10	34	...	25	1	4	20	...
		Total, Group (a)	*75*	*7*	*14*	*54*	...	*50*	*6*	*10*	*34*	...	*25*	*1*	*4*	*20*	...
		Group (b).—Conjuring, fortune-telling and other exhibitions.															
		216. Story and ballad reciters	15	4	2	9	...	6	2	...	4	...	9	2	2	5	...
		217. Exhibitors of puppets	15	3	4	8	...	5	1	2	2	...	10	2	2	6	...
		218. Conjurors and fortune-tellers	2	...	...	2	...	2	...	...	2	...	...	...	...	...	...
		Total, Group (b)	*32*	*7*	*6*	*19*	...	*13*	*3*	*2*	*8*	...	*19*	*4*	*4*	*11*	...
		Group (c).—Acrobatics and Athletics.															
		219. Tumblers, acrobats, wrestlers, etc.	...	...	...	...	...	...	...	...	...	...	...	...	...	...	...
		Total, Group (c)	...	...	...	...	...	...	...	...	...	...	...	...	...	...	...
		Group (d).—Service of places of entertainment.															
		220. Tennis and racquet court service	2	...	1	1	...	...	...	...	...	...	2	...	1	1	...
		Total, Group (d)	*2*	...	*1*	*1*	...	...	...	...	...	...	*2*	...	*1*	*1*	...
		Total, Sub-order 73	109	14	21	74	...	63	9	12	42	...	46	5	9	32	...
		Total, Order XXI	**126**	**18**	**23**	**85**	...	**74**	**11**	**13**	**50**	...	**52**	**7**	**10**	**35**	...
		Total, Class F.	**2,321**	**236**	**360**	**1,725**	...	**1,492**	**120**	**185**	**1,187**	...	**829**	**116**	**175**	**538**	...
G.—INDEFINITE AND INDEPENDENT.	XXIII.—INDEFINITE.	**Sub-order 74.—Unskilled Labour.**															
		Group (a).—Special Branches.															
		221. Well sinkers	30	7	4	19	...	23	5	3	15	...	7	2	1	4	...
		222. Road, canal, etc., labourers	277	13	39	225	...	197	5	16	176	...	80	8	23	49	...
		223. Quarrymen	22	...	...	22	...	20	...	...	20	...	2	...	...	2	...
		224. Rice-pounders and huskers	757	88	139	530	...	126	35	35	56	...	631	53	104	474	...
		Total, Group (a)	*1,086*	*108*	*182*	*796*	...	*366*	*45*	*54*	*267*	...	*720*	*63*	*128*	*529*	
		Group (b).—General.															
		225. General labour	8,780	942	1,581	6,250	7	5,029	463	833	3,726	7	3,751	479	748	2,524	...
		Total, Group (b)	*8,780*	*942*	*1,581*	*6,250*	*7*	*5,029*	*463*	*833*	*3,726*	*7*	*3,751*	*470*	*748*	*2,524*	...
		Total, Sub-order 74	9,866	1,050	1,763	7,046	7	5,395	508	887	3,993	7	4,471	542	876	3,053	...
		Sub-order 75.—Undefined, etc.															
		226. Disreputable means of livelihood	24	5	5	14	...	4	3	1	...	...	20	2	4	14	...
		227. Undefined means of livelihood	173	42	50	80	1	104	26	31	47	...	69	16	19	33	1
		Total, Sub-order 75	197	47	55	94	1	108	29	32	47	...	89	18	23	47	1
		Total, Order XXIII	**10,063**	**1,097**	**1,818**	**7,140**	**8**	**5,508**	**537**	**919**	**4,040**	**7**	**4,560**	**560**	**899**	**3,100**	**1**

Table XVII—Part A.—Occupations by Age.—Coorg.

TABLE XVII—Part A.— Occupations by Age—*contd.*

Class.	Order.	Sub-order, Group and Occupation.	PROVINCIAL TOTAL.														
			Total.					Males.					Females.				
			Total.	0—4.	5—14.	15 and over.	Not stated	Total.	0—4.	5—14.	15 and over.	Not stated	Total.	0—4.	5—14.	15 and over.	Not stated.
1	2	3	4	5	6	7	8	9	10	11	12	13	14	15	16	17	18
G.—INDEFINITE AND INDEPENDENT—*contd.*	XXIV.—INDEPENDENT OF WORK.	Sub-order 76.—Property and Alms.															
		Group (a).—Property and Allowances.															
		228. House-rent, shares and other property	8	1	1	6	...	5	1	1	3	...	3	...	...	3	...
		229. Allowances from patrons or relatives	4	...	1	3	...	2	...	1	1	...	2	...	...	2	...
		Total, Group (a)	*12*	*1*	*2*	*9*	...	*7*	*1*	*2*	*4*	...	*5*	...	...	*5*	...
		Group (b).—Charity and Endowment.															
		230. Educational or other endowments	4	...	...	4	...	2	...	...	2	...	2	...	...	2	...
		231. Mendicancy	716	65	128	523	...	374	31	61	282	...	342	34	67	241	...
		Total, Group (b)	*720*	*65*	*128*	*527*	...	*376*	*31*	*61*	*284*	...	*344*	*34*	*67*	*243*	...
		Total, Sub-order 76	732	66	130	536	...	383	32	63	288	...	349	34	67	248	...
		Sub-order 77.—Supported at the public charge.															
		Group (a).—Pension.															
		232. Pension, civil services	86	8	20	58	...	43	4	10	29	...	43	4	10	29	...
		233. Pension, military services	27	2	6	19	...	14	2	1	11	...	13	...	5	8	...
		Total, Group (a)	*113*	*10*	*26*	*77*	...	*57*	*6*	*11*	*40*	...	*56*	*4*	*15*	*37*	...
		Group (b).—Prisoners.															
		234. Prisoners, under trial	18	...	...	18	...	16	...	...	16	...	2	...	...	2	...
		235. Prisoners, for debt	4	...	...	4	...	4	...	...	4	...	...	...	...	...	1
		236. Prisoners, convicted or in reformatories	96	...	4	92	...	89	...	4	85	...	7	...	...	7	...
		Total, Group (b)	*118*	...	*4*	*114*	...	*109*	...	*4*	*105*	...	*9*	...	...	*9*	...
		Total, Sub-order 77	231	10	30	191	...	166	6	15	145	...	65	4	15	46	...
		Total, Order XXIV	**963**	**76**	**160**	**727**	...	**549**	**38**	**78**	**433**	...	**414**	**38**	**82**	**294**	...
		Total, Class G	**12,926**	**1,364**	**2,316**	**9,238**	**8**	**7,025**	**663**	**1,169**	**5,186**	**7**	**5,901**	**701**	**1,147**	**4,052**	**1**
		GRAND TOTAL	**173,055**	**21,903**	**38,334**	**112,769**	**49**	**95,907**	**10,677**	**20,006**	**65,192**	**32**	**77,148**	**11,226**	**18,328**	**47,577**	**17**

TABLE XVII—Part A.—Occupations by Age—*contd.*

Class.	Order.	Sub-order, Group and Occupation.	TOWN. Total. Total.					Males. Total.					Females. Total.				
			Total.	0—4.	5—14.	15 and over.	Not stated	Total.	0—4.	5—14.	15 and over.	Not stated	Total.	0—4.	5—14.	15 and over.	Not stated
			19	20	21	22	23	24	25	26	27	28	29	30	31	32	33
G.—INDEFINITE AND INDEPENDENT—*contd.*	XXIV.—INDEPENDENT OF WORK.	**Sub-order 76.—Property and Alms.**															
		Group (a).—Property and Allowances.															
		228. House-rent, shares and other property	7	1	1	5	...	4	1	1	2	...	3	...	...	3	...
		229. Allowances from patrons or relatives	4	...	1	3	...	2	...	1	1	...	2	...	...	2	...
		Total, Group (a)	*11*	*1*	*2*	*8*	...	*6*	*1*	*2*	*3*	...		...	...	*5*	...
		Group (b).—Charity and Endowment.															
		230. Educational or other endowments	4	...	...	4	...	2	...	...	2	...	2	...	...	2	...
		231. Mendicancy	200	15	36	149	...	206	9	20	77	...	94	6	16	72	...
		Total, Group (b)	*204*	*15*	*36*	*153*	...	*208*	*9*	*20*	*79*	...	*96*	*6*	*16*	*74*	...
		Total, Sub-order 76	215	16	38	161	...	214	10	22	82	...	101	6	16	79	...
		Sub-order 77.—Supported at the public charge.															
		Group (a).—Pension.															
		232. Pension, civil services	61	6	14	41	...	32	3	7	22	...	29	3	7	19	...
		233. Pension, military services	23	2	5	16	...	12	2	1	9	...	11	...	4	7	...
		Total, Group (a)	*84*	*8*	*19*	*57*	...	*44*	*5*	*8*	*31*	...	*40*	*3*	*11*	*26*	...
		Group (b).—Prisoners.															
		234. Prisoners, under trial	18	...	...	18	...	16	...	...	16	...	2	...	...	2	...
		235. Prisoners, for debt	4	...	...	4	...	4	...	...	4	...	...	...	...	...	...
		236. Prisoners, convicted or in reformatories	96	...	4	92	...	89	...	4	85	...	7	...	...	7	...
		Total, Group (b)	*118*	...	*4*	*114*	...	*109*	...	*4*	*105*	...	*9*	...	...	*9*	...
		Total, Sub-order 77	202	8	23	171	...	153	5	12	136	...	49	3	11	35	...
		Total, Order XXIV	**417**	**24**	**61**	**332**	...	**267**	**15**	**34**	**218**	...	**150**	**9**	**27**	**114**	...
		Total, Class G	**2,317**	**215**	**399**	**1,708**	...	**1,240**	**103**	**206**	**931**	...	**1,077**	**112**	**193**	**772**	...
		GRAND TOTAL	**15,511**	**1,756**	**3,174**	**10,577**	**4**	**[illegible],630**	**853**	**1,662**	**6,112**	**3**	**6,881**	**903**	**1,512**	**4,435**	**1**

TABLE XVII—Part A.—Occupations by Age—*contd.*

Class.	Order.	Sub-order, Group and Occupation.	COUNTRY. Total. Total.	Total. 0—4.	Total. 5—14.	Total. 15 and over.	Total. Not stated	Males. Total.	Males. 0—4.	Males. 5—14.	Males. 15 and over.	Males. Not stated	Females. Total.	Females. 0—4.	Females. 5—14.	Females. 15 and over.	Females. Not stated.
			34	35	36	37	38	39	40	41	42	43	44	45	46	47	48
G.—INDEFINITE AND INDEPENDENT.—*contd.*	XXIV.—INDEPENDENT OF WORK.	SUB-ORDER 76.—PROPERTY AND ALMS.															
		Group (a).—Property and Allowances.															
		228. House-rent, shares and other property	1	...	...	1	...	1	...	...	1	...	...	...	...	...	...
		229. Allowances from patrons or relatives	...	...	...	...	...	...	...	...	...	...	...	...	...	...	...
		Total, Group (a)	*1*	...	...	*1*	...	*1*	...	...	*1*	...	...	...	...	...	...
		Group (b).—Charity and Endowment.															
		230. Educational or other endowments	...	...	...	...	...	...	...	...	...	...	...	...	...	...	...
		231. Mendicancy	516	50	92	374	...	268	22	41	205	...	248	28	51	169	...
		Total, Group (b)	*516*	*50*	*92*	*374*	...	*268*	*22*	*41*	*205*	...	*248*	*28*	*51*	*169*	...
		TOTAL, SUB-ORDER 76	517	50	92	375	...	269	22	41	206	...	248	28	51	169	...
		SUB-ORDER 77.—SUPPORTED at the PUBLIC CHARGE.															
		Group (a).—Pension.															
		232. Pension, civil services	25	2	6	17	...	11	1	3	7	...	14	1	3		...
		233. Pension, military services	4	...	1	3	...	2	...	...	2	...	2	...	1		...
		Total, Group (a)	*29*	*2*	*7*	*20*	...	*13*	*1*	*3*	*9*	...	*16*	*1*	*4*	*11*	...
		Group (b).—Prisoners.															
		234. Prisoners, under trial	...	...	...	...	...	...	...	...	...	...	...	...	...	...	...
		235. Prisoners, for debt	...	...	...	...	...	...	...	...	...	...	...	...	...	...	...
		236. Prisoners, convicted or in reformatories	...	...	...	...	...	...	...	...	...	...	...	...	...	...	...
		Total, Group (b)	...	...	...	...	...	...	...	...	...	...	...	...	...	...	...
		TOTAL, SUB-ORDER 77	29	2	7	20	...	13	1	3	9	...	16	1	4	11	...
		Total, Order XXIV	**546**	**52**	**99**	**395**	...	**282**	**23**	**44**	**215**	...	**264**	**29**	**55**	**180**	...
		Total, Class G	**10,609**	**1,149**	**1,917**	**7,585**	**8**	**5,785**	**560**	**963**	**4,255**	**7**	**4,824**	**589**	**954**	**3,280**	**1**
		GRAND TOTAL	**157,544**	**20,147**	**35,160**	**102192**	**45**	**87,277**	**9,824**	**18,344**	**59,080**	**29**	**70,267**	**10,323**	**16,816**	**43,112**	**16**

TABLE XVII—Part C.—Occupations combined with Agriculture.

Sub-order.	Occupation.	Land Occupants.				Tenants.				Farm-servants and Field Labourers.	
		Non-Cultivating.		Cultivating.		Non-cultivating.		Cultivating.			
		Males.	Females.	Males.	Females.	Males.	Females.	Males.	Females.	Males.	Females.
1	2	3	4	5	6	7	8	9	10	11	12
1.—Government Service.	Officers	19	4	6	8	...	...	21	21	...	...
	Office superintendents and clerical establishments, police and excise inspectors, sub-registrars, etc.	22	27	15	7	...	...	58	44	...	...
	Messengers, constables, bailiffs, warders, menials, etc.	5	2	17	10	...	...	37	4	...	...
	Total, Sub-order 1	**46**	**33**	**38**	**25**	...	...	**116**	**69**	...	...
2.—Local and Municipal Service.	Clerical establishments	1	...	4	2	...	...	...	...	...	...
	Menials	5	3	...	...	...	...	...	...	...	...
	Total, Sub-order 2	**6**	**3**	**4**	**2**	...	...	...	...	...	...
3.—Village Service.	Headmen, when not agriculturists	61	48	346	248	...	...	222	163	...	...
	Accountants	2	...	1	...	...	...	3	...	...	...
	Watchmen and other menials	19	17	210	114	...	...	48	46	5	4
	Total, Sub-order 3	**82**	**65**	**557**	**362**	...	...	**273**	**209**	**5**	**4**
4.—Army	Non-commissioned officers and privates	...	...	...	...	...	...	...	1	...	...
	Total, Sub-order 4	...	...	...	...	...	...	...	**1**	...	...
8.—Stock breeding and dealing.	Cattle breeders and dealers, and commissariat farm establishment	...	...	...	2	...	...	...	...	...	...
	Herdsmen	...	...	2	...	...	...	22	...	...	...
	Sheep and goat breeders and dealers	...	...	1	...	...	...	...	...	...	...
	Total, Sub-order 8	...	...	**3**	**2**	...	...	**22**	...	...	...
9.—Subsidiary Services to Stock.	Horse, bullock and elephant breakers and trainers, etc.	2	4	3	...	...	...	7	...	...	...
	Total, Sub-order 9	**2**	**4**	**3**	...	...	...	**7**	...	...	...
14.—Personal and Domestic Services.	Barbers	...	...	39	22	...	...	46	50	...	...
	Washermen	2	...	55	18	...	...	72	95	1	1
	Cooks	...	...	1	...	...	...	4	11	...	1
	Indoor servants	...	1	6	11	...	...	...	6	...	...
	Grooms, coachmen and dog-boys, etc.	...	...	...	...	...	...	4	2	...	...
	Total, Sub-order 14	**2**	**1**	**101**	**51**	...	...	**126**	**164**	**1**	**2**
16.—Sanitation	Sweepers and scavengers	...	...	...	...	...	...	4	...	...	...
	Total, Sub-order 16	...	...	...	...	...	...	**4**	...	...	...
17.—Animal Food	Cow and buffalo keepers and milk and butter sellers	...	...	4	3	...	...	2	...	...	...
	Butchers	...	...	...	...	...	...	3	2	...	...
	Fishermen and fish curers	1	...	1	...	...	...	1	...	...	...
	Total, Sub-order 17	**1**	...	**5**	**3**	...	...	**6**	**2**	...	...
18.—Vegetable Food.	Grain dealers	7	18	32	12	...	...	45	23	...	...
	Grain parchers	...	...	3	...	...	...	...	...	...	...
	Vegetable sellers	...	...	...	...	...	...	4	9	...	...
	Cocoanut dealers	...	...	...	...	...	...	2	...	...	...
	Confectioners and sweetmeat makers and sellers	...	3	...	...	...	...	2	5	...	...
	Sweetmeat pedlars	...	...	...	4	...	...	1	...	...	...
	Total, Sub-order 18	**7**	**21**	**35**	**16**	...	...	**54**	**37**	...	...

TABLE XVII—Part C.—Occupations combined with Agriculture —*contd.*

Sub-order.	Occupation.	Land Occupants.				Tenants.				Farm-servants and Field Labourers.	
		Non-Cultivating.		Cultivating.		Non-Cultivating.		Cultivating.			
		Males.	Females.	Males.	Females.	Males.	Females.	Males.	Females.	Males.	Females.
1	2	3	4	5	6	7	8	9	10	11	12
19. Drink, Condiments and Narcotics.	Country spirits distillers and sellers	5	1	1	1	...	...	...	...	...	...
	Toddy drawers and sellers	3	...	...	...	...	...	12	9	...	...
	Foreign wine and spirit dealers	4	5	...		...	...	...	...	...	...
	Coffee preparers and sellers (not planters)	26	26	13	16	...	...	15	15	...	...
	Grocers and general condiment dealers	18	29	4	3	...	...	8	...	...	...
	Betel-leaf and areca-nut sellers	8	6	9	11	...	...	21	4	...	...
	Tobacco and snuff manufacturers and sellers	14	19	5	6	...	...	1	...	...	...
	Total, Sub-order 19	**78**	**86**	**32**	**37**	...	...	**57**	**28**	...	...
20. Lighting	Oil pressers and sellers	1	...	3	1	...	...	6	5	...	...
	Total, Sub-order 20	**1**	...	**3**	**1**	...	...	**6**	**5**	...	...
22. Building Meterials.	Lime, chunam and shell burners and sellers	...	...	3	3	...	...	6	6	...	...
	Total, Sub-order 22	...	...	**3**	**3**	...	...	**6**	**6**	...	...
23. Artificers in Building.	Stone and marble workers	...	...	20	...	...	...	7	3	...	...
	Masons	...	...	...	...	...	...	3	2	...	...
	Plasterers and house painters	1	...	..	...	...	...	...	...	...	...
	Mud wall and roof builders	...	...	...	...	...	...	3	...	1	...
	Total, Sub-order 23	**1**	...	**20**	...	...	...	**13**	**5**	**1**	...
33. Necklaces, etc.	Bangle makers and sellers in glass	1	5	3	...	...	...	28	8	...	...
	Total, Sub-order 33	**1**	**5**	**3**	...	...	...	**28**	**8**	...	...
36. Tools and Machinary.	Knife and tool makers and sellers	...	...	...	1	...	...	...	...	...	...
	Total, Sub-order 36	...	...	...	**1**	...	...	...	...	...	...
40. Cotton	Cotton weavers, mill owners and managers	1	...	10	2	...	...	33	19	...	...
	Total, Sub-order 40	**1**	...	**10**	**2**	...	...	**33**	**19**	...	...
42. Dress	Outfitters and clothes and quilt dealers	24	15	6	6	...	...	1	3	...	...
	Total, Sub-order 42	**24**	**15**	**6**	**6**	...	...	**1**	**3**	...	...
43. Gold, Silver and Precious Stones.	Gold and silver workers	22	21	84	72	...	...	43	17	...	...
	Coral dealers	...	...	8	...	...	...	1	...	...	...
	Total, Sub-order 43	**22**	**21**	**92**	**72**	...	...	**44**	**17**	...	...
44. Brass, Copper, and Bell-metal.	Copper workers and sellers	2	...	...	...	...	...	...	...	...	...
	Bell-metal workers and sellers	...	...	1	...	...	...	2	...	...	...
	Brass and copper dealers	...	...	2	...	...	...	...	...	...	...
	Total, Sub-order 44	**2**	...	**3**	...	...	...	**2**	...	...	...
46. Iron and Steel	Blacksmiths	5	2	71	35	...	...	63	26	...	...
	Total, Sub-order 46	**5**	**2**	**71**	**35**	...	...	**63**	**26**	...	...
48. Earthen and Stoneware.	Potters and pot and pipe-bowl makers and sellers	1	1	18	2	...	...	22	15	...	...
	Total, Sub-order 48	**1**	**1**	**18**	**2**	...	...	**22**	**15**	...	...

TABLE XVII.—Part(C).—Occupations combined with Agriculture—*contd.*

Sub-order.	Occupation.	Land Occupants. Non-Cultivating. Males.	Land Occupants. Non-Cultivating. Females.	Land Occupants. Cultivating. Males.	Land Occupants. Cultivating. Females.	Tenants. Non-Cultivating. Males.	Tenants. Non-Cultivating. Females.	Tenants. Cultivating. Males.	Tenants. Cultivating. Females.	Farm-servants and Field Labourers. Males.	Farm-servants and Field Labourers. Females.
1	2	3	4	5	6	7	8	9	10	11	12
49—Timber and Wood.	Timber and bamboo agents and dealers	1	2	...	...	...	...	2	1	...	...
	Wood cutters and sawyers	...	...	6	...	...	...	8	4	...	...
	Carpenters	...	...	6	2	...	...	20	21	...	...
	Total, Sub-order 49	**1**	**2**	**12**	**2**	...	...	**30**	**26**	...	...
50.—Cane work, Matting and Leaves, etc.	Basket weavers and winnowing-pan makers and sellers	...	...	37	8	...	...	23	6	15	...
	Brush and comb makers and sellers	...	...	...	...	...	...	3	...	...	...
	Total, Sub-order 50	...	...	**37**	**8**	...	...	**26**	**6**	**15**	...
52.—Drugs, Dyes, Pigments, etc.	Indigo workers and dealers (not planters)	...	...	...	1	...	...	...	...	...	...
	Total, Sub-order 52	...	...	...	**1**	...	...	...	...	...	...
53.—Leather, etc.	Shoe, sandal, boot, etc., makers and sellers	...	...	1	15	...	...	7	1	...	...
	Total, Sub-order 53	...	...	**1**	**15**	...	...	**7**	**1**	...	...
55.—General Merchandise.	Merchants' managers, accountants, clerks, assistants, etc.	...	...	...	...	...	...	1	...	...	...
	Total, Sub-order 55	...	...	...	...	...	...	**1**	...	...	...
56.—Dealing unspecified.	Shop-keepers, otherwise unspecified	...	...	5	1	...	...	...	1	...	...
	Total, Sub-order 56	...	...	**5**	**1**	...	...	...	**1**	...	...
57.—Middlemen, etc.	Brokers, agents, dubash	1	6	...	...	...	...	...	...	...	...
	Farmers of liquor, opium, etc.	2	...	...	...	...	...	1	...	...	...
	Contractors, otherwise unspecified	12	10	...	...	...	...	1	...	...	...
	Total, Sub-order 57	**15**	**16**	...	...	...	...	**2**	...	...	...
59.—Road	Cart owners and drivers, carting agents, etc.	9	3	81	...	...	...	52	3	...	...
	Palki, etc., owners, bearers, etc.	...	...	1	...	...	...	...	...	...	...
	Pack bullock owners, drivers, etc.	...	...	...	...	...	...	8	...	...	...
	Total, Sub-order 59	**9**	**3**	**82**	...	...	...	**60**	**3**	...	...
61.—Messages	Postal directors, postmasters and clerks	...	...	...	...	...	...	2	...	...	...
	Postal messengers, runners, etc.	...	...	3	...	...	...	7	2	...	...
	Messengers (unspecified)	...	...	1	...	...	...	1	...	...	...
	Signallers and messengers	3	...	...	...	...	...	...	...	...	...
	Total, Sub-order 61	**3**	...	**4**	...	...	...	**10**	**2**	...	...
62.—Storage and Weighing.	Weighmen and measurers	...	...	...	...	...	...	...	2	...	...
	Total, Sub-order 62	...	...	...	...	...	...	...	**2**	...	...
63.—Religion	Priests, ministers, preachers, missionaries, etc.	10	27	17	8	...	...	61	43	...	...
	Catechists, readers, zanána mission service, etc.	...	...	...	...	...	...	1	...	...	...
	Exorcists, hail-averters, amulettiers, etc.	...	...	2	1	...	...	1	4	...	...
	Religious mendicants, inmates of monasteries, convents, etc.	...	...	4	3	...	...	...	...	...	...
	Church, temple, masjid, pagoda, ghat, burial or burning-ground service, pilgrim conductors, and undertakers	...	...	...	...	...	...	1	1	...	...
	Total, Sub-order 63	**10**	**27**	**23**	**12**	...	...	**64**	**48**	...	...

TABLE XVII.-Part (C).—Occupations combined with Agriculture—contd.

Sub-order.	Occupation.	Land Occupants. Non-Cultivating. Males.	Land Occupants. Non-Cultivating. Females.	Land Occupants. Cultivating. Males.	Land Occupants. Cultivating. Females.	Tenants. Non-Cultivating. Males.	Tenants. Non-Cultivating. Females.	Tenants. Cultivating. Males.	Tenants. Cultivating. Females.	Farm-Servants and Field Labourers. Males.	Farm-Servants and Field Labourers. Females.
1	2	3	4	5	6	7	8	9	10	11	12
64. Education	Principals, professors and teachers in colleges, etc., schools, etc.	2	...	6	1	...	...	37	11	...	...
	Total, Sub-order 64	2	...	6	1	...	...	37	11	...	...
65. Literature	Private secretaries and clerks	7	...	5	5	...	...	12	1	...	...
	Total, Sub-order 65	7	...	5	5	...	...	12	1	...	...
66. Law	Barristers, advocates and pleaders	7	6	1	...	...	...	1	5	...	...
	Stamp-vendors	...	...	1	...	...	...	4	3	...	...
	Petition-writers	1	1	1	...	...	...	1	...	...	...
	Total, Sub-order 66	8	7	3	...	..	...	6	8	...	...
67. Medicine	Practitioners without diploma	2	3	1	...	...	...	4	...	..	...
	Total, Sub-order 67	2	3	1	...	...	...	4	...	...	...
68. Engineering and Surveying	Topographical, Archæological and Revenue Surveyors	...	...	1	...	...	...	3	...	...	...
	Draughtsmen and operators in survey offices, overseers, etc.	...	...	...	...	...	...	...	2	...	...
	Clerks, etc., in offices of the above	3	1	1	...	...	...	9	...	...	...
	Total, Sub-order 68	3	1	2	...	...	...	12	2	...	...
69. Other Sciences	Astrologers, genealogists and horoscope casters	1	...	...	...	...	...	...	...	...	...
	Total, Sub-order 69	1	...	...	...	...	...	...	...	...	...
71. Music, Acting, Dancing	Bandmasters and players (not military)	2	...	2	...	...	...	9	7	...	...
	Actors, singers and dancers and their accompanists	...	...	1	...	...	...	...	...	...	...
	Total, Sub-order 71	2	...	3	...	...	...	9	7	...	...
74. Unskilled Labour.	Well sinkers	...	...	...	...	...	...	1	...	...	...
	Rice-pounders and huskers	...	...	...	1	...	...	2	1	...	...
	General labour	3	...	47	18	1	...	69	18	...	...
	Total, Sub-order 74	3	...	47	19	1	...	72	19	...	...
76. Property and Alms.	Mendicancy (not being affiliated to a religious order)	5	3	4	...	...	...	9	...	...	...
	Total, Sub-order 76	5	3	4	...	...	...	9	...	...	...
77. Supported at the Public Charge.	Pension, Civil services	3	3	3	4	...	...	...	2	...	...
	Total, Sub-order 77	3	3	3	4	...	...	...	2	...	...
	Grand Total	356	322	1,245	688	1	...	1,244	753	22	6

TABLE A.—Christians by Sect and Race.

Sect.	Males.				Females.			
	Total.	Foreign.	Eurasian.	Native.	Total.	Foreign.	Eurasian.	Native.
1	2	3	4	5	6	7	8	9
Armenian	1	...	...	1	...	...	...	...
Baptist	1	...	1	...	...	...	...	...
Church of England	185	118	36	31	120	56	24	40
Church of Scotland	...	...	...	...	2	1	...	1
Congregationalist	1	1	...	...	...	...	...	...
Episcopalian	1	1	...	...	...	...	...	...
Free Church of Scotland	2	2	...	...	...	...	...	...
Heathen	1	...	...	1	1	...	1	...
Independent	...	...	...	...	1	1	...	...
Lutheran	16	6	1	9	13	5	...	8
Presbyterian	40	10	...	30	21	5	...	16
Protestant	76	6	7	63	76	4	5	67
Roman Catholic	1,391	9	57	1,325	1,197	7	55	1,135
Sarvéswaranamatha	2	...	...	2	1	...	...	1
Unitarian	1	1	...	...	...	...	...	...
Unsectarian	10	9	1	...	1	...	1	...
Wesleyan	21	...	10	11	28	...	11	17
Not stated	119	4	1	114	63	3	1	59
Total	1,868	167	114	1,587	1,524	82	98	1,344

TABLE B.—Europeans, Eurasians and Armenians by age.

Ages.	Males.				Females.			
	Total.	Europeans.	Eurasians.	Armenians.	Total.	Europeans.	Eurasians.	Armenians.
1	2	3	4	5	6	7	8	9
0-14	77	36	38	3	79	25	47	7
15-34	115	68	44	3	72	32	37	3
35-49	77	48	27	2	31	20	10	1
50 and over	21	15	5	1	9	5	4	...
Not stated	...	...	...	...	...	...	...	...
Total	290	167	114	9	191	82	98	11

TABLE C.—Castes, Tribes and Races by Education.

Class.	Group.	Caste, Tribe or Race.	Religion.	MALES. Total.	Learning.	Literate.	English Literate.	Illiterate.	Not stated.	FEMALES. Total.	Learning.	Literate.	English Literate.	Illiterate.	Not stated.
1	2	3	4	5	6	7	8	9	10	11	12	13	14	15	16
A.—AGRICULTURAL.	1.—Military and Dominant.	Agamudaiyan	Hindu	6	...	1	...	1	4	2	...	...	...	...	2
		Arasu	Do.	17	2	3	1	12	...	13	...	...	...	13	...
		Aré	Do.	54	2	3	...	49	...	20	...	...	...	20	...
		Kailan	Do.	...	...	...	...	...	...	1	...	...	...	1	...
		Kápála	Do.	71	...	...	...	71	...	79	...	...	...	79	...
		Kodagu	Do.	16,527	2,162	3,755	249	10,518	92	16,084	380	249	1	15,343	112
		Kshatriya	Do.	127	8	37	...	82	...	92	...	...	...	92	...
			Jain	2	...	1	...	1	...	2	...	...	...	2	...
		Maráthi	Hindu	1,388	23	83	...	1,272	10	996	1	1	...	989	5
		Náyar	Do.	953	2	164	1	783	4	144	4	43	...	97	...
		Pindári	Musalman	31	1	1	...	29	...	22	...	...	...	21	1
		Ráchevár	Hindu	13	2	1	...	10	...	16	...	...	...	16	...
		Rájpinde	Do.	1	...	...	...	1	...	2	...	...	...	2	...
		Rájput	Do.	188	14	52	8	122	...	149	1	2	...	145	1
		Rávuta	Do.	1	...	...	...	1	...	...	...	...	...	...	...
		Sérvégára	Do.	70	2	3	...	65	...	31	...	...	...	31	...
		Tirtha Kshatriya	Jain	21	4	8	...	9	...	27	...	1	...	26	...
		Total, Group A—1	...	19,470	2,222	4,112	259	13,026	110	17,680	386	296	1	16,877	121
	2 (a).—Cultivators.	Aruchi	Hindu	...	...	...	...	...	...	1	...	...	...	1	...
		Ayyambokkalu	Do.	2	...	...	...	2	...	2	...	...	...	2	...
		Badaga	Do.	1	...	...	...	1	...	...	...	...	...	...	...
		Bálólikára	Do.	7	...	2	...	5	...	2	...	...	...	2	...
		Banta	Do.	734	24	61	5	638	11	333	3	2	...	324	4
		Binepatta	Do.	55	...	3	...	46	6	46	...	1	...	45	...
		Gauda	Do.	7,001	372	551	...	6,030	48	6,322	25	7	...	6,251	39
			Christian	1	...	...	...	1	...	1	...	...	...	1	...
		Hallikára	Hindu	2	...	...	...	2	...	...	...	...	...	...	...
		Jain	Jain	32	1	14	...	17	...	30	...	1	...	29	...
		Kárgóli	Hindu	3	...	1	...	2	...	4	...	...	...	4	...
		Kávudi	Do.	22	...	3	...	19	...	15	...	...	...	15	...
		Kóvinajáti	Do.	2	...	...	...	2	...	6	...	...	...	6	...
		Kunchiga	Do.	14	...	10	...	4	...	10	...	...	...	10	...
		Púluvan	Do.	1	...	...	...	1	...	3	...	...	...	3	...
		Rájapuri	Do.	26	...	4	...	21	1	27	...	...	...	27	...
		Reddi	Do.	33	4	7	...	22	...	28	...	1	...	27	...
		Súdra	Do.	18	2	1	...	15	...	13	...	1	...	12	...
		Vádári	Do.	12	...	...	...	12	...	15	...	...	...	15	...
		Vakkaliga	Do.	7,131	151	259	2	6,677	44	5,290	4	1	...	5,239	46
			Christian	2	...	...	...	2	...	2	...	...	...	2	...
		Vellála	Hindu	655	69	205	29	375	6	575	9	46	...	517	3
			Christian	4	...	1	...	3	...	5	...	...	...	5	...
		Total, Group A—2(a)	...	15,808	623	1,122	36	13,947	116	12,730	41	60	...	12,537	92
	2 (b).—Cattle-breeders, Graziers, etc.	Gandhári	Hindu	3	...	3	...	...	...	...	...	...	...	...	...
		Gauliga	Do.	94	...	1	...	93	...	85	...	...	...	84	1
		Total, Group A—2(b)	...	97	...	4	...	93	...	85	...	...	...	84	1
	2 (c).—Field Labourers.	Adiyán	Hindu	303	...	...	...	302	1	234	...	...	...	234	...
		Agnáni	Do.	16	...	4	...	12	...	14	...	...	...	14	...
			Christian	2	...	...	...	2	...	2	...	...	...	2	...
		Ajala	Hindu	1	...	...	...	1	...	...	...	...	...	...	...
		Ánekula	Do.	4	...	...	...	4	...	5	...	...	...	5	...
		Bákuda	Do.	5	...	...	...	5	...	1	...	...	...	1	...
		Bhaira	Do.	40	...	...	...	40	...	18	...	...	...	18	...
		Holeya	Do.	13,724	25	89	2	13,489	121	10,357	...	8	...	10,260	89
			Christian	2	...	...	...	2	...	2	...	...	...	2	...
		Káládi	Hindu	2	...	...	...	2	...	3	...	...	...	3	...
		Máyava	Do.	1	...	...	...	1	...	...	...	...	...	...	...
		Máyila	Do.	91	...	...	...	91	...	39	...	...	...	39	...
		Méra	Do.	4	...	...	...	4	...	8	...	...	...	8	...
		Pále	Do.	2,693	...	2	...	2,660	31	1,352	...	...	...	1,341	11
		Pallan	Do.	30	...	2	...	28	...	38	...	...	...	38	...
		Paniyan	Do.	1	...	...	...	1	...	...	...	...	...	...	...
		Paraiyan	Do.	35	1	10	...	24	...	39	...	...	...	39	...
			Christian	...	...	...	...	...	...	3	...	...	...	3	...
		Parava	Hindu	6	...	...	...	6	...	5	...	...	...	5	...
		Tigala	Do.	16	...	...	...	16	...	7	...	...	...	7	...
			Christian	...	...	...	...	...	...	1	...	1	...	...	...
		Total, Group A—2(c)	...	16,976	26	107	2	16,690	153	12,128	...	9	...	12,019	100
	4.—Forest and Hill Tribes.	Betta	Hindu	2	...	...	...	2	...	1	...	...	...	1	...
		Koraga	Do.	7	...	...	...	7	...	1	...	...	...	1	...
			Christian	1	...	1	...	...	...	2	...	...	...	2	...
		Kudiya	Hindu	321	...	1	...	310	10	321	...	...	...	310	11
		Malasar	Do.	6	...	...	...	6	...	10	...	...	...	10	...
		Yerava	Do.	7,376	...	4	...	7,297	75	6,833	...	1	...	6,754	78
		Total, Group A—(4)	...	7,713	...	6	...	7,622	85	7,168	...	1	...	7,078	89
		Total, Class A	...	60,064	2,871	5,351	297	51,378	464	49,791	427	366	1	48,595	403
B.—PROFESSIONAL.	5.—Priests.	Bráhman Advaita	Hindu	1	...	...	...	1	...	3	...	...	...	3	...
		„ Aitála	Do.	2	...	2	...	...	...	...	...	...	...	...	...
		„ Ándhra	Do.	10	...	8	...	2	...	3	...	...	...	3	...
		„ Árádhya	Do.	...	...	...	...	...	...	2	...	...	...	2	...
		„ Aravattuvakkalu	Do.	5	2	3	2	...	...	9	2	...	...	7	...
		„ Áruvélu	Do.	6	...	5	2	1	...	5	...	...	...	5	...
		„ Babbúru Kamme	Do.	8	1	3	...	4	...	4	...	...	...	4	...
		„ Badaganádu	Do.	37	6	22	9	9	...	38	4	1	...	33	...
		„ Bettadapurada Sankéti	Do.	1	...	1	...	...	...	...	...	...	...	...	...
		„ Brahacharanam	Do.	1	...	1	...	...	...	...	...	...	...	...	...
		„ Bráhman	Do.	30	2	16	...	12	...	17	...	...	...	17	...
		„ Chittapávana	Do.	1	...	...	...	1	...	...	...	...	...	...	...
		„ Chólamandala	Do.	3	...	2	...	1	...	1	...	...	...	1	...
		„ Désasta	Do.	31	7	19	9	5	...	32	2	1	...	29	...

TABLE C.—Castes, Tribes and Races by Education—*contd.*

Class.	Group.	Caste, Tribe or Race.	Religion.	MALES. Total.	Learning.	Literate.	English Literate.	Illiterate.	Not stated.	FEMALES. Total.	Learning.	Literate.	English Literate.	Illiterate.	Not stated.
1	2	3	4	5	6	7	8	9	10	11	12	13	14	15	16
B.—PROFESSIONAL—*contd.*	5.—Priests—*contd.*	Bráhman Drávida	Hindu	11	2	8	2	1	...	3	...	...	...	3	...
		" Gauda	Do.	16	1	3	...	12	...	17	...	...	...	17	...
		" Golkonda	Do.	1	...	...	...	1	...	...	...	...	...	...	...
		" Hale Kannadiga	Do.	2	...	2	...	...	...	4	...	...	...	4	...
		" Hale Karnátaka	Do.	5	...	2	...	3	...	1	...	...	...	1	...
		" Havig	Do.	319	55	159	22	103	2	281	5	5	...	265	6
		" Hebbára	Do.	4	...	3	...	1	...	3	...	...	...	3	...
		" Hemmige	Do.	1	...	1	...	...	...	1	...	...	...	1	...
		" Hoisala Karnátaka	Do.	63	15	34	4	14	...	52	...	1	...	51	...
		" Hosanádu Karnátaka	Do.	3	1	1	...	1	...	3	...	...	...	3	...
		" Kamme	Do.	13	8	5	...	...	...	6	...	...	...	6	...
		" Kanauj	Do.	4	1	1	...	2	...	4	...	...	...	4	...
		" Kandavara	Do.	1	...	...	...	1	...	...	...	...	...	...	...
		" Kannada	Do.	3	1	2	...	...	...	1	...	...	...	1	...
		" Karnátaka	Do.	94	10	57	2	26	1	64	3	4	...	56	1
		" Kónasímai Drávida	Do.	4	...	2	...	2	...	3	...	...	...	3	...
		" Konkanasta	Do.	16	3	6	...	7	...	16	2	2	...	12	...
		" Kóta	Do.	11	1	7	...	3	...	10	...	...	...	10	...
		" Kudlukára	Do.	2	...	...	...	2	...	...	...	...	...	...	...
		" Mádhva	Do.	1	...	1	1	...	...	...	...	...	...	...	...
		" Maharáshtra	Do.	1	...	...	...	1	...	...	...	...	...	...	...
		" Malanádu Kamme	Do.	3	1	2	...	...	...	2	...	...	...	2	...
		" Malanádu Karnátaka	Do.	3	...	...	...	3	...	...	...	...	...	...	...
		" Márvádi	Do.	1	...	1	...	...	...	...	...	...	...	...	...
		" Pralákalyana vamsa	Do.	1	...	...	...	1	...	3	...	...	...	3	...
		" Rámánuja matam	Do.	1	...	1	...	...	...	...	...	...	...	...	...
		" Sankéti	Do.	42	1	34	...	7	...	25	...	...	...	25	...
		" Sárasvata	Do.	55	4	32	7	19	...	41	1	4	...	36	...
		" Shivalli	Do.	302	35	164	2	101	2	265	2	4	...	258	1
		" Smárta	Do.	51	2	36	4	13	...	56	...	...	...	54	2
		" Smárta Karnátaka	Do.	22	4	12	...	6	...	31	...	...	...	30	1
		" Srívaishnava	Do.	61	9	36	12	16	...	45	3	6	...	36	...
		" Tengalai	Do.	3	...	3	...	...	...	2	...	...	...	2	...
		" Tulu	Do.	9	...	7	...	2	...	11	...	1	...	10	...
		" Ulucha Kamme	Do.	1	...	1	...	...	...	...	...	...	...	...	...
		" Uttaráji	Do.	2	...	2	...	...	...	2	...	...	...	2	...
		" Vadagalai	Do.	73	16	38	16	19	...	87	6	6	...	75	...
		" Vadama	Do.	9	2	3	...	4	...	9	...	...	...	9	...
		" Vaidíki	Do.	4	1	3	...	...	...	2	...	...	...	2	...
		" Vaishnava	Do.	10	1	7	...	2	...	9	...	...	...	9	...
		" Vélanádu Ándhra	Do.	3	...	2	1	1	...	1	...	...	...	1	...
		TOTAL, BRÁHMANS	...	1,367	192	760	95	410	5	1,174	30	35	...	1,098	11
		Jangam	Hindu	495	44	111	...	339	1	486	1	1	...	481	3
		Pandáram	Do.	4	...	3	...	1	...	2	...	...	...	2	...
		Total, Group B—5	...	1,866	236	874	95	750	6	1,662	31	36	...	1,581	14
	6.—Devotees	Gósáyi	Hindu	4	...	...	...	4	...	3	...	1	...	2	...
		Sanyási	Do.	2	...	1	...	1	...	...	...	...	...	...	...
		Total, Group B—6	...	6	...	1	...	5	...	3	...	1	...	2	...
	7.—Temple-Servants	Ambalavási	Hindu	5	...	...	...	5	...	...	...	...	...	...	...
		Devadiga	Do.	1	...	1	...	...	...	2	...	...	...	2	...
		Moyili	Do.	8	...	...	...	8	...	...	...	...	...	...	...
		Mukkáti	Do.	12	2	3	...	7	...	11	...	...	...	11	...
		Padárti	Do.	109	15	33	...	61	...	96	...	...	...	96	...
		Sátáni	Do.	30	...	12	...	18	...	27	...	...	...	27	...
		Siva Bráhman	Do.	3	...	1	...	2	...	4	...	...	...	4	...
		Sivadvija	Do.	14	5	9	4	...	...	7	1	...	...	6	...
		Stalada Bráhman	Do.	77	8	39	...	28	2	100	...	...	...	96	4
		Stalada vartaka Bráhman	Do.	6	...	...	...	6	...	5	...	...	...	5	...
		Stánika	Do.	73	8	43	...	22	...	67	...	...	...	67	...
		Total, Group, B—7	...	338	38	141	4	157	2	319	1	...	...	314	4
	10.—Astrologers, etc.	Kaniya	Hindu	124	7	54	...	60	3	82	...	...	...	76	6
		Panika	Do.	80	5	12	...	62	1	77	...	1	...	76	...
		Total, Group B—10	...	204	12	66	...	122	4	159	...	1	...	152	6
	11.—Musicians, etc.	Batta	Hindu	12	...	...	...	12	...	6	...	...	...	6	...
		Sappaliga	Do.	2	...	...	...	2	...	...	...	...	...	...	...
		Total, Group B—11	...	14	...	...	...	14	...	6	...	...	...	6	...
	12.—Dancers and Singers.	Basavi	Hindu	9	...	1	...	8	...	8	...	...	...	8	...
		Total, Group B—12	...	9	...	1	...	8	...	8	...	...	...	8	...
		Total, Class B.	...	2,437	286	1,083	99	1,056	12	2,157	32	38	...	2,063	24

TABLE C.—Castes. Tribes and Races by Education—*contd.*

Class.	Group.	Caste, Tribe or Race.	Religion.	MALES. Total.	MALES. Learning.	MALES. Literate.	MALES. English Literate.	MALES. Illiterate.	MALES. Not stated.	FEMALES. Total.	FEMALES. Learning.	FEMALES. Literate.	FEMALES. English Literate.	FEMALES. Illiterate.	FEMALES. Not stated.
1	2	3	4	5	6	7	8	9	10	11	12	13	14	15	16
C.—COMMERCIAL.	14.—Traders	Agravála	Hindu	2	...	2	...	...	...	...	...	...	...	...	...
		Banajiga	Do.	830	45	188	11	596	1	719	8	8	...	702	1
		Baniya	Do.	14	...	2	...	11	1	8	...	...	...	8	...
		Chetti	Do.	34	5	3	...	25	1	23	...	...	...	23	...
			Christian	15	...	1	...	14	...	15	...	...	...	15	...
		Dèsiyatvani	Hindu	9	...	...	...	9	...	...	...	...	...	...	...
		Kavarai	Do.	15	6	5	...	4	...	17	1	1	...	15	...
		Kómati	Do.	11	1	7	...	3	...	6	...	1	...	5	...
		Labbai	Musalman	425	9	178	...	235	3	98	...	...	...	94	4
		Ládar	Hindu	3	...	...	...	3	...	4	...	...	...	4	...
		Máppilla	Musalman	3,466	57	438	...	2,933	38	1,704	8	8	...	1,671	17
		Méman	Do.	40	2	28	...	10	...	2	...	...	...	2	...
		Naváyat	Do.	265	13	107	1	139	6	60	3	1	...	56	...
		Vaisya	Hindu	136	14	70	1	52	...	117	...	1	...	116	...
		Total, Group C—14	...	5,255	152	1,029	13	4,024	50	2,773	20	20	...	2,711	22
	16.—Carriers	Lambádi	Hindu	114	...	1	...	113	...	42	...	...	...	42	...
		Total, Group C—16	...	114	...	1	...	113	...	42	...	...	...	42	...
		Total, Class C.	...	**5,369**	**152**	**1,030**	**13**	**4,137**	**50**	**2,815**	**20**	**20**	...	**2,753**	**22**
D.—ARTISAN AND VILLAGE MENIAL.	17.—Goldsmiths	Akkasále	Hindu	685	30	100	4	549	6	506	1	2	...	500	3
			Christian	3	...	...	...	3	...	2	...	...	...	2	...
		Chinnavára	Hindu	2	...	2	...	...	...	...	...	...	...	...	...
		Sonégára	Do.	51	1	16	...	34	...	12	...	...	...	12	...
		Súrya Bráhman	Do.	3	...	3	...	...	...	...	...	...	...	...	...
		Tattán	Do.	5	...	...	...	5	...	...	...	...	...	...	...
		Total, Group D—17	...	749	31	121	4	591	6	520	1	2	...	514	3
	17(a).—Artisans	Ásári	Hindu	131	...	72	...	59	...	29	...	...	...	28	1
		Kuláchári	Do.	2	...	...	...	2	...	...	...	...	...	...	...
		Pánchála	Do.	395	13	71	...	307	4	330	...	...	...	326	4
		Visvakarma	Do.	119	6	29	...	83	1	116	...	...	...	116	...
		Total, Group D—17(a)	...	647	19	172	...	451	5	475	...	...	...	470	5
	18.—Barbers	Hajám	Hindu	451	7	27	...	416	1	435	2	...	...	433	...
		Kahauraka	Do.	1	...	...	...	1	...	1	...	...	...	1	...
		Náyinda	Do.	26	...	...	...	26	...	28	...	...	...	28	...
		Total, Group D—18	...	478	7	27	...	443	1	464	2	...	...	462	...
	19.—Blacksmiths	Ayaakári	Hindu	2	...	2	...	...	...	1	...	...	...	1	...
		Gejjegárá	Do.	3	...	...	...	3	...	1	...	...	...	1	...
		Kammara	Do.	...	...	...	...	...	...	2	...	...	...	2	...
		Kollan	Do.	65	...	9	...	56	...	31	...	...	...	30	1
		Total, Group D—19	...	70	...	11	...	59	...	35	...	...	...	34	1
	20.—Carpenters, Masons and Turners.	Áyiri	Hindu	601	17	113	...	471	...	406	...	...	...	403	3
		Badagi	Do.	306	6	17	...	280	3	275	...	...	...	274	1
		Chàrodi	Do.	4	...	...	...	4	...	...	...	...	...	...	...
		Cheptégára	Do.	28	1	10	1	17	...	26	...	...	...	26	...
		Gudigára	Do.	2	...	...	...	2	...	...	...	...	...	...	...
		Kallukutti	Do.	34	2	7	...	24	1	44	1	...	...	43	...
		Kóláyiri	Do.	239	2	12	...	223	2	153	...	...	...	152	1
		Maniyáni	Do.	92	2	21	...	67	2	15	...	...	...	15	...
		Moyáyiri	Do.	4	...	...	...	4	...	...	...	...	...	...	...
		Pudála	Do.	3	...	1	...	2	...	...	...	...	...	...	...
		Total, Group D—20	...	1,313	30	181	1	1,094	8	919	1	...	...	913	5
	21.—Brass and Coppersmiths.	Chembukutti	Hindu	23	...	12	...	9	2	...	...	...	...	...	...
		Kanchugára	Do.	7	...	...	...	7	...	2	...	...	...	2	...
		Total, Group D—21	...	30	...	12	...	16	2	2	...	...	...	2	...
	22.—Tailors	Darji	Hindu	34	2	5	...	27	...	24	1	...	...	23	...
		Námdév	Do.	17	...	2	...	15	...	10	...	...	...	10	...
		Total, Group D—22	...	51	2	7	...	42	...	34	1	...	...	33	...
	22(c).—Flour Sellers	Huvvadiga	Hindu	1	...	...	...	1	...	1	...	...	...	1	...
		Total, Group D—22(c)	...	1	...	...	...	1	...	1	...	...	...	1	...

TABLE C.—Castes, Tribes and Races by Education—*contd.*

Class.	Group.	Caste, Tribe or Race.	Religion.	Males. Total.	Learning.	Literate.	English Literate.	Illiterate.	Not stated.	Females. Total.	Learning.	Literate.	English Literate.	Illiterate.	Not stated.
1	2	3	4	5	6	7	8	9	10	11	12	13	14	15	16
D.—Artisan and Village Menial—*contd.*	23.—Weavers, Calenderers and Dyers.	Bilimagga	Hindu	567	30	81	...	452	4	536	1	...	...	526	9
		Chaliya	Do.	98	...	2	...	95	1	31	...	...	...	31	...
		Dêvânga	Do.	1,207	96	240	8	867	4	1,154	8	5	...	1,136	5
		Jâda	Do.	7	...	...	...	7	...	3	...	...	...	3	...
		Kaikôlan	Do.	2	...	...	...	2	...	...	...	...	...	...	...
		Maggadava	Do.	11	...	1	...	10	...	4	...	...	...	4	...
		Pattusâle	Do.	3	...	1	...	2	...	...	...	...	...	...	...
		Rangâri	Do.	18	...	2	...	16	...	23	...	...	...	23	...
		Sâle	Do.	10	...	...	...	10	...	8	...	...	...	8	...
		Togata	Do.	1	...	...	...	1	...	...	...	...	...	...	...
		Total, Group D—23	...	1,924	126	327	8	1,462	9	1,759	9	5	...	1,731	14
	24.—Washermen	Agasa	Hindu	715	9	6	...	699	1	652	...	...	...	652	...
		Dhôbi	Do.	7	...	...	...	7	...	8	...	...	...	8	...
		Madivâla	Do.	187	6	2	...	179	...	148	...	...	...	148	...
		Total, Group D—24	...	909	15	8	...	885	1	808	...	...	...	808	...
	25.—Cotton-Cleaners	Pinjâri	Musalman	3	...	...	...	3	...	...	...	...	...	...	...
		Total, Group D—25	...	3	...	...	...	3	...	...	...	...	...	...	...
	26.—Shepherds, etc.	Golla	Hindu	475	13	33	...	429	...	448	2	1	...	444	1
		Heggade	Do.	696	35	50	2	610	1	611	1	3	...	606	1
		Kavâdi	Do.	2	1	...	...	1	...	1	...	...	...	1	...
		Kurikalu	Do.	1	...	...	...	1	...	...	...	...	...	...	...
		Kuruba	Do.	4,123	9	15	...	4,079	20	3,498	...	1	...	3,474	23
		Total, Group D—26	...	5,297	58	98	2	5,120	21	4,558	3	5	...	4,525	25
	27.—Oil-pressers	Gâniga	Hindu	290	7	20	...	261	2	195	2	1	...	192	...
		Vâniya	Do.	85	1	1	...	83	...	4	...	...	...	4	...
		Total, Group D—27	...	375	8	21	...	344	2	199	2	1	...	196	...
	28.—Potters	Koyava	Hindu	173	1	13	...	159	...	150	...	...	...	150	...
		Kumbâra	Do.	495	7	3	1	484	1	413	...	...	...	413	...
		Total, Group D—28	...	668	8	16	1	643	1	563	...	...	...	563	...
	29.—Glass workers	Balegâra	Hindu	2	...	...	...	2	...	6	...	...	...	6	...
		Total, Group D—29	...	2	...	...	...	2	...	6	...	...	...	6	...
	30.—Salt workers	Uppâra	Hindu	210	3	1	...	206	...	129	...	...	...	129	...
		Total, Group D—30	...	210	3	1	...	206	...	129	...	...	...	129	...
	35.—Fishermen, Boatmen, Palki-bearers, Cooks, etc.	Besta	Hindu	329	3	3	...	323	...	298	...	...	...	297	1
		Bôyi	Do.	482	13	4	...	464	1	476	...	...	...	475	1
		Kabbêra	Do.	3	...	...	...	3	...	...	...	...	...	...	...
		Mogêr	Do.	1	...	...	...	1	...	...	...	...	...	...	...
		Toreya	Do.	249	2	2	...	244	1	179	...	...	...	179	...
		Total, Group D—35	...	1,064	18	9	...	1,035	2	953	...	...	...	951	2
	35(a).—Personal service.	Mukkâri	Hindu	8	...	...	...	8	...	...	...	...	...	...	...
		Total, Group D—35(a)	...	8	...	...	...	8	...	...	...	...	...	...	...
	36.—Distillers and Toddy-drawers.	Billava	Hindu	998	8	30	...	952	8	368	...	...	...	357	11
		Biruva	Do.	10	...	...	...	10	...	2	...	...	...	2	...
		Dîvâr	Do.	377	9	15	...	350	3	326	...	...	...	325	1
		Halepaik	Do.	16	...	...	...	16	...	12	...	...	...	12	...
		Hummaliga	Do.	9	...	...	...	9	...	6	...	...	...	6	...
		Idiga	Do.	17	...	1	...	16	...	...	...	...	...	...	...
		Tiyyan	Do.	814	3	116	4	689	6	118	...	4	...	112	2
		Total, Group D—36		2,241	20	162	4	2,042	17	832	...	4	...	814	14
	37.—Butchers	Kasâyi	Hindu	5	...	...	...	5	...	3	...	...	...	3	...
		Total, Group D—37	...	5	...	...	...	5	...	3	...	...	...	3	...
	38.—Leather workers.	Mâdiga	Hindu	920	3	...	...	905	12	629	...	...	...	620	9
		Muc'chi	Do.	8	...	...	...	8	...	6	...	...	...	6	...
		Total, Group D—38	...	928	3	...	...	913	12	635	...	...	...	626	9
		Total, Class D	...	16,973	348	1,173	20	15,365	87	12,895	19	17	...	12,781	78

TABLE C.—Castes, Tribes and Races by Education—*contd.*

Class.	Group.	Caste, Tribe or Race.	Religion.	MALES. Total.	Learning.	Literate.	English Literate.	Illiterate.	Not stated.	FEMALES. Total.	Learning.	Literate.	English Literate.	Illiterate.	Not stated.
1	2	3	4	5	6	7	8	9	10	11	12	13	14	15	16
E.—Vagrants, Minor Artisans and Performers, etc.	41.—Earth workers	Odde	Hindu	260	...	...	...	260	...	181	...	...	...	180	1
		Total, Group E—41	...	260	...	...	...	260	...	181	...	...	...	180	1
	42.—Knife Grinders.	Sikligára	Hindu	1	...	...	...	1	...	...	...	...	...	...	...
		Total, Group E—42	...	1	...	...	...	1	...	...	...	...	...	...	...
	43.—Mat-makers, Cane-splitters, etc.	auriga	Hindu	186	1	1	...	184	...	176	...	...	...	176	...
		Korama	Do.	154	...	4	...	150	...	170	...	...	...	168	2
		Méda	Do.	134	...	...	...	134	...	127	...	...	...	127	...
		Total, Group E—43	...	474	1	5	...	468	...	473	...	...	...	471	2
	44.—Hunters, etc.	Bédar	Hindu	129	1	6	...	121	1	94	...	1	...	93	...
		Total, Group E—44	...	129	1	6	...	121	1	94	...	1	...	93	...
	45.—Miscellaneous and disreputable Vagrants.	Mále or Maleya	Hindu	107	1	28	...	78	...	88	...	...	...	87	1
		Súle	Do.	1	...	1	...	...	...	...	...	...	...	...	...
		Total, Group E—45	...	108	1	29	...	78	...	88	...	...	...	87	1
	45(*a*).—Beggars, etc.	Banna	Hindu	81	1	8	...	72	...	66	...	...	...	66	...
		Dásari	Do.	10	...	...	...	10	...	8	...	...	...	8	...
		Helava	Do.	1	...	...	...	1	...	...	...	...	...	...	...
		Jógi	Do.	66	3	...	...	63	...	38	1	...	...	37	...
		Kutuna	Do.	34	...	...	...	34	...	40	...	...	...	40	...
		Paradési	Do.	2	...	2	...	...	...	1	...	...	...	1	...
		Siddha	Do.	10	...	...	...	10	...	10	...	...	...	10	...
		Total, Group E—45(*a*)	...	204	4	10	...	190	...	163	1	...	...	162	...
	46.—Tumblers and Acrobats.	Domba	Hindu	17	...	...	...	17	...	12	...	...	...	12	...
		Jetti	Do.	1	...	...	...	1	...	2	...	...	...	2	...
		Total, Group E—46.	...	18	...	...	...	18	...	14	...	...	...	14	...
		Total, Class E	...	**1,194**	**7**	**50**	...	**1,136**	**1**	**1,018**	**1**	**1**	...	**1,007**	**4**
F.—Races and Nationalities.	48.—Non-Indian Asiatic races.	Armenian	Christian	9	...	5	4	3	1	11	...	3	1	8	...
		Duráni	Musalman	6	...	5	...	1	...	2	...	...	...	2	...
		Ehóda	Christian	1	...	...	...	1	...	...	...	...	...	...	...
		Khurési	Musalman	2	1	1	...	...	...	5	1	3	...	1	...
		Lódi Pathán	Do.	2	...	...	...	2	...	1	...	...	...	1	...
		Moghal	Do.	58	3	11	...	44	...	43	2	3	...	38	...
		Pársi	Pársi	24	5	11	5	8	...	15	2	6	...	7	...
		Pathán	Musalman	465	20	55	3	388	2	408	3	3	...	400	2
		Saiyad	Do.	411	15	65	...	331	...	314	1	4	...	308	1
		Sheik	Do.	1,889	96	350	6	1,439	4	1,484	12	23	...	1,447	2
		Total, Group F—48	...	2,867	140	503	18	2,217	7	2,283	21	45	1	2,210	5
	50.—Non-Asiatic races.	Celtic	Christian	...	...	...	...	...	...	1	...	...	...	1	...
		English	Do.	3	1	2	2	...	...	1	...	...	...	1	...
		European	Do.	163	23	124	120	12	4	79	13	51	40	12	3
		Portuguese	Do.	13	1	11	3	...	1	8	2	1	...	5	...
		Scotch	Do.	1	...	1	1	...	...	1	...	1	1	...	...
		Total, Group F—50	...	180	25	138	126	12	5	90	15	53	50	19	3
	51.—Eurasians.	Eurasian	Christian	114	11	73	73	30	...	98	15	49	44	33	1
		Total, Group F—51	...	114	11	73	73	30	...	98	15	49	44	33	1
	52.—Christian Converts.	Native Christian	Christian	1,460	86	400	58	956	18	1,245	44	68	6	1,119	14
		Total, Group F—52	...	1,460	86	400	58	956	18	1,245	44	68	6	1,119	14
		Total, Class F	...	**4,621**	**262**	**1,114**	**275**	**3,215**	**30**	**3,716**	**95**	**215**	**101**	**3,388**	**22**

TABLE C.—Castes, Tribes and Races by Education—*contd.*

Class.	Group.	Caste, Tribe or Race.	Religion.	MALES.						FEMALES.					
				Total.	Learning.	Literate.	English Literate.	Illiterate.	Not stated	Total.	Learning.	Literate.	English Literate.	Illiterate.	Not stated
1	2	3	4	5	6	7	8	9	10	11	12	13	14	15	16
G.—INDEFINITE AND UNKNOWN.	53.—Titular names.	Mudali	Hindu	19	2	5	1	12	...	19	...	2	...	17	...
		Náyaka	Do.	57	1	3	...	53	...	23	...	...	...	23	...
		Náyudu	Do.	9	...	4	4	5	...	3	...	...	...	3	...
		Pillai	Do.	6	...	6	1	...	...	8	...	...	...	8	...
		Total, Group G—53		91	3	18	6	70	...	53	...	2	...	51	...
	54.—Territorial, Linguistic and Sectarian names	Ándhra	Hindu	3	...	2	...	1	...	2	...	1	...	1	...
		Cháptia Sunni	Musalmán	2	...	...	...	2	...	1	...	...	...	1	...
		Hanafi	Do.	39	2	10	...	27	...	50	...	...	...	50	...
		Islám	Do.	6	...	1	...	5	...	7	...	...	...	7	...
		Karnàtaka	Hindu	18	...	3	...	15	...	19	...	...	...	19	...
		Konga	Do.	51	...	5	2	46	...	35	...	...	...	34	1
		Konkani	Do.	364	19	78	...	264	3	248	...	5	...	243	...
			Christian	73	5	17	...	51	...	45	1	...	...	44	...
		Krishnamata	Hindu	1	...	1	...	...	...	...	...	...	...	...	...
		Lingáyat	Do.	1,785	75	271	...	1,436	3	1,754	4	2	...	1,743	5
		Malayáli	Do.	143	...	22	...	121	...	8	...	...	...	8	...
		Multáni	Do.	3	...	3	...	...	...	...	...	...	...	...	...
		Musalman	Musalman	770	13	95	...	654	8	555	1	...	...	550	4
		Panchácbára	Hindu	244	12	25	...	205	2	259	...	...	...	256	3
		Rámánuja	Do.	2	...	1	...	1	...	3	...	...	...	3	...
		Saiva	Do.	115	5	16	1	94	...	141	...	...	...	140	1
		Sháfi	Musalman	14	...	5	...	9	...	1	...	...	...	1	...
		Sunni	Do.	12	...	5	1	7	...	2	...	...	...	2	...
		Tamil	Hindu	14	...	...	...	14	...	15	...	...	...	15	...
		Telugu	Do.	597	33	90	...	469	5	563	3	3	...	554	3
		Tuluva	Do.	31	2	...	...	29	...	14	...	...	...	14	...
		Turakaru	Musalman	5	...	1	1	4	...	...	...	...	...	...	...
		Vaishnava	Hindu	75	2	15	1	58	...	49	1	...	...	48	...
		Vírasaiva	Do.	709	56	190	1	463	...	871	1	1	...	866	3
		Total, Group G—54		5,076	224	856	7	3,975	21	4,642	11	12	...	4,599	20
	55.—Unclassified Castes.	Bánava	Hindu	1	...	...	...	1	...	...	...	...	...	...	...
		Bandára	Do.	4	...	...	...	4	...	4	...	...	...	4	...
		Chaniya	Do.	1	...	...	...	1	...	1	...	...	...	1	...
		Chauriya	Do.	1	...	...	...	1	...	...	...	...	...	...	...
		Chipira	Musalman	...	...	...	...	...	...	1	...	...	...	1	...
		Davala	Hindu	...	...	...	...	...	...	1	...	...	...	...	1
		Gópi	Do.	1	...	...	...	1	...	1	...	...	...	1	...
		Kurchi	Do.	10	...	...	...	10	...	2	...	...	...	2	...
		Low caste	Christian	1	...	...	...	1	...	...	...	...	...	...	...
		Mahale	Hindu	3	...	...	...	3	...	...	...	...	...	...	...
		Malkara	Do.	...	...	...	...	...	...	1	...	...	...	1	...
		Massadi	Musalmán	2	1	...	...	1	...	2	...	...	...	2	...
		Native	Hindu	...	...	...	...	...	...	1	...	...	...	1	...
		Palinga	Do.	3	...	...	...	3	...	2	...	...	...	2	...
		Total, Group G—55		27	1	...	...	26	...	16	...	...	...	15	1
		Total, Class G		5,194	228	874	13	4,071	21	4,711	11	14	...	4,665	21
NOT STATED.	Not stated.	Caste—Not returned	Hindu	55	1	4	...	41	9	50	...	...	...	50	...
		Grand Total		95,907	4,155	10,679	717	80,399	674	77,148	605	671	102	75,297	575

TABLE E.—Castes, Tribes and Races by Civil Condition.

MALES.

Class.	Group.	Caste, Tribe, etc.	Religion.	All Ages. Total.	All Ages. Single.	All Ages. Married.	All Ages. Widowed.	All Ages. Not stated.	0–9. Total.	0–9. Single.	0–9. Married.	0–9. Widowed.	0–9. Not stated.	10–14. Total.	10–14. Single.	10–14. Married.	10–14. Widowed.	10–14. Not stated.	15–39. Total.	15–39. Single.	15–39. Married.	15–39. Widowed.	15–39. Not stated.	40 and over. Total.	40 and over. Single.	40 and over. Married.	40 and over. Widowed.	40 and over. Not stated.	Not stated. Total.	Not stated. Single.	Not stated. Married.	Not stated. Widowed.	Not stated. Not stated.
1	2	3	4	5	6	7	8	9	10	11	12	13	14	15	16	17	18	19	20	21	22	23	24	25	26	27	28	29	30	31	32	33	34
A—AGRICULTURAL.	1.—Military and Dominant.	Agamodaiyan	Hindu	6	4	1	1	...	1	1	...	...	...	...	...	...	...	...	3	3	...	...	...	2	...	1	1	...	...	...	...	...	...
		Arasu	Do.	17	13	4	...	...	1	1	...	...	...	3	3	...	...	...	10	8	2	...	...	3	1	2	...	...	...	...	...	...	...
		Áré	Do.	54	23	29	2	...	3	3	...	...	...	8	7	...	1	...	36	13	22	1	...	7	...	7	...	...	...	...	...	...	...
		Kailan	Do.	...	...	...	...	...	...	...	...	...	...	...	...	...	...	...	...	...	...	...	...	...	...	...	...	...	...	...	...	...	...
		Kápála	Do.	71	36	34	1	...	19	19	...	...	...	8	8	...	...	...	28	9	18	1	...	16	...	16	...	...	...	...	...	...	...
		Kodagu	Do.	16,527	10,366	5,584	547	30	6,521	6,504	6	...	11	1,993	1,986	5	...	2	5,439	1,846	3,406	180	7	2,557	21	2,166	366	4	17	9	1	1	6
		Kshatriya	Do.	127	55	65	7	...	9	9	...	...	...	10	8	2	...	...	80	36	42	2	...	28	2	21	5	...	...	...	...	...	...
			Jain	2	...	2	...	...	...	...	...	...	...	...	...	...	...	...	1	...	1	...	...	1	...	1	...	...	...	...	...	...	...
		Maráthi	Hindu	1,388	685	640	61	1	258	254	4	...	...	121	116	5	...	...	761	306	437	17	1	248	9	194	45	...	...	...	...	...	...
		Náyar	Do.	953	330	595	28	...	40	39	1	...	...	19	19	...	...	...	688	264	414	10	...	206	8	180	18	...	...	...	...	...	...
		Pindári	Musalman	31	16	15	...	...	6	6	...	...	...	4	4	...	...	...	17	6	11	...	...	4	...	4	...	...	...	...	...	...	...
		Ráchevár	Hindu	13	10	2	1	...	...	...	...	...	...	4	4	...	...	...	6	6	...	...	...	3	...	2	1	...	...	...	...	...	...
		Rávuta	Do.	1	...	1	...	...	...	...	...	...	...	...	...	...	...	...	...	...	...	...	...	1	...	1	...	...	...	...	...	...	...
		Rájput	Do.	188	107	73	8	...	37	37	...	...	...	16	16	...	...	...	100	50	47	3	...	35	4	26	5	...	...	...	...	...	...
		Rájpinde	Do.	1	1	...	...	...	...	...	...	...	...	...	...	...	...	...	...	...	...	...	...	1	1	...	...	...	...	...	...	...	...
		Sérvégára	Do.	70	30	36	4	...	8	8	...	...	...	5	5	...	...	...	46	17	28	1	...	11	...	8	3	...	...	...	...	...	...
		Tírtha Kshatriya	Jain	21	15	6	...	...	7	7	...	...	...	2	2	...	...	...	10	6	4	...	...	2	...	2	...	...	...	...	...	...	...
		Total, Group A—1		29,470	21,691	7,087	661	31	6,910	6,888	11	...	11	2,193	2,178	12	1	2	7,225	2,570	4,432	215	8	3,125	46	2,631	444	4	17	9	1	1	6
	2(a).—Cultivators.	Aruchi	Hindu	...	...	...	...	...	...	...	...	...	...	...	...	...	...	...	...	...	...	...	...	...	...	...	...	...	...	...	...	...	...
		Ayyambokkalu	Do.	2	2	...	...	...	...	...	...	...	...	2	2	...	...	...	...	...	...	...	...	...	...	...	...	...	...	...	...	...	...
		Bádaga	Do.	1	...	1	...	...	...	...	...	...	...	...	...	...	...	...	1	...	1	...	...	...	...	...	...	...	...	...	...	...	...
		Bátólikára	Do.	7	7	...	...	...	1	1	...	...	...	1	1	...	...	...	5	5	...	...	...	...	...	...	...	...	...	...	...	...	...
		Banta	Do.	784	389	369	26	...	90	90	...	...	...	52	52	...	...	...	515	246	258	11	...	127	1	111	15	...	...	...	...	...	...
		Binepatta	Do.	55	34	18	3	...	18	18	...	...	...	8	8	...	...	...	25	8	15	2	...	4	...	3	1	...	...	...	...	...	...
		Gauda	Do.	7,001	3,883	2,852	264	2	1,974	1,956	16	...	2	826	796	29	1	...	3,128	1,109	1,873	146	...	1,073	22	934	117	...	...	...	...	...	...
			Christian	1	1	...	...	...	...	...	...	...	...	...	...	...	...	...	1	1	...	...	...	...	...	...	...	...	...	...	...	...	...
		Hallikára	Hindu	2	2	...	...	...	...	...	...	...	...	...	...	...	...	...	2	2	...	...	...	...	...	...	...	...	...	...	...	...	...
		Jain	Jain	32	14	17	1	...	2	2	...	...	...	1	1	...	...	...	19	11	7	1	...	10	...	10	...	...	...	...	...	...	...
		Kárgóli	Hindu	3	1	2	...	...	...	...	...	...	...	...	...	...	...	...	3	1	2	...	...	...	...	...	...	...	...	...	...	...	...
		Kávudi	Do.	22	13	6	3	...	3	3	...	...	...	1	1	...	...	...	13	9	4	...	...	5	...	2	3	...	...	...	...	...	...
		Kóvinajáti	Do.	2	1	1	...	...	...	...	...	...	...	1	1	...	...	...	...	...	...	...	...	1	...	1	...	...	...	...	...	...	...
		Kunchiga	Do.	14	9	5	...	...	...	...	...	...	...	7	7	...	...	...	4	1	3	...	...	3	1	2	...	...	...	...	...	...	...
		Púluvan	Do.	1	...	1	...	...	...	...	...	...	...	...	...	...	...	...	...	...	...	...	...	1	...	1	...	...	...	...	...	...	...
		Rájapuri	Do.	26	15	10	1	...	5	5	...	...	...	3	3	...	...	...	11	7	4	...	...	7	...	6	1	...	...	...	...	...	...
		Reddi	Do.	33	23	10	...	...	9	9	...	...	...	7	7	...	...	...	17	7	10	...	...	...	...	...	...	...	...	...	...	...	...
		Súdra	Do.	18	13	5	...	...	6	6	...	...	...	1	1	...	...	...	7	6	1	...	...	4	...	4	...	...	...	...	...	...	...
		Vádári	Do.	12	6	6	...	...	3	3	...	...	...	3	2	1	...	...	3	1	2	...	...	3	...	3	...	...	...	...	...	...	...
		Vakkaliga	Do.	7,132	3,701	3,163	268	...	1,154	1,149	5	...	...	892	884	8	...	...	4,018	1,645	2,276	97	...	1,066	23	873	170	...	1	...	...	1	...
			Christian	2	...	2	...	...	...	...	...	...	...	...	...	...	...	...	2	...	2	...	...	...	...	...	...	...	...	...	...	...	...
		Vellála	Hindu	655	427	199	29	...	169	169	...	...	...	93	93	...	...	...	300	161	130	9	...	93	4	69	20	...	...	...	...	...	...
			Christian	4	4	...	...	...	1	1	...	...	...	1	1	...	...	...	2	2	...	...	...	...	...	...	...	...	...	...	...	...	...
		Total, Group A—2 (a)		15,808	8,545	6,666	595	2	3,435	3,412	21	...	2	1,899	1,860	38	1	...	8,076	3,222	4,588	266	...	2,397	52	2,039	307	...	1	...	...	1	...
	2 (b).—Cattle Breeders, Graziers, etc.	Gandhári	Hindu	3	...	3	...	...	...	...	...	...	...	...	...	...	...	...	2	...	2	...	...	1	...	1	...	...	...	...	...	...	...
		Ganiga	Do.	94	48	38	8	...	22	22	...	...	...	15	15	...	...	...	45	11	32	2	...	12	...	6	5	...	...	...	...	...	...
		Total, Group A—2 (b)		97	48	41	8	...	22	22	...	...	...	15	15	...	...	...	47	11	34	2	...	13	...	7	6	...	...	...	...	...	...

Table E.—Castes by Civil Condition and Age.—Coorg.

Class.	Group.	Caste, Tribe, etc.	Religion.	FEMALES. All Ages.					0–9.					10–14.					15–39.					40 and over.					Not stated.				
				Total.	Single.	Married.	Widowed.	Not stated.	Total.	Single.	Married.	Widowed.	Not stated.	Total.	Single.	Married.	Widowed.	Not stated.	Total.	Single.	Married.	Widowed.	Not stated.	Total.	Single.	Married.	Widowed.	Not stated.	Total.	Single.	Married.	Widowed.	Not stated.
				35	36	37	38	39	40	41	42	43	44	45	46	47	48	49	50	51	52	53	54	55	56	57	58	59	60	61	62	63	64
A.—Agricultural.	1.—Military and Dominant.	Agamudaiyan	Hindu	2	1	1	...	...	1	1	...	...	...	...	...	...	...	...	1	...	1	...	...	...	...	...	...	...	...	...	...	...	...
		Arásu	Do.	13	3	6	4	...	2	2	...	...	...	...	...	...	...	...	4	1	1	2	...	7	...	5	2	...	...	...	...	...	...
		Áré	Do.	20	5	15	...	...	4	4	...	...	...	1	1	...	...	...	7	...	7	...	...	8	...	8	...	...	...	...	...	...	...
		Kallan	Do.	1	...	...	1	...	...	...	...	...	...	...	...	...	...	...	1	...	...	1	...	...	...	...	...	...	...	...	...	...	...
		Kápála	Do.	79	33	37	9	...	18	18	...	...	...	11	11	...	...	...	42	4	32	6	...	8	...	5	3	...	...	...	...	...	...
		Kodagu	Do.	16,084	8,363	5,638	2,058	25	5,982	5,957	10	...	15	1,994	1,940	53	...	1	5,710	453	4,751	501	5	2,389	9	821	1,557	2	9	4	3	...	2
		Kshatriya	Do.	92	34	34	24	...	23	23	...	...	...	5	4	1	...	...	49	7	30	12	...	15	...	3	12	...	...	...	...	...	...
			Jain	2	1	1	...	...	1	1	...	...	...	...	...	...	...	...	1	...	1	...	...	...	...	...	...	...	...	...	...	...	...
		Maráthi	Hindu	996	361	430	205	...	249	243	6	...	...	86	74	11	1	...	474	43	368	63	...	187	1	45	141	...	...	...	...	...	...
		Náyar	Do.	144	66	67	11	...	43	43	...	...	...	14	13	1	...	...	71	9	60	2	...	16	1	6	9	...	...	...	...	...	...
		Pindári	Musalman	22	7	9	6	...	5	5	...	...	...	2	2	...	...	...	9	...	9	...	...	6	...	...	6	...	...	...	...	...	...
		Ráchevár	Hindu	16	5	4	7	...	3	3	...	...	...	2	2	...	...	...	7	...	3	4	...	4	...	1	3	...	...	...	...	...	...
		Rájpinde	Do.	2	...	...	2	...	...	...	...	...	...	...	...	...	...	...	1	...	...	1	...	1	...	...	1	...	...	...	...	...	...
		Rájput	Do.	149	43	76	30	...	32	32	...	...	...	10	7	3	...	...	78	2	63	13	...	29	2	10	17	...	...	...	...	...	...
		Rávuta	Do.	...	...	...	...	...	...	...	...	...	...	...	...	...	...	...	...	...	...	...	...	...	...	...	...	...	...	...	...	...	...
		Sérvégára	Do.	31	11	15	5	...	5	5	...	...	...	4	4	...	...	...	20	2	15	3	...	2	...	...	2	...	...	...	...	...	...
		Tírtha Kshatriya	Jain	27	3	7	17	...	3	3	...	...	...	2	...	2	...	...	12	...	5	7	...	10	...	...	10	...	...	...	...	...	...
		Total, Group A—1	...	17,680	8,936	6,340	2,379	25	6,371	6,340	16	...	15	2,131	2,058	71	1	1	6,487	521	5,346	615	5	2,682	13	904	1,763	2	9	4	3	...	2
	2 (a)—Cultivators	Arechi	Hindu	1	...	...	1	...	...	...	...	...	...	...	...	...	...	...	...	...	...	...	...	1	...	...	1	...	...	...	...	...	...
		Ayyambokkalu	Do.	2	2	...	...	...	2	2	...	...	...	...	...	...	...	...	...	...	...	...	...	...	...	...	...	...	...	...	...	...	...
		Badaga	Do.	...	...	...	...	...	...	...	...	...	...	...	...	...	...	...	...	...	...	...	...	...	...	...	...	...	...	...	...	...	...
		Bálólikára	Do.	2	...	1	1	...	...	...	...	...	...	...	...	...	...	...	1	...	1	...	...	1	...	...	1	...	...	...	...	...	...
		Banta	Do.	333	131	145	57	...	94	94	...	...	...	28	23	5	...	...	142	11	119	12	...	69	3	21	45	...	...	...	...	...	...
		Binepatta	Do.	46	20	17	9	...	13	13	...	...	...	4	4	...	...	...	19	3	15	1	...	10	...	2	8	...	...	...	...	...	...
		Gauda	Do.	6,322	2,649	2,769	904	...	1,990	1,957	33	...	...	623	512	110	1	...	2,832	177	2,290	365	...	876	2	336	538	...	1	1	...	...	...
			Christian	1	...	...	1	...	...	...	...	...	...	...	...	...	...	...	...	...	...	...	...	1	...	...	1	...	...	...	...	...	...
		Hallikára	Hindu	...	...	...	...	...	...	...	...	...	...	...	...	...	...	...	...	...	...	...	...	...	...	...	...	...	...	...	...	...	...
		Jain	Jain	30	6	12	12	...	4	4	...	...	...	1	1	...	...	...	13	1	8	4	...	12	...	4	8	...	...	...	...	...	...
		Kárgóli	Hindu	4	2	...	2	...	1	1	...	...	...	...	...	...	...	...	2	1	...	1	...	1	...	...	1	...	...	...	...	...	...
		Kávudi	Do.	15	9	5	1	...	6	6	...	...	...	2	2	...	...	...	7	1	5	1	...	...	...	...	...	...	...	...	...	...	...
		Kóvinajáti	Do.	6	2	1	3	...	1	1	...	...	...	1	1	...	...	...	4	...	1	3	...	...	...	...	...	...	...	...	...	...	...
		Kunchiga	Do.	10	1	1	8	...	...	...	...	...	...	...	...	...	...	...	3	1	1	1	...	7	...	...	7	...	...	...	...	...	...
		Púlluvan	Do.	3	...	2	1	...	...	...	...	...	...	...	...	...	...	...	2	...	2	...	...	1	...	...	1	...	...	...	...	...	...
		Rájapuri	Do.	27	6	10	11	...	4	4	...	...	...	1	1	...	...	...	15	1	8	6	...	7	...	2	5	...	...	...	...	...	...
		Reddi	Do.	28	14	6	8	...	8	8	...	...	...	2	2	...	...	...	12	4	5	3	...	6	...	1	5	...	...	...	...	...	...
		Súdra	Do.	13	5	4	4	...	4	4	...	...	...	1	1	...	...	...	7	...	4	3	...	1	...	...	1	...	...	...	...	...	...
		Vádári	Do.	15	7	6	2	...	5	5	...	...	...	1	...	1	...	...	7	2	4	1	...	2	...	1	1	...	...	...	...	...	...
		Vakkaliga	Do.	5,290	2,038	2,052	1,200	...	1,224	1,218	6	...	...	685	633	46	6	...	2,508	172	1,801	535	...	872	15	198	659	...	1	...	1	...	...
			Christian	2	1	1	...	...	...	...	...	...	...	1	1	...	...	...	1	...	1	...	...	...	...	...	...	...	...	...	...	...	...
		Vellála	Hindu	575	240	188	147	...	174	173	1	...	...	53	44	8	1	...	225	22	154	49	...	122	...	25	97	...	1	1	...	...	...
			Christian	5	2	...	3	...	1	1	...	...	...	1	1	...	...	...	1	...	...	1	...	2	...	...	2	...	...	...	...	...	...
		Total, Group A—2 (a)		12,730	5,135	5,220	2,375	...	3,531	3,491	40	...	...	1,404	1,226	170	8	...	5,801	396	4,429	986	...	1,991	20	590	1,381	...	3	2	1	...	...
	2 (b)—Cattle-breeders, Graziers, etc.	Gandhári	Hindu	...	...	...	...	...	...	...	...	...	...	...	...	...	...	...	...	...	...	...	...	...	...	...	...	...	...	...	...	...	...
		Gauliga	Do.	85	23	34	28	...	16	16	...	...	...	16	3	13	...	...	37	4	19	14	...	16	...	2	14	...	...	...	...	...	...
		Total, Group A—2 (b)		85	23	34	28	...	16	16	...	...	...	16	3	13	...	...	37	4	19	14	...	16	...	2	14	...	...	...	...	...	...

TABLE E.—Castes, Tribes and Races by Civil Condition—*contd.*

Class.	Group.	Caste, Tribe, etc.	Religion.	MALES. All Ages. Total.	Single.	Married.	Widowed.	Not stated.	0—9. Total.	Single.	Married.	Widowed.	Not stated.	10—14. Total.	Single.	Married.	Widowed.	Not stated.	15—39. Total.	Single.	Married.	Widowed.	Not stated.	40 and over. Total.	Single.	Married.	Widowed.	Not stated.	Not stated. Total.	Single.	Married.	Widowed.	Not stated.
1	2	3	4	5	6	7	8	9	10	11	12	13	14	15	16	17	18	19	20	21	22	23	24	25	26	27	28	29	30	31	32	33	34
A.—AGRICULTURAL—*contd.*	2 (c).—Field Labourers.	Adiyán	Hindu	303	123	165	15	...	63	63	...	...	...	21	20	1	...	...	160	39	117	4	...	59	1	47	11	—	...	...	...	...	...
		Agnáni	Do.	16	8	6	2	...	4	4	...	...	...	2	2	...	...	...	3	1	2	...	...	7	1	4	2	...	...	...	...	...	...
			Christian	2	1	...	1	...	...	...	...	...	...	...	...	...	...	...	1	1	...	...	...	1	...	...	1	...	...	...	...	...	...
		Ajala	Hindu	1	1	...	...	...	1	1	...	...	...	...	...	...	...	...	...	...	...	...	...	...	...	...	...	...	...	...	...	...	...
		Aneku'a	Do.	4	3	...	1	...	1	1	...	...	...	1	1	...	...	...	2	1	...	1	...	...	...	...	...	...	...	...	...	...	...
		Bákuda	Do.	5	...	5	...	...	...	...	...	...	...	...	...	...	...	...	4	...	4	...	...	1	...	1	...	...	...	...	...	...	...
		Biraira	Do.	40	21	18	1	...	11	11	...	...	...	3	3	...	...	...	24	7	16	1	...	2	...	2	...	...	...	...	...	...	...
		Holeya	Do.	13,724	7,109	6,165	448	2	2,794	2,781	11	1	1	1,142	1,115	27	...	...	7,825	3,158	4,444	222	1	1,961	54	1,683	224	...	2	1	...	1	...
			Christian	2	...	...	2	...	...	...	...	...	...	...	...	...	...	...	2	...	...	2	...	...	...	...	...	...	...	...	...	...	...
		Káládi	Hindu	2	1	1	...	...	1	1	...	...	...	...	...	...	...	...	...	...	...	...	...	1	...	1	...	...	...	...	...	...	...
		Máyava	Do.	1	...	1	...	...	...	...	...	...	...	...	...	...	...	...	1	...	1	...	...	...	...	...	...	...	...	...	...	...	...
		Máyila	Do.	91	51	35	5	...	18	18	...	...	...	5	5	...	...	...	52	28	22	2	...	16	...	13	3	...	...	...	...	...	...
		Méra	Do.	4	3	1	...	...	2	2	...	...	...	1	1	...	...	...	1	...	1	...	...	...	...	...	...	...	...	...	...	...	...
		Pále	Do.	2,693	1,134	1,420	137	2	353	319	4	...	...	222	213	9	...	...	1,717	561	1,097	57	2	401	11	310	80	...	...	...	...	...	...
		Pallan	Do.	30	14	15	1	...	4	4	...	...	...	1	1	...	...	...	23	9	14	...	...	2	...	1	1	...	...	...	...	...	...
		Paniyan	Do.	1	...	1	...	...	...	...	...	...	...	...	...	...	...	...	1	...	1	...	...	...	...	...	...	...	...	...	...	...	...
		Paraiyan	Do.	35	13	21	1	...	8	8	...	...	...	1	1	...	...	...	21	4	17	...	...	5	...	4	1	...	...	...	...	...	...
			Christian	...	...	...	...	...	...	...	...	...	...	...	...	...	...	...	...	...	...	...	...	...	...	...	...	...	...	...	...	...	...
		Parava	Hindu	6	2	3	1	...	...	...	...	...	...	1	1	...	...	...	3	1	1	1	...	2	...	2	...	...	...	...	...	...	...
		Tigala	Do.	16	9	6	1	...	...	...	...	...	...	1	1	...	...	...	11	7	3	1	...	4	1	3	...	...	...	...	...	...	...
			Christian	...	...	...	...	...	...	...	...	...	...	...	...	...	...	...	...	...	...	...	...	...	...	...	...	...	...	...	...	...	...
		Total, Group A—2 (c)		16,976	8,493	7,863	616	4	3,260	3,243	15	1	1	1,401	1,364	37	...	...	9,851	3,817	5,740	291	3	2,462	68	2,071	323	...	2	1	...	1	...
	4.—Forest and Hill Tribes.	Betta	Hindu	2	...	2	...	...	...	...	...	...	...	...	...	...	...	...	1	...	1	...	...	1	...	1	...	...	...	...	...	...	...
		Koraga	Do.	7	4	3	...	...	...	...	...	...	...	1	1	...	...	...	6	3	3	...	...	...	...	...	...	...	...	...	...	...	...
			Christian	1	...	1	...	...	...	...	...	...	...	...	...	...	...	...	1	...	1	...	...	...	...	...	...	...	...	...	...	...	...
		Kudiya	Hindu	321	191	116	14	...	92	92	...	...	...	37	36	1	...	...	149	62	79	8	...	43	1	36	6	...	...	...	...	...	...
		Malasar	Do.	6	5	1	...	...	2	2	...	...	...	2	2	...	...	...	2	1	1	...	...	...	...	...	...	...	...	...	...	...	...
		Yerava	Do.	7,376	3,803	3,220	353	...	942	934	8	...	...	319	310	9	...	...	4,817	2,495	2,169	153	...	1,297	63	1,034	200	...	1	1	...	...	...
		Total, Group A—4		7,713	4,003	3,343	367	...	1,036	1,028	8	...	...	359	349	10	...	...	4,976	2,561	2,254	162	...	1,341	64	1,071	206	...	1	1	...	...	...
		Total, Class A		60,064	32,780	25,000	2,247	37	14,663	14,593	55	1	14	5,867	5,766	97	2	2	30,175	12,181	17,048	935	11	9,338	229	7,799	1,306	4	21	11	1	3	6
B.—PROFESSIONAL.	5.—Priests	Bráhman Advaita	Hindu	1	1	...	...	...	1	1	...	...	...	...	...	...	...	...	...	...	...	...	...	...	...	...	...	...	...	...	...	...	...
		" Aitála	Do.	2	2	...	...	...	...	...	...	...	...	...	...	...	...	...	1	1	...	...	...	1	1	...	...	...	...	...	...	...	...
		" Ándhra	Do.	10	5	4	1	...	1	1	...	...	...	1	1	...	...	...	5	2	3	...	...	3	1	1	1	...	...	...	...	...	...
		" Árádhya	Do.	...	...	...	...	...	...	...	...	...	...	...	...	...	...	...	...	...	...	...	...	...	...	...	...	...	...	...	...	...	...
		" Aravattuvakkalu	Do.	5	3	2	...	...	...	...	...	...	...	2	2	...	...	...	3	1	2	...	...	...	...	...	...	...	...	...	...	...	...
		" Áruvélu	Do.	6	1	4	1	...	...	...	...	...	...	1	1	...	...	...	3	...	3	...	...	2	...	1	1	...	...	...	...	...	...
		" Babbúru Kamme	Do.	8	3	5	...	...	2	2	...	...	...	1	1	...	...	...	4	...	4	...	...	1	...	1	...	...	...	...	...	...	...
		" Badaganádu	Do.	37	16	21	...	...	7	7	...	...	...	3	3	...	...	...	15	5	10	...	...	12	1	11	...	...	...	...	...	...	...
		" Bettadapurada Sankéti	Do.	1	...	1	...	...	...	...	...	...	...	...	...	...	...	...	1	...	1	...	...	...	...	...	...	...	...	...	...	...	...
		" Brahacharanam	Do.	1	...	1	...	...	...	...	...	...	...	...	...	...	...	...	1	...	1	...	...	...	...	...	...	...	...	...	...	...	...
		" Bráhman	Do.	30	14	12	4	...	5	5	...	...	...	3	3	...	...	...	16	6	6	4	...	6	...	6	...	...	...	...	...	...	...
		" Chittapávana	Do.	1	1	...	...	...	...	...	...	...	...	...	...	...	...	...	1	1	...	...	...	...	...	...	...	...	...	...	...	...	...
		" Chólamandala	Do.	3	1	1	1	...	...	...	...	...	...	1	1	...	...	...	2	...	1	1	...	...	...	...	...	...	...	...	...	...	...
		" Désasta	Do.	31	16	12	3	...	8	8	...	...	...	1	1	...	...	...	17	7	7	3	...	5	...	5	...	...	...	...	...	...	...

Table E.—Castes by Civil Condition and Age.—Coorg.

Class.	Group.	Caste, Tribe, etc.	Religion.	FEMALES.																													
				All Ages.					0–9.					10–14.					15–39.					40 and over.					Not stated.				
				Total.	Single.	Married.	Widowed.	Not stated.	Total.	Single.	Married.	Widowed.	Not stated.	Total.	Single.	Married.	Widowed.	Not stated.	Total.	Single.	Married.	Widowed.	Not stated.	Total.	Single.	Married.	Widowed.	Not stated.	Total.	Single.	Married.	Widowed.	Not stated.
				35	36	37	38	39	40	41	42	43	44	45	46	47	48	49	50	51	52	53	54	55	56	57	58	59	60	61	62	63	64
A.—AGRICULTURAL—contd.	2 (c)—Field Labourers.	Adiyán	Hindu	234	86	134	13	1	62	62	...	...	...	22	15	7	...	...	126	9	115	1	1	24	...	12	12	...	...	...	...	...	...
		Agnáni	Do.	14	3	9	2	...	3	3	...	...	...	...	...	...	...	...	9	...	8	1	...	2	...	1	1	...	...	...	...	...	...
			Christian	2	...	...	2	...	...	...	...	...	...	...	...	...	...	...	1	...	...	1	...	1	...	...	1	...	...	...	...	...	...
		Ajala	Hindu	...	...	...	...	...	...	...	...	...	...	...	...	...	...	...	...	...	...	...	...	...	...	...	...	...	...	...	...	...	...
		Anekula	Do.	5	4	...	1	...	3	3	...	...	...	...	...	...	...	...	2	1	...	1	...	...	...	...	...	...	...	...	...	...	...
		Bákuda	Do.	1	...	1	...	...	...	...	...	...	...	...	...	...	...	...	...	...	...	...	...	1	...	1	...	...	...	...	...	...	...
		Bhaira	Do.	18	5	9	4	...	3	3	...	...	...	...	...	...	...	...	9	2	7	...	...	6	...	2	4	...	...	...	...	...	...
		Holeya	Do.	10,357	4,075	4,439	1,840	3	2,885	2,864	17	2	2	932	772	157	3	...	5,150	415	3,842	893	...	1,389	24	423	942	...	1	...	...	...	1
			Christian	2	...	...	2	...	...	...	...	...	...	...	...	...	...	...	1	...	...	1	...	1	...	...	1	...	...	...	...	...	...
		Káládi	Do.	3	1	1	1	...	1	1	...	...	...	...	...	...	...	...	1	...	1	...	...	1	...	...	1	...	...	...	...	...	...
		Máyava	Do.	...	...	...	...	...	...	...	...	...	...	...	...	...	...	...	...	...	...	...	...	...	...	...	...	...	...	...	...	...	...
		Máylia	Do.	39	16	20	3	...	14	13	1	...	...	2	2	...	...	...	17	1	15	1	...	6	...	4	2	...	...	...	...	...	...
		Méra	Do.	8	6	1	1	...	2	2	...	...	...	2	2	...	...	...	3	2	1	...	...	1	...	...	1	...	...	...	...	...	...
		Pále	Do.	1,352	516	677	159	...	335	333	2	...	...	123	101	22	...	...	723	82	584	57	...	171	...	69	102	...	...	...	...	...	...
		Palian	Do.	38	10	16	12	...	3	3	...	...	...	2	2	...	...	...	26	5	15	6	...	7	...	1	6	...	...	...	...	...	...
		Paniya	Hindu	...	...	...	...	...	...	...	...	...	...	...	...	...	...	...	...	...	...	...	...	...	...	...	...	...	...	...	...	...	...
		Paraiyan	Do.	39	15	17	7	...	7	7	...	...	...	3	3	...	...	...	21	4	14	3	...	8	1	3	4	...	...	...	...	...	...
			Christian	3	1	2	...	...	...	...	...	...	...	1	1	...	...	...	2	...	2	...	...	...	...	...	...	...	...	...	...	...	...
		Parva	Hindu	5	2	3	...	...	2	2	...	...	...	...	...	...	...	...	3	...	3	...	...	...	...	...	...	...	...	...	...	...	...
		Tigala	Do	7	...	4	3	...	...	...	...	...	...	...	...	...	...	...	4	...	4	...	...	3	...	...	3	...	...	...	...	...	...
			Christian	1	...	1	...	...	...	...	...	...	...	...	...	...	...	...	1	...	1	...	...	...	...	...	...	...	...	...	...	...	...
		Total, Group A—2(c).		12,128	4,740	5,334	2,050	4	3,320	3,296	20	2	2	1,087	898	186	3	...	6,099	521	4,612	965	1	1,621	25	516	1,080	...	1	...	...	...	1
	4.—Forest and Hill Tribes.	Betta	Hindu	1	...	1	...	...	...	...	...	...	...	...	...	...	...	...	1	...	1	...	...	...	...	...	...	...	...	...	...	...	...
		Koraga	Do	1	...	...	1	...	...	...	...	...	...	...	...	...	...	...	...	...	...	...	...	1	...	...	1	...	...	...	...	...	...
			Christian	2	...	1	1	...	...	...	...	...	...	...	...	...	...	...	1	...	1	...	...	1	...	...	1	...	...	...	...	...	...
		Kudiya	Hindu	321	168	114	39	...	105	104	1	...	...	30	28	2	...	...	145	35	97	13	...	40	...	14	26	...	1	1	...	...	...
		Malasar	Do.	10	4	4	2	...	1	1	...	...	...	1	1	...	...	...	6	2	4	...	...	2	...	...	2	...	...	...	...	...	...
		Yerava	Do.	6,833	3,067	3,157	609	...	1,387	1,381	5	1	...	357	297	59	1	...	4,209	1,371	2,638	200	...	880	18	455	407	...	...	...	...	...	...
		Total, Group A—4.		7,168	3,239	3,277	652	...	1,493	1,486	6	1	...	388	326	61	1	...	4,362	1,408	2,741	213	...	924	18	469	437	...	1	1	...	...	...
		Total, Class A		40,791	22,073	20,205	7,484	29	14,731	14,629	82	3	17	5,026	4,511	501	13	1	22,786	2,850	17,137	2,793	6	7,234	76	2,481	4,675	2	14	7	4	...	3
B.—PROFESSIONAL.	5.—Priests	Bráhman Advaita	Hindu	3	...	...	3	...	...	...	...	...	...	1	...	...	1	...	1	...	...	1	...	1	...	...	1	...	...	...	...	...	...
		" Ajitála	Do.	...	...	...	...	...	...	...	...	...	...	...	...	...	...	...	...	...	...	...	...	...	...	...	...	...	...	...	...	...	...
		" Andhra	Do.	3	1	2	...	...	1	1	...	...	...	...	...	...	...	...	2	...	2	...	...	...	...	...	...	...	...	...	...	...	...
		" Arádya	Do.	2	...	...	2	...	...	...	...	...	...	...	...	...	...	...	1	...	...	1	...	1	...	...	1	...	...	...	...	...	...
		" Aravattu-vakkalu	Do.	9	3	4	2	...	3	3	...	...	...	...	...	...	...	...	4	...	3	1	...	2	...	1	1	...	...	...	...	...	...
		" Áruvélu	Do.	5	1	4	...	...	1	1	...	...	...	...	...	...	...	...	3	...	3	...	...	1	...	1	...	...	...	...	...	...	...
		" Babbúru Kamme	Do.	4	...	3	1	...	...	...	...	...	...	...	...	...	...	...	3	...	3	...	...	1	...	...	1	...	...	...	...	...	...
		" Badaganádu	Do.	38	11	18	9	...	11	11	...	...	...	1	...	1	...	...	15	...	14	1	...	10	...	2	8	...	1	...	1	...	...
		" Bettadapurada Sankéti	Do.	...	...	...	...	...	...	...	...	...	...	...	...	...	...	...	...	...	...	...	...	...	...	...	...	...	...	...	...	...	...
		" Bráhacharanam	Do.	...	...	...	...	...	...	...	...	...	...	...	...	...	...	...	...	...	...	...	...	...	...	...	...	...	...	...	...	...	...
		" Bráhman	Do.	17	6	7	4	...	5	5	...	...	...	1	1	...	...	...	10	...	7	3	...	1	...	...	1	...	...	...	...	...	...
		" Chittapávana	Do.	...	...	...	...	...	...	...	...	...	...	...	...	...	...	...	...	...	...	...	...	...	...	...	...	...	...	...	...	...	...
		" Chólamandala	Do.	1	...	...	1	...	...	...	...	...	...	...	...	...	...	...	...	...	...	...	...	1	...	...	1	...	...	...	...	...	...
		" Désasta	Do.	32	9	15	8	...	8	8	...	...	...	2	1	1	...	...	13	...	11	2	...	9	...	3	6	...	...	...	...	...	...

TABLE E.—Castes, Tribes and Races by Civil Condition—*contd.*

Class.	Group.	Caste, Tribe, etc.	Religion.	MALES. All Ages. Total.	Single.	Married.	Widowed.	Not stated.	0—9. Total.	Single.	Married.	Widowed.	Not stated.	10—14. Total.	Single.	Married.	Widowed.	Not stated.	15—39. Total.	Single.	Married.	Widowed.	Not stated.	40 and over. Total.	Single.	Married.	Widowed.	Not stated.	Not stated. Total.	Single.	Married.	Widowed.	Not stated.
1	2	3	4	5	6	7	8	9	10	11	12	13	14	15	16	17	18	19	20	21	22	23	24	25	26	27	28	29	30	31	32	33	34
B.—PROFESSIONAL—*contd.*	5.—Priests—*contd.*	Bráhman Drávida	Hindu	11	3	7	1	...	...	...	...	...	...	...	...	...	...	...	9	3	6	...	...	2	...	1	1	...	...	...	...	...	...
		" Gauda	Do.	16	12	4	...	...	6	6	...	...	...	4	4	...	...	...	4	2	2	...	...	2	...	2	...	...	...	...	...	...	...
		" Golkonda	Do.	1	...	1	...	...	...	...	...	...	...	...	...	...	...	...	1	...	1	...	...	...	...	...	...	...	...	...	...	...	...
		" Hale Kannadiga	Do.	2	...	2	...	...	...	...	...	...	...	...	...	...	...	...	2	...	2	...	...	...	...	...	...	...	...	...	...	...	...
		" Hale Karnátaka	Do.	5	...	5	...	...	...	...	...	...	...	...	...	...	...	...	3	...	3	...	...	2	...	2	...	...	...	...	...	...	...
		" Havig	Do.	319	143	127	49	...	50	50	...	...	...	26	15	1	...	...	163	74	83	6	...	90	4	43	43	...	...	...	...	...	...
		" Hebbára	Do.	4	2	2	...	...	1	1	...	...	...	...	...	...	...	...	2	1	1	...	...	1	...	1	...	...	...	...	...	...	...
		" Hemmige	Do.	1	...	1	...	...	...	...	...	...	...	...	...	...	...	...	1	...	1	...	...	...	...	...	...	...	...	...	...	...	...
		" Hoisala Karnátaka	Do.	63	32	25	6	...	15	15	...	...	...	8	8	...	...	...	24	9	14	1	...	16	...	11	5	...	...	...	...	...	...
		" Hosanádu Karnátaka	Do.	3	2	1	...	...	1	1	...	...	...	1	1	...	...	...	...	...	...	...	...	1	...	1	...	...	...	...	...	...	...
		" Kamme	Do.	13	7	6	...	...	3	3	...	...	...	2	2	...	...	...	7	2	5	...	...	1	...	1	...	...	...	...	...	...	...
		" Kanauj	Do.	4	2	2	...	...	2	2	...	...	...	...	...	...	...	...	2	...	2	...	...	...	...	...	...	...	...	...	...	...	...
		" Kandavara	Do.	1	1	...	...	...	...	...	...	...	...	...	...	...	...	...	1	1	...	...	...	...	...	...	...	...	...	...	...	...	...
		" Kannada	Do.	3	1	2	...	...	...	...	...	...	...	...	...	...	...	...	1	1	...	...	...	2	...	2	...	...	...	...	...	...	...
		" Karnátaka	Do.	94	43	46	5	...	19	19	...	...	...	4	4	...	...	...	52	20	28	4	...	19	...	18	1	...	...	...	...	...	...
		" Kónasímai Drávida	Do.	4	3	1	...	...	2	2	...	...	...	...	...	...	...	...	2	1	1	...	...	...	...	...	...	...	...	...	...	...	...
		" Konkanasta	Do.	16	8	6	2	...	6	6	...	...	...	...	...	...	...	...	6	2	4	...	...	4	...	2	2	...	...	...	...	...	...
		" Kóta	Do.	11	7	4	...	...	3	3	...	...	...	1	1	...	...	...	5	3	2	...	...	2	...	2	...	...	...	...	...	...	...
		" Kudlukára	Do.	2	1	1	...	...	1	1	...	...	...	...	...	...	...	...	1	...	1	...	...	...	...	...	...	...	...	...	...	...	...
		" Mádhva	Do.	1	...	...	1	...	...	...	...	...	...	...	...	...	...	...	1	...	...	1	...	...	...	...	...	...	...	...	...	...	...
		" Maharáshtra	Do.	1	...	1	...	...	...	...	...	...	...	...	...	...	...	...	...	...	...	...	...	1	...	1	...	...	...	...	...	...	...
		" Málanádu Kamme	Do.	3	1	2	...	...	...	...	...	...	...	...	...	...	...	...	2	...	2	...	...	1	1	...	...	...	...	...	...	...	...
		" Malanádu Karnátaka	Do.	3	2	1	...	...	...	...	...	...	...	...	...	...	...	...	3	2	1	...	...	...	...	...	...	...	...	...	...	...	...
		" Márvádi	Do.	1	...	1	...	...	...	...	...	...	...	...	...	...	...	...	1	...	1	...	...	...	...	...	...	...	...	...	...	...	...
		" Pralákalyana Vámsa	Do.	1	...	1	...	...	...	...	...	...	...	...	...	...	...	...	...	...	...	...	...	1	...	1	...	...	...	...	...	...	...
		" Rámánujamatam	Do.	1	...	...	1	...	...	...	...	...	...	...	...	...	...	...	...	...	...	...	...	1	...	...	1	...	...	...	...	...	...
		" Sankéti	Do.	42	13	27	2	...	4	4	...	...	...	4	4	...	...	...	25	5	19	1	...	9	...	8	1	...	...	...	...	...	...
		" Sárasvata	Do.	55	29	26	...	...	9	9	...	...	...	3	3	...	...	...	36	17	19	...	...	7	...	7	...	...	...	...	...	...	...
		" Shivalli	Do.	302	175	101	25	1	59	59	...	...	...	28	27	1	...	...	158	85	67	5	1	57	4	33	20	...	...	...	...	...	...
		" Smárta	Do.	51	18	32	1	...	8	8	...	...	...	1	1	...	...	...	35	9	26	...	...	7	...	6	1	...	...	...	...	...	...
		" Smárta Karnátaka	Do.	22	13	8	1	...	7	7	...	...	...	3	3	...	...	...	9	3	6	...	...	3	...	2	1	...	...	...	...	...	...
		" Srívaishnava	Do.	61	30	30	1	...	15	15	...	...	...	8	5	3	...	...	29	10	19	...	...	9	...	8	1	...	...	...	...	...	...
		" Tengalai	Do.	3	2	1	...	...	...	...	...	...	...	...	...	...	...	...	1	1	...	...	...	2	1	1	...	...	...	...	...	...	...
		" Tulu	Do.	9	1	8	...	...	1	1	...	...	...	...	...	...	...	...	7	...	7	...	...	1	...	1	...	...	...	...	...	...	...
		" Ulucha Kamme	Do.	1	1	...	...	...	...	...	...	...	...	...	...	...	...	...	1	1	...	...	...	...	...	...	...	...	...	...	...	...	...
		" Uttaráji	Do.	2	...	2	...	...	...	...	...	...	...	...	...	...	...	...	1	...	1	...	...	1	...	1	...	...	...	...	...	...	...
		" Vadagalai	Do.	73	35	35	2	...	20	20	...	...	...	10	8	2	...	...	28	6	21	1	...	15	1	13	1	...	...	...	...	...	...
		" Vadama	Do.	9	5	4	...	...	2	2	...	...	...	1	1	...	...	...	5	2	3	...	...	1	...	1	...	...	...	...	...	...	...
		" Vaidíki	Do.	4	2	2	...	...	...	...	...	...	...	1	1	...	...	...	3	1	2	...	...	...	...	...	...	...	...	...	...	...	...
		" Vaishnava	Do.	10	3	6	1	...	2	2	...	...	...	1	1	...	...	...	4	...	4	...	...	3	...	2	1	...	...	...	...	...	...
		" Vélanádu Ándhra	Do.	3	1	2	...	...	1	1	...	...	...	...	...	...	...	...	2	...	2	...	...	...	...	...	...	...	...	...	...	...	...
		Total, Bráhmans	. . .	1,367	661	597	108	1	261	261	...	...	...	109	102	7	...	...	706	284	394	27	1	291	14	196	81	...	...	...	...	...	...
		Jangam	Hindu	495	288	176	31	..	141	138	2	1	...	59	59	...	...	...	206	87	109	10	...	88	4	64	20	...	1	...	1	...	...
		Pandáram	Do.	4	3	1	...	...	...	...	...	...	...	...	...	...	...	...	3	3	...	...	...	1	...	1	...	...	...	...	...	...	...
		Total, Group B—5.		1,866	952	774	139	1	402	399	2	1	...	168	161	7	...	...	915	374	503	37	1	380	18	261	101	...	1	...	1	...	...

Table E.—Castes by Civil Condition and Age.—Coorg

B.—PROFESSIONAL—*contd.*

5.—Priests—*contd.*

Caste, Tribe, etc.	Religion	FEMALES. All Ages. Total.	Single.	Married.	Widowed.	Not stated.	0–9. Total.	Single.	Married.	Widowed.	Not stated.	10–14. Total.	Single.	Married.	Widowed.	Not stated.	15–39. Total.	Single.	Married.	Widowed.	Not stated.	40 and over. Total.	Single.	Married.	Widowed.	Not stated.	Not Stated. Total.	Single.	Married.	Widowed.	Not stated.
		35	36	37	38	39	40	41	42	43	44	45	46	47	48	49	50	51	52	53	54	55	56	57	58	59	60	61	62	63	64
Bráhman Drávida	Hindu	3	...	2	1	...	...	...	...	...	...	...	...	...	...	...	3	...	2	1	...	...	...	...	...	...	...	...	...	...	...
" Gauda	Do.	17	5	5	7	...	4	4	...	...	...	...	...	...	...	...	8	1	5	2	...	5	...	...	5	...	...	...	...	...	...
" Golkonda	Do.	...	...	...	...	...	...	...	...	...	...	...	...	...	...	...	...	...	...	...	...	...	...	...	...	...	...	...	...	...	...
" Hale Kannadiga	Do.	4	...	4	...	...	...	...	...	...	...	...	...	...	...	...	2	...	2	...	...	2	...	2	...	...	...	...	...	...	...
" Hale Karnátaka	Do.	1	...	1	...	...	...	...	...	...	...	...	...	...	...	...	1	...	1	...	...	...	...	...	...	...	...	...	...	...	...
" Havig	Do.	281	86	120	74	1	80	79	...	...	1	11	6	5	...	...	124	1	106	17	...	66	...	9	57	...	...	...	...	...	...
" Hebbára	Do.	3	...	2	1	...	...	...	...	...	...	...	...	...	...	...	2	...	2	...	...	1	...	...	1	...	...	...	...	...	...
" Hemmige	Do.	1	...	1	...	...	...	...	...	...	...	...	...	...	...	...	1	...	1	...	...	...	...	...	...	...	...	...	...	...	...
" Hoisala Karnátaka	Do.	52	16	24	12	...	15	15	...	...	...	3	1	2	...	...	23	...	20	3	...	11	...	2	9	...	...	...	...	...	...
" Hosanádu Karnátaka	Do.	3	...	2	1	...	...	...	...	...	...	...	...	...	...	...	2	...	2	...	...	1	...	...	1	...	...	...	...	...	...
" Kamme	Do.	6	3	2	1	...	3	3	...	...	...	...	...	...	...	...	3	...	2	1	...	...	...	...	...	...	...	...	...	...	...
" Kannuj	Do.	4	2	2	...	...	2	2	...	...	...	...	...	...	...	...	1	...	1	...	...	1	...	1	...	...	...	...	...	...	...
" Kandavara	Do.	...	...	...	...	...	...	...	...	...	...	...	...	...	...	...	...	...	...	...	...	...	...	...	...	...	...	...	...	...	...
" Kannada	Do.	1	...	1	...	...	...	...	...	...	...	...	...	...	...	...	1	...	1	...	...	...	...	...	...	...	...	...	...	...	...
" Karnátaka	Do.	64	18	23	23	...	13	13	...	...	...	6	5	1	...	...	23	...	17	6	...	22	...	5	17	...	...	...	...	...	...
" Kónasimai Drávida	Do.	3	1	2	...	...	...	...	...	...	...	1	1	...	...	...	2	...	2	...	...	...	...	...	...	...	...	...	...	...	...
" Konkanasta	Do.	16	4	7	5	...	4	4	...	...	...	1	...	1	...	...	6	...	6	...	...	5	...	...	5	...	...	...	...	...	...
" Kóta	Do.	10	4	6	...	...	3	3	...	...	...	2	...	2	...	...	5	1	4	...	...	...	...	...	...	...	...	...	...	...	...
" Kudlukára	Do.	...	...	...	...	...	...	...	...	...	...	...	...	...	...	...	...	...	...	...	...	...	...	...	...	...	...	...	...	...	...
" Mádhva	Do.	...	...	...	...	...	...	...	...	...	...	...	...	...	...	...	...	...	...	...	...	...	...	...	...	...	...	...	...	...	...
" Maharáshtra	Do.	...	...	...	...	...	...	...	...	...	...	...	...	...	...	...	...	...	...	...	...	...	...	...	...	...	...	...	...	...	...
" Malanádu Kamme	Do.	2	...	1	1	...	...	...	...	...	...	...	...	...	...	...	1	...	1	...	...	1	...	...	1	...	...	...	...	...	...
" Malanádu Karnátaka	Do.	...	...	...	...	...	...	...	...	...	...	...	...	...	...	...	...	...	...	...	...	...	...	...	...	...	...	...	...	...	...
" Márvádi	Do.	...	...	...	...	...	...	...	...	...	...	...	...	...	...	...	...	...	...	...	...	...	...	...	...	...	...	...	...	...	...
" Pratákaiyana Vamsa	Do.	3	1	1	1	...	1	1	...	...	...	...	...	...	...	...	1	...	1	...	...	1	...	...	1	...	...	...	...	...	...
" Rámánujamatam	Do.	...	...	...	...	...	...	...	...	...	...	...	...	...	...	...	...	...	...	...	...	...	...	...	...	...	...	...	...	...	...
" Sankéti	Do.	25	8	14	3	...	5	5	...	...	...	5	1	4	...	...	13	2	9	2	...	2	...	1	1	...	...	...	...	...	...
" Sárasvata	Do.	41	9	19	13	...	8	8	...	...	...	2	1	1	...	...	18	...	16	2	...	13	...	2	11	...	...	...	...	...	...
" Shivalli	Do.	266	74	99	93	...	64	61	3	...	...	29	10	19	...	...	109	3	77	29	...	63	...	...	63	...	...	...	...	...	...
" Smárta	Do.	56	11	22	23	...	10	10	...	...	...	3	1	2	...	...	27	...	20	7	...	16	...	...	16	...	...	...	...	...	...
" Smárta Karnátaka	Do.	31	10	9	12	...	9	9	...	...	...	2	1	1	...	...	11	...	6	5	...	9	...	2	7	...	...	...	...	...	...
" Srívaishnava	Do.	45	15	17	13	...	14	14	...	...	...	3	1	2	...	...	18	...	15	3	...	10	...	...	10	...	...	...	...	...	...
" Tengalai	Do.	2	1	1	...	...	...	...	...	...	...	1	1	...	...	...	...	...	...	...	...	1	...	1	...	...	...	...	...	...	...
" Tulu	Do.	11	4	3	4	...	5	4	...	1	...	...	...	...	...	...	3	...	2	1	...	3	...	1	2	...	...	...	...	...	...
" Utucha Kamme	Do.	...	...	...	...	...	...	...	...	...	...	...	...	...	...	...	...	...	...	...	...	...	...	...	...	...	...	...	...	...	...
" Uttaráji	Do.	2	1	1	...	...	1	1	...	...	...	...	...	...	...	...	1	...	1	...	...	...	...	...	...	...	...	...	...	...	...
" Vadagalai	Do.	87	33	33	21	...	29	29	...	...	...	9	4	5	...	...	30	...	25	5	...	19	...	3	16	...	...	...	...	...	...
" Vadama	Do.	9	5	4	...	...	4	4	...	...	...	1	1	...	...	...	4	...	4	...	...	...	...	...	...	...	...	...	...	...	...
" Vaidíki	Do.	2	...	1	1	...	...	...	...	...	...	...	...	...	...	...	...	...	...	...	...	2	...	1	1	...	...	...	...	...	...
" Vaishnava	Do.	9	1	5	3	...	2	1	1	...	...	1	...	1	...	...	4	...	2	2	...	2	...	1	1	...	...	...	...	...	...
" Vélanádu-Andhra	Do.	1	...	1	...	...	...	...	...	...	...	...	...	...	...	...	1	...	1	...	...	...	...	...	...	...	...	...	...	...	...
Total, Bráhmans		1,174	343	488	342	1	305	299	4	1	1	85	36	48	1	...	500	8	387	95	...	283	...	38	245	...	1	...	1	...	...
Jangam	Hindu	486	186	181	119	...	124	124	...	...	...	50	43	7	...	...	220	19	147	54	...	92	...	27	65	...	...	...	...	...	...
Pandáram	Do.	2	1	1	...	...	...	...	...	...	...	...	...	...	...	...	1	1	...	...	...	1	...	1	...	...	...	...	...	...	...
Total, Group B—5.		1,662	530	670	461	1	429	423	4	1	1	135	79	55	1	...	721	28	544	149	...	376	...	66	310	...	1	...	1	...	...

TABLE E.—Castes, Tribes and Races by Civil Condition—*contd.*

Class.	Group.	Caste, Tribe, etc.	Religion.	MALES. All Ages. Total.	Single.	Married.	Widowed.	Not stated.	0—9. Total.	Single.	Married.	Widowed.	Not stated.	10—14. Total.	Single.	Married.	Widowed.	Not stated.	15—39. Total.	Single.	Married.	Widowed.	Not stated.	40 and over. Total.	Single.	Married.	Widowed.	Not stated.	Not Stated. Total.	Single.	Married.	Widowed.	Not stated.
1	2	3	4	5	6	7	8	9	10	11	12	13	14	15	16	17	18	19	20	21	22	23	24	25	26	27	28	29	30	31	32	33	34
B.—PROFESSIONAL—contd.	6.—Devotees	Gósáyi	Hindu	4	2	2	...	...	1	1	...	...	...	...	...	...	...	...	2	1	1	...	...	1	...	1	...	...	...	...	...	...	...
		Sanyási	Do.	2	...	2	...	...	...	...	...	...	...	...	...	...	...	...	2	...	2	...	...	...	...	...	...	...	...	...	...	...	...
		Total, Group B—6		6	2	4	...	...	1	1	...	...	...	...	...	...	...	...	4	1	3	...	...	1	...	1	...	...	...	...	...	...	...
	7.—Temple-Servants.	Ambalavási	Hindu	5	4	1	...	...	...	...	...	...	...	...	...	...	...	...	4	4	...	...	...	1	...	1	...	...	...	...	...	...	...
		Dévadiga	Do.	1	1	...	...	...	...	...	...	...	...	...	...	...	...	...	1	1	...	...	...	...	...	...	...	...	...	...	...	...	...
		Moyili	Do.	8	3	4	1	...	...	...	...	...	...	...	...	...	...	...	7	3	3	1	...	1	...	1	...	...	...	...	...	...	...
		Mukkáti	Do.	12	6	5	1	...	2	3	...	...	...	2	2	...	...	...	4	1	2	1	...	3	...	3	...	...	...	...	...	...	...
		Padárti	Do.	109	61	43	5	...	32	32	...	...	...	11	10	1	...	...	43	19	23	1	...	23	...	19	4	...	...	...	...	...	...
		Sátáni	Do.	30	10	14	6	...	2	2	...	...	...	...	...	...	...	...	18	8	10	...	...	10	...	4	6	...	...	...	...	...	...
		Siva Bráhman	Do.	3	...	1	2	...	...	...	...	...	...	...	...	...	...	...	2	...	1	1	...	1	...	...	1	...	...	...	...	...	...
		Sivadvija	Do.	14	8	4	2	...	2	2	...	...	...	4	4	...	...	...	6	2	4	...	...	2	...	...	2	...	...	...	...	...	...
		Stalada Bráhman	Do.	77	49	27	1	...	28	28	...	...	...	7	7	...	...	...	33	14	19	...	...	9	...	8	1	...	...	...	...	...	...
		Staladavartaka Bráhman	Do.	6	2	3	1	...	2	2	...	...	...	...	...	...	...	...	2	...	2	...	...	2	...	1	1	...	...	...	...	...	...
		Stánika	Do.	73	39	26	8	...	16	16	...	...	...	7	7	...	...	...	29	11	17	1	...	21	5	9	7	...	...	...	...	...	...
		Total, Group B—7		338	183	128	27	...	85	85	...	...	...	31	30	1	...	...	149	63	81	5	...	73	5	46	22	...	...	...	...	...	...
	10.—Astrologers, etc.	Kaniya	Hindu	124	45	77	2	...	18	18	...	...	...	7	7	...	...	...	72	18	53	1	...	27	2	24	1	...	...	...	...	...	...
		Panika	Do.	80	48	27	5	...	22	22	...	...	...	9	9	...	...	...	38	17	16	5	...	11	...	11	...	...	...	...	...	...	...
		Total, Group B—10		204	93	104	7	...	40	40	...	...	...	16	16	...	...	...	110	35	69	6	...	38	2	35	1	...	...	...	...	...	...
	11.—Musicians, etc.	Batta	Hindu	12	8	3	1	...	2	2	...	...	...	1	1	...	...	...	7	5	2	...	...	2	...	1	1	...	...	...	...	...	...
		Sappaliga	Do.	2	2	...	...	...	1	1	...	...	...	1	1	...	...	...	...	...	...	...	...	...	...	...	...	...	...	...	...	...	...
		Total, Group B—11		14	10	3	1	...	3	3	...	...	...	2	2	...	...	...	7	5	2	...	...	2	...	1	1	...	...	...	...	...	...
	12.—Dancers and Singers.	Basavi	Hindu	9	5	3	1	...	2	2	...	...	...	1	1	...	...	...	4	2	1	1	...	2	...	2	...	...	...	...	...	...	...
		Total, Group B—12		9	5	3	1	...	2	2	...	...	...	1	1	...	...	...	4	2	1	1	...	2	...	2	...	...	...	...	...	...	...
		Total, Class B		2,437	1,245	1,016	175	1	533	530	2	1	...	218	210	8	...	...	1,189	480	659	49	1	496	25	346	125	...	4	...	1	...	...

Table E.—Castes by Civil Condition and Age.—Coorg.

Class.	Group.	Caste, Tribe, etc.	Religion.	FEMALES.																													
				All Ages.					0—9.					10—14.					15—39.					40 and over.					Not stated.				
				Total.	Single.	Married.	Widowed.	Not stated.	Total.	Single.	Married.	Widowed.	Not stated.	Total.	Single.	Married.	Widowed.	Not stated.	Total.	Single.	Married.	Widowed.	Not stated.	Total.	Single.	Married.	Widowed.	Not stated.	Total.	Single	Married.	Widowed.	Not stated.
				35	36	37	38	39	40	41	42	43	44	45	46	47	48	49	50	51	52	63	54	55	56	57	58	59	60	61	62	63	64
B.—PROFESSIONAL—contd.	6.—Devotees	Gósáyi	Hindu	3	...	...	3	...	...	...	...	...	...	...	...	...	...	...	1	...	...	1	...	2	...	...	2	...	...	...	...	...	...
		Sanyási	Do.	...	...	...	...	...	...	...	...	...	...	...	...	...	...	...	...	...	...	...	...	...	...	...	...	...	...	...	...	...	...
		Total, Group B—6.		3	...	...	3	...	...	...	...	...	...	...	...	...	...	...	1	...	...	1	...	2	...	...	2	...	...	...	...	...	...
	7.—Temple-Servants	Ambalavási	Hindu	...	...	...	...	...	...	...	...	...	...	...	...	...	...	...	...	...	...	...	...	...	...	...	...	...	...	...	...	...	...
		Dévadiga	Do.	2	...	...	2	...	...	...	...	...	...	...	...	...	...	...	2	...	...	2	...	...	...	...	...	...	...	...	...	...	...
		Moyili	Do.	...	...	...	...	...	...	...	...	...	...	...	...	...	...	...	...	...	...	...	...	...	...	...	...	...	...	...	...	...	...
		Mukkáti	Do.	11	2	7	2	...	1	1	...	...	...	...	...	...	...	...	8	1	6	1	...	2	...	1	1	...	...	...	...	...	...
		Padárti	Do.	96	41	40	15	...	27	27	...	...	...	13	11	2	...	...	41	3	33	5	...	15	...	5	10	...	...	...	...	...	...
		Sátáni	Do.	27	9	14	4	...	5	5	...	...	...	1	1	...	...	...	17	3	13	1	...	4	...	1	3	...	...	...	...	...	...
		Siva Bráhman	Do.	4	...	1	3	...	...	...	...	...	...	1	...	1	...	...	...	...	...	...	...	3	...	...	3	...	...	...	...	...	...
		Sivadvija	Do.	7	1	4	2	...	1	1	...	...	...	...	...	...	...	...	4	...	4	...	...	2	...	...	2	...	...	...	...	...	...
		Stalada Bráhman	Do.	100	31	35	34	...	26	26	...	...	...	5	4	1	...	...	48	1	31	16	...	21	...	3	18	...	...	...	...	...	...
		Staladavartaka Bráhman	Do.	5	2	1	2	...	...	...	...	...	...	2	2	...	...	...	1	...	1	...	...	2	...	...	2	...	...	...	...	...	...
		Stánika	Do.	67	19	27	21	...	16	16	...	...	...	2	2	...	...	...	28	1	23	4	...	21	...	4	17	...	...	...	...	...	...
		Total, Group B—7.		319	105	129	85	...	76	76	...	...	...	24	20	4	...	...	149	9	111	29	...	70	...	14	56	...	...	...	...	...	...
	10.—Astrologers, etc.	Kaniya	Hindu	82	30	42	10	...	21	21	...	...	...	8	7	1	...	...	41	2	37	2	...	12	...	4	8	...	...	...	...	...	...
		Panika	Do.	77	37	32	8	...	27	25	2	...	...	4	3	1	...	...	37	9	26	2	...	9	...	3	6	...	...	...	...	...	...
		Total, Group B—10.		159	67	74	18	...	48	46	2	...	...	12	10	2	...	...	78	11	63	4	...	21	...	7	14	...	...	...	...	...	...
	11.—Musicians, etc.	Batta	Hindu	6	3	2	1	...	3	3	...	...	...	...	...	...	...	...	2	...	2	...	...	1	...	...	1	...	...	...	...	...	...
		Sappaliga	Do.	...	...	...	...	...	...	...	...	...	...	...	...	...	...	...	...	...	...	...	...	...	...	...	...	...	...	...	...	...	...
		Total, Group B—11.		6	3	2	1	...	3	3	...	...	...	...	...	...	...	...	2	...	2	...	...	1	...	...	1	...	...	...	...	...	...
	12.—Dancers and Singers.	Basavi	Hindu	8	5	3	...	...	2	2	...	...	...	...	...	...	...	...	5	3	2	...	...	1	...	1	...	...	...	...	...	...	...
		Total, Group B—12.		8	5	3	...	...	2	2	...	...	...	...	...	...	...	...	5	3	2	...	...	1	...	1	...	...	...	...	...	...	...
		Total, Class B		2,157	710	878	568	1	558	550	6	1	1	171	109	61	1	...	956	51	722	183	...	471	...	88	383	...	1	...	1	...	...

Table E.—Castes by Civil Condition and Age.—Coorg.

TABLE E.—Castes, Tribes and Races by Civil Condition—*contd.*

MALES.

Class.	Group.	Caste, Tribe, etc.	Religion.	All Ages. Total.	All Ages. Single.	All Ages. Married.	All Ages. Widowed.	All Ages. Not stated.	0—9. Total.	0—9. Single.	0—9. Married.	0—9. Widowed.	0—9. Not stated.	10—14. Total.	10—14. Single.	10—14. Married.	10—14. Widowed.	10—14. Not stated.	15—39. Total.	15—39. Single.	15—39. Married.	15—39. Widowed.	15—39. Not stated.	40 and over. Total.	40 and over. Single.	40 and over. Married.	40 and over. Widowed.	40 and over. Not stated.	Not stated. Total.	Not stated. Single.	Not stated. Married.	Not stated. Widowed.	Not stated. Not stated.
1	2	3	4	5	6	7	8	9	10	11	12	13	14	15	16	17	18	19	20	21	22	23	24	25	26	27	28	29	30	31	32	33	34
C.—COMMERCIAL.	14.—Traders	Agravála	Hindu	2	...	2	...	...	...	...	...	...	...	...	...	...	...	...	2	...	2	...	...	...	...	...	...	...	...	...	...	...	...
		Banajiga	Do.	830	466	315	49	...	163	163	...	...	...	79	79	...	...	...	441	210	216	15	...	146	13	99	34	...	1	1	...	...	...
		Baniya	Do.	14	8	6	...	...	2	2	...	...	...	1	1	...	...	...	11	5	6	...	...	...	...	...	...	...	...	...	...	...	...
		Chetti	Do.	34	22	12	...	...	16	16	...	...	...	3	3	...	...	...	13	3	10	...	...	2	...	2	...	...	...	...	...	...	...
			Christian	15	6	9	...	...	3	3	...	...	...	3	3	...	...	...	5	...	5	...	...	4	...	4	...	...	...	...	...	...	...
		Désiyatvani	Hindu	9	2	7	...	...	...	...	...	...	...	...	...	...	...	...	6	2	4	...	...	3	...	3	...	...	...	...	...	...	...
		Kavarai	Do.	15	11	3	1	...	3	3	...	...	...	3	3	...	...	...	7	5	2	...	...	2	...	1	1	...	...	...	...	...	...
		Kómati	Do.	11	4	7	...	...	2	2	...	...	...	2	2	...	...	...	4	...	4	...	...	3	...	3	...	...	...	...	...	...	...
		Labbai	Musalman	415	216	191	8	...	20	20	...	...	...	38	38	...	...	...	292	155	132	5	...	65	3	59	3	...	...	...	...	...	...
		Ládar	Hindu	3	1	2	...	...	...	...	...	...	...	...	...	...	...	...	3	1	2	...	...	...	...	...	...	...	...	...	...	...	...
		Máppilla	Musalman	3,466	1,649	1,780	35	2	500	498	1	...	1	302	299	3	...	...	2,084	842	1,219	22	1	579	10	556	13	...	1	...	1	...	...
		Méman	Do.	40	9	31	...	...	...	...	...	...	...	...	...	...	...	...	26	3	23	...	...	14	6	8	...	...	...	...	...	...	...
		Naráyat	Do.	265	121	139	5	...	12	12	...	...	...	25	25	...	...	...	179	84	94	1	...	49	...	45	4	...	...	...	...	...	...
		Vaisya	Hindu	136	60	63	13	...	35	35	...	...	...	11	11	...	...	...	63	12	42	9	...	27	2	21	4	...	...	...	...	...	...
		Total, Group C—14		5,255	2,575	2,567	111	2	756	754	1	...	1	467	464	3	...	...	3,136	1,322	1,761	52	1	894	34	801	59	...	2	1	1	...	...
	16.—Carriers	Lambádi	Hindu	114	35	71	8	...	1	1	...	...	...	7	6	1	...	...	82	25	51	6	...	24	3	19	2	...	...	...	...	...	...
		Total, Group C—16		114	35	71	8	...	1	1	...	...	...	7	6	1	...	...	82	25	51	6	...	24	3	19	2	...	...	...	...	...	...
		Total, Class C	...	5,369	2,610	2,638	119	2	757	755	1	...	1	474	470	4	...	...	3,218	1,347	1,812	58	1	918	37	820	61	...	2	1	1	...	...
D.—ARTISAN AND VILLAGE MENIAL.	17.—Goldsmiths	Akkasále	Hindu	685	354	306	25	...	131	130	1	...	...	59	59	...	...	...	379	160	207	12	...	116	5	98	13	...	...	...	...	...	...
			Christian	3	2	1	...	...	2	2	...	...	...	...	...	...	...	...	1	...	1	...	...	...	...	...	...	...	...	...	...	...	...
		Chinnavára	Hindu	2	...	2	...	...	...	...	...	...	...	...	...	...	...	...	2	...	2	...	...	...	...	...	...	...	...	...	...	...	...
		Sonégára	Do.	51	27	24	...	...	5	5	...	...	...	3	3	...	...	...	35	19	16	...	...	8	...	8	...	...	...	...	...	...	...
		Súrya Bráhman	Do.	3	3	...	...	...	...	...	...	...	...	...	...	...	...	...	3	3	...	...	...	...	...	...	...	...	...	...	...	...	...
		Tattán	Do.	5	...	4	1	...	...	...	...	...	...	...	...	...	...	...	4	...	4	...	...	1	...	...	1	...	...	...	...	...	...
		Total, Group D—17		749	386	337	26	...	138	137	1	...	...	62	62	...	...	...	424	182	230	12	...	125	5	106	14	...	...	...	...	...	...
	17(a).—Artisans.	Ásári	Hindu	131	47	84	...	...	7	7	...	...	...	2	2	...	...	...	96	38	58	...	...	26	...	26	...	...	...	...	...	...	...
		Kuláchári	Do.	2	...	2	...	...	...	...	...	...	...	...	...	...	...	...	2	...	2	...	...	...	...	...	...	...	...	...	...	...	...
		Pánchála	Do.	395	212	165	18	...	69	69	...	...	...	49	45	4	...	...	217	95	110	12	...	60	3	51	6	...	...	...	...	...	...
		Visvakarma	Do.	119	45	65	9	...	21	21	...	...	...	10	10	...	...	...	52	12	39	1	...	36	2	26	8	...	...	...	...	...	...
		Total, Group D—17 (a)		647	304	316	27	...	97	97	...	...	...	61	57	4	...	...	367	145	209	13	...	122	5	103	14	...	...	...	...	...	...
	18.—Barbers	Hajám	Hindu	451	228	205	17	1	110	108	1	...	1	32	32	...	...	...	234	86	140	8	...	75	2	64	9	...	...	...	...	...	...
		Kshauraka	Do.	1	...	1	...	...	...	...	...	...	...	...	...	...	...	...	...	...	...	...	...	1	...	1	...	...	...	...	...	...	...
		Náyinda	Do.	26	15	10	1	...	9	9	...	...	...	3	3	...	...	...	11	3	7	1	...	3	...	3	...	...	...	...	...	...	...
		Total, Group D—18		478	243	216	18	1	119	117	1	...	1	35	35	...	...	...	245	89	147	9	...	79	2	68	9	...	...	...	...	...	...

Table E.—Castes by Civil Condition and Age.—Coorg.

Class.	Group.	Caste, Tribe, etc.	Religion.	FEMALES.																													
				All Ages					0—9.					10—14.					15—39.					40 and over.					Not stated.				
				Total.	Single.	Married.	Widowed.	Not stated.	Total.	Single.	Married.	Widowed.	Not stated.	Total.	Single.	Married.	Widowed.	Not stated.	Total.	Single.	Married.	Widowed.	Not stated.	Total.	Single.	Married.	Widowed.	Not stated.	Total.	Single.	Married.	Widowed.	Not stated.
				35	36	37	38	39	40	41	42	43	44	45	46	47	48	49	50	51	52	53	54	55	56	57	58	59	60	61	62	63	64
C.—Commercial.	14.—Traders	Agravála	Hindu	...	...	...	...	...	...	...	...	...	...	...	...	...	...	...	...	...	...	...	...	...	...	...	...	...	...	...	...	...	...
		Banajiga	Do.	719	264	245	209	1	167	165	1	...	1	56	53	3	...	...	328	40	204	84	...	168	6	37	125	...	...	...	...	...	...
		Baniya	Do.	8	4	4	...	...	3	3	...	...	...	...	...	...	...	...	5	1	4	...	...	...	...	...	...	...	...	...	...	...	...
		Chetti	Do.	23	12	7	4	...	10	10	...	...	...	1	1	...	...	...	10	1	6	3	...	2	...	1	1	...	...	...	...	...	...
			Christian	15	8	7	...	...	3	3	...	...	...	4	4	...	...	...	7	1	6	...	...	1	...	1	...	...	...	...	...	...	...
		Désiyatvani	Hindu	...	...	...	...	...	...	...	...	...	...	...	...	...	...	...	...	...	...	...	...	...	...	...	...	...	...	...	...	...	...
		Kavárai	Do.	17	12	3	2	...	4	4	...	...	...	5	5	...	...	...	6	3	3	...	...	2	...	...	2	...	...	...	...	...	...
		Kómati	Do.	6	2	3	1	...	2	2	...	...	...	...	...	...	...	...	3	...	3	...	...	1	...	...	1	...	...	...	...	...	...
		Labbai	Musalman	98	37	49	12	...	27	27	...	...	...	8	7	1	...	...	48	3	42	3	...	15	...	6	9	...	...	...	...	...	...
		Ládar	Hindu	4	1	2	1	...	1	1	...	...	...	...	...	...	...	...	2	...	2	...	...	1	...	...	1	...	...	...	...	...	...
		Máppilla	Musalman	1,704	659	805	240	...	474	473	1	...	...	172	144	25	3	...	837	38	718	81	...	221	4	61	156	...	...	...	...	...	...
		Méman	Do.	2	1	1	...	...	1	1	...	...	...	...	...	...	...	...	1	...	1	...	...	...	...	...	...	...	...	...	...	...	...
		Naváyat	Do.	60	22	26	12	...	18	18	...	...	...	6	4	2	...	...	21	...	19	2	...	15	...	5	10	...	...	...	...	...	...
		Valeya	Hindu	117	33	59	25	...	31	30	1	...	...	9	2	7	...	...	53	1	42	10	...	24	...	9	15	...	...	...	...	...	...
		Total, Group C—14.		2,773	1,055	1,211	506	1	741	737	3	...	1	261	220	38	3	...	1,321	88	1,050	183	...	450	10	120	320	...	...	...	...	...	...
	16.—Carriers	Lambádi	Hindu	42	13	23	6	...	8	8	...	...	...	2	2	...	...	...	23	3	18	2	...	9	...	5	4	...	...	...	...	...	...
		Total, Group C—16.		42	13	23	6	...	8	8	...	...	...	2	2	...	...	...	23	3	18	2	...	9	...	5	4	...	...	...	...	...	...
		Total, Class C.		**2,815**	**1,068**	**1,234**	**512**	**1**	**749**	**745**	**3**	...	**1**	**263**	**222**	**38**	**3**	...	**1,344**	**91**	**1,068**	**185**	...	**459**	**10**	**125**	**324**	...	...	...	...	...	...
D.—Artisan and Village Menial.	17.—Goldsmiths	Akkasále	Hindu	506	187	210	109	...	118	118	...	...	...	55	46	8	1	...	228	23	170	35	...	105	...	32	73	...	...	...	...	...	...
			Christian	2	2	...	...	...	2	2	...	...	...	...	...	...	...	...	...	...	...	...	...	...	...	...	...	...	...	...	...	...	...
		Chinnavára	Hindu	...	...	...	...	...	...	...	...	...	...	...	...	...	...	...	...	...	...	...	...	...	...	...	...	...	...	...	...	...	...
		Sonegára	Do.	12	1	8	3	...	1	1	...	...	...	...	...	...	...	...	8	...	6	2	...	3	...	2	1	...	...	...	...	...	...
		Súrya Bráhman	Do.	...	...	...	...	...	...	...	...	...	...	...	...	...	...	...	...	...	...	...	...	...	...	...	...	...	...	...	...	...	...
		Tattán	Do.	...	...	...	...	...	...	...	...	...	...	...	...	...	...	...	...	...	...	...	...	...	...	...	...	...	...	...	...	...	...
		Total, Group D—17.		520	190	218	112	...	121	121	...	...	...	55	46	8	1	...	236	23	176	37	...	108	...	34	74	...	...	...	...	...	...
	17(a).—Artisans	Ásári	Hindu	29	14	12	3	...	10	10	...	...	...	2	2	...	...	...	15	2	12	1	...	2	...	...	2	...	...	...	...	...	...
		Kuláchári	Do.	...	...	...	...	...	...	...	...	...	...	...	...	...	...	...	...	...	...	...	...	...	...	...	...	...	...	...	...	...	...
		Pánchála	Do.	330	121	142	66	1	74	74	...	...	...	40	31	9	...	...	164	16	121	27	...	52	...	12	39	1	...	...	...	...	...
		Visvakarma	Do.	116	31	70	15	...	21	20	1	...	...	9	7	2	...	...	44	4	36	4	...	42	...	31	11	...	...	...	...	...	...
		Total, Group D—17(a).		475	166	224	84	1	105	104	1	...	...	51	40	11	...	...	223	22	169	32	...	96	...	43	52	1	...	...	...	...	...
	18.—Barbers	Hajám	Hindu	435	162	196	77	...	95	95	...	...	...	67	61	6	...	...	186	6	155	25	...	87	...	35	52	...	...	...	...	...	...
		Kshauraka	Do.	1	...	1	...	...	...	...	...	...	...	...	...	...	...	...	1	...	1	...	...	...	...	...	...	...	...	...	...	...	...
		Náyinda	Do.	28	13	12	3	...	9	9	...	...	...	4	4	...	...	...	11	...	10	1	...	4	...	2	2	...	...	...	...	...	...
		Total, Group D—18.		464	175	209	80	...	104	104	...	...	...	71	65	6	...	...	198	6	166	26	...	91	...	37	54	...	...	...	...	...	...

TABLE E.—Castes, Tribes and Races by Civil Condition—*contd.*

Class.	Group.	Caste, Tribe, etc.	Religion.	MALES. All Ages. Total.	All Ages. Single.	All Ages. Married.	All Ages. Widowed.	All Ages. Not stated.	0–9. Total.	0–9. Single.	0–9. Married.	0–9. Widowed.	0–9. Not stated.	10–14. Total.	10–14. Single.	10–14. Married.	10–14. Widowed.	10–14. Not stated.	15–39. Total.	15–39. Single.	15–39. Married.	15–39. Widowed.	15–39. Not stated.	40 and over. Total.	40 and over. Single.	40 and over. Married.	40 and over. Widowed.	40 and over. Not stated.	Not stated. Total.	Not stated. Single.	Not stated. Married.	Not stated. Widowed.	Not stated. Not stated.
1	2	3	4	5	6	7	8	9	10	11	12	13	14	15	16	17	18	19	20	21	22	23	24	25	26	27	28	29	30	31	32	33	34
D.—ARTISAN AND VILLAGE MENIAL—*contd.*	19.—Blacksmiths	Ayaskári	Hindu	2	2	...	...	...	...	...	...	...	...	...	...	...	...	...	2	2	...	...	...	...	...	...	...	...	...	...	...	...	...
		Gejjegára	Do.	3	3	...	...	...	...	...	...	...	...	...	...	...	...	...	1	1	...	...	...	2	2	...	...	...	...	...	...	...	...
		Kammara	Do.	...	...	...	...	...	...	...	...	...	...	...	...	...	...	...	...	...	...	...	...	...	...	...	...	...	...	...	...	...	...
		Kollan	Do.	65	27	34	4	...	13	13	...	...	...	2	2	...	...	...	39	11	27	1	...	11	1	7	3	...	...	...	...	...	...
		Total, Group D.—19		70	32	34	4	...	13	13	...	...	...	2	2	...	...	...	42	14	27	1	...	13	3	7	3	...	...	...	...	...	...
	20.—Carpenters, Masons and Turners.	Áyiri	Hindu	601	282	302	17	...	113	113	...	...	...	58	58	...	...	...	305	108	191	6	...	125	3	111	11	...	...	...	...	...	...
		Badagi	Do.	306	168	124	14	...	72	71	1	...	...	32	31	...	1	...	155	65	85	5	...	47	1	38	8	...	...	...	...	...	...
		Chárodi	Do.	4	...	4	...	...	...	...	...	...	...	...	...	...	...	...	4	...	4	...	...	...	...	...	...	...	...	...	...	...	...
		Cheptégára	Do.	28	14	14	...	...	1	1	...	...	...	2	2	...	...	...	19	11	8	...	...	6	...	6	...	...	...	...	...	...	...
		Gudigára	Do.	2	1	1	...	...	1	1	...	...	...	...	...	...	...	...	1	...	1	...	...	...	...	...	...	...	...	...	...	...	...
		Kallukutti	Do.	34	16	16	2	...	4	4	...	...	...	3	3	...	...	...	25	8	16	1	...	2	1	...	1	...	...	...	...	...	...
		Kóláyiri	Do.	239	99	131	9	...	45	45	...	...	...	21	20	1	...	...	125	32	88	5	...	48	2	42	4	...	...	...	...	...	...
		Maniyáni	Do.	92	18	72	2	...	3	3	...	...	...	1	1	...	...	...	58	14	43	1	...	30	...	29	1	...	...	...	...	...	...
		Muyáyiri	Do.	4	...	4	...	...	...	...	...	...	...	...	...	...	...	...	3	...	3	...	...	1	...	1	...	...	...	...	...	...	...
		Pudála	Do.	3	...	3	...	...	...	...	...	...	...	...	...	...	...	...	2	...	2	...	...	1	...	1	...	...	...	...	...	...	...
		Total, Group D.—20		1,313	598	671	44	...	239	238	1	...	...	117	115	1	1	...	697	238	441	18	...	260	7	228	25	...	...	...	...	...	...
	21.—Brass and Copper Smiths.	Chembukutti	Hindu	23	10	13	...	...	...	...	...	...	...	2	2	...	...	...	16	8	8	...	...	5	...	5	...	...	...	...	...	...	...
		Kanchugára	Do.	7	1	4	2	...	1	1	...	...	...	...	...	...	...	...	3	...	2	1	...	3	...	2	1	...	...	...	...	...	...
		Total, Group D.—21		30	11	17	2	...	1	1		...	...	2	2	...	...	...	19	8	10	1	...	8	...	7	1	...	...	...	...	...	...
	22.—Tailors	Darji	Hindu	34	21	11	2	...	13	13	...	...	...	1	1	...	...	...	14	7	7	...	...	6	...	4	2	...	...	...	...	...	...
		Námdév	Do.	17	8	7	2	...	4	4	...	...	...	...	...	...	...	...	10	4	5	1	...	3	...	2	1	...	...	...	...	...	...
		Total, Group D.—22		51	29	18	4	...	17	17	...	...	...	1	1	...	...	...	24	11	12	1	...	9	...	6	3	...	...	...	...	...	...
	22(c).—Flower Sellers	Huvvadigi	Hindu	1	...	1	...	...	...	...	...	...	...	...	...	...	...	...	1	...	1	...	...	...	...	...	...	...	...	...	...	...	...
		Total, Group D.—22 (c)		1	...	1	...	...	...	...	...	...	...	...	...	...	...	...	1	...	1	...	...	...	...	...	...	...	...	...	...	...	...
	23.—Weavers, Calenderers and Dyers.	Billmagga	Hindu	567	314	237	16	...	150	150	...	...	...	61	60	1	...	...	244	101	140	3	...	112	3	96	13	...	...	...	...	...	...
		Cháliya	Do.	98	39	58	1	...	13	13	...	...	...	7	5	2	...	...	57	20	37	...	...	21	1	19	1	...	...	...	...	...	...
		Dévánga	Do.	1,207	683	450	74	...	292	291	1	...	...	144	139	5	...	...	563	245	286	32	...	208	8	158	42	...	...	...	...	...	...
		Jáda	Do.	7	7	...	...	...	1	1	...	...	...	1	1	...	...	...	5	5	...	...	...	...	...	...	...	...	...	...	...	...	...
		Kaikólan	Do.	2	...	2	...	...	...	...	...	...	...	...	...	...	...	...	...	...	...	...	...	2	...	2	...	...	...	...	...	...	...
		Maggadava	Do.	11	7	3	1	...	3	3	...	...	...	...	...	...	...	...	7	4	2	1	...	1	...	1	...	...	...	...	...	...	...
		Pattusále	Do.	3	...	1	2	...	...	...	...	...	...	...	...	...	...	...	2	...	1	1	...	1	...	...	1	...	...	...	...	...	...
		Rangári	Do.	18	10	8	...	...	4	4	...	...	...	...	...	...	...	...	12	6	6	...	...	2	...	2	...	...	...	...	...	...	...
		Sále	Do.	10	3	7	...	...	2	2	...	...	...	1	1	...	...	...	5	...	5	...	...	2	...	2	...	...	...	...	...	...	...
		Toganta	Do.	1	1	...	...	...	...	...	...	...	...	...	...	...	...	...	1	1	...	...	...	...	...	...	...	...	...	...	...	...	...
		Total, Group D.—23		1,924	1,064	766	94	...	465	464	1	...	...	214	206	8	...	...	896	382	477	37	...	349	18	280	57	...	...	...	...	...	...

Table E.—Castes by Civil Condition and Age.—Coorg.

Class.	Group.	Caste, Tribe, etc.	Religion.	FEMALES. All Ages. Total.	All Ages. Single.	All Ages. Married.	All Ages. Widowed.	All Ages. Not stated.	0—9. Total.	0—9. Single.	0—9. Married.	0—9. Widowed.	0—9. Not stated.	10—14. Total.	10—14. Single.	10—14. Married.	10—14. Widowed.	10—14. Not stated.	15—39. Total.	15—39. Single.	15—39. Married.	15—39. Widowed.	15—39. Not stated.	40 and over. Total.	40 and over. Single.	40 and over. Married.	40 and over. Widowed.	40 and over. Not stated.	Not stated. Total.	Not stated. Single.	Not stated. Married.	Not stated. Widowed.	Not stated. Not stated.
				35	36	37	38	39	40	41	42	43	44	45	46	47	48	49	50	51	52	53	54	55	56	57	58	59	60	61	62	63	64
D.—ARTISAN AND VILLAGE MENIAL—contd.	19.—Blacksmiths	Ayaskári	Hindu	1	1	...	...	...	1	1	...	...	...	...	...	...	...	...	...	...	...	...	...	...	...	...	...	...	...	...	...	...	...
		Gejjegára	Do.	1	...	1	...	...	...	...	...	...	...	...	...	...	...	...	...	...	...	...	...	1	...	1	...	...	...	...	...	...	...
		Kammara	Do.	2	2	...	...	...	2	2	...	...	...	...	...	...	...	...	...	...	...	...	...	...	...	...	...	...	...	...	...	...	...
		Kollan	Do.	31	11	14	6	...	9	9	...	...	...	2	2	...	...	...	13	...	11	2	...	7	...	3	4	...	...	...	...	...	...
		Total, Group D.—19.		35	14	15	6	...	12	12	...	...	...	2	2	...	...	...	13	...	11	2	...	8	...	4	4	...	...	...	...	...	...
	20.—Carpenters, Masons and Turners.	Áyiri	Hindu	406	202	156	47	1	139	137	1	...	1	40	37	3	...	...	162	26	124	12	...	65	2	28	35	...	...	...	...	...	...
		Badagi	Do.	275	113	108	54	...	64	63	1	...	...	42	40	2	...	...	134	10	99	25	...	35	...	6	29	...	...	...	...	...	...
		Chárödi	Do.	...	...	...	...	...	...	...	...	...	...	...	...	...	...	...	...	...	...	...	...	...	...	...	...	...	...	...	...	...	...
		Cheptégára	Do.	26	8	8	10	...	6	6	...	...	...	1	1	...	...	...	8	1	7	...	...	11	...	1	10	...	...	...	...	...	...
		Gudigára	Do.	...	...	...	...	...	...	...	...	...	...	...	...	...	...	...	...	...	...	...	...	...	...	...	...	...	...	...	...	...	...
		Kallu kutti	Do.	44	21	14	9	...	15	15	...	...	...	5	5	...	...	...	12	1	9	2	...	12	...	5	7	...	...	...	...	...	...
		Kólâyiri	Do.	153	61	68	24	...	43	43	...	...	...	15	13	2	...	...	75	5	56	14	...	20	...	10	10	...	...	...	...	...	...
		Maniyáni	Do.	15	5	8	2	...	3	3	...	...	...	1	1	...	...	...	8	1	7	...	...	3	...	1	2	...	...	...	...	...	...
		Muvâyiri	Do.	...	...	...	...	...	...	...	...	...	...	...	...	...	...	...	...	...	...	...	...	...	...	...	...	...	...	...	...	...	...
		Pudála	Do.	...	...	...	...	...	...	...	...	...	...	...	...	...	...	...	...	...	...	...	...	...	...	...	...	...	...	...	...	...	...
		Total, Group D.—20.		919	420	362	146	1	270	267	2	...	1	104	97	7	...	...	399	44	302	53	...	146	2	51	93	...	...	...	...	...	...
	21.—Brass and Copper Smiths.	Chembukutti	Hindu	...	...	...	...	...	...	...	...	...	...	...	...	...	...	...	...	...	...	...	...	...	...	...	...	...	...	...	...	...	...
		Kanchugára	Do.	2	...	1	1	...	...	...	...	...	...	...	...	...	...	...	1	...	1	...	...	1	...	...	1	...	...	...	...	...	...
		Total, Group D.—21.		2	...	1	1	...	...	...	...	...	...	...	...	...	...	...	1	...	1	...	...	1	...	...	1	...	...	...	...	...	...
	22.—Tailors	Darji	Hindu	24	8	10	6	...	5	5	...	...	...	2	2	...	...	...	12	1	9	2	...	5	...	1	4	...	...	...	...	...	...
		Námdév	Do.	10	2	6	2	...	1	1	...	...	...	3	1	2	...	...	3	...	2	1	...	3	...	2	1	...	...	...	...	...	...
		Total, Group D.—22.		34	10	16	8	...	6	6	...	...	...	5	3	2	...	...	15	1	11	3	...	8	...	3	5	...	...	...	...	...	...
	22(c).—Flower Sellers	Huvvadiga	Hindu	1	...	1	...	...	...	...	...	...	...	...	...	...	...	...	1	...	1	...	...	...	...	...	...	...	...	...	...	...	...
		Total, Group D.—22c.		1	...	1	...	...	...	...	...	...	...	...	...	...	...	...	1	...	1	...	...	...	...	...	...	...	...	...	...	...	...
	23.—Weavers, Calenderers and Dyers	Billimagga	Hindu	536	311	230	95	...	150	148	2	...	...	51	43	8	...	...	238	19	192	27	...	97	1	28	68	...	...	...	...	...	...
		Châliya	Do.	31	14	13	4	...	6	6	...	...	...	5	5	...	...	...	16	3	11	2	...	4	...	2	2	...	...	...	...	...	...
		Dévánga	Do.	1,154	410	434	310	...	282	278	3	1	...	123	99	21	3	...	532	32	362	138	...	217	1	48	168	...	...	...	...	...	...
		Jáda	Do.	3	...	3	...	...	...	...	...	...	...	...	...	...	...	...	...	...	...	...	...	3	...	3	...	...	...	...	...	...	...
		Kaikólan	Do.	...	...	...	...	...	...	...	...	...	...	...	...	...	...	...	...	...	...	...	...	...	...	...	...	...	...	...	...	...	...
		Maggadava	Do.	4	...	3	1	...	...	...	...	...	...	...	...	...	...	...	3	...	2	1	...	1	...	1	...	...	...	...	...	...	...
		Pattusále	Do.	...	...	...	...	...	...	...	...	...	...	...	...	...	...	...	...	...	...	...	...	...	...	...	...	...	...	...	...	...	...
		Rangári	Do.	23	12	8	3	...	7	7	...	...	...	2	2	...	...	...	13	3	8	2	...	1	...	...	1	...	...	...	...	...	...
		Sále	Do.	8	2	3	3	...	2	2	...	...	...	...	...	...	...	...	3	...	3	...	...	3	...	...	3	...	...	...	...	...	...
		Togata	Do.	...	...	...	...	...	...	...	...	...	...	...	...	...	...	...	...	...	...	...	...	...	...	...	...	...	...	...	...	...	...
		Total, Group D.—23.		1,759	649	694	416	...	447	441	5	1	...	181	149	29	3	...	805	57	578	170	...	326	2	82	242	...	...	...	...	...	...

TABLE E.—Castes, Tribes and Races by Civil Condition—*contd.*

Class.	Group.	Caste, Tribe, etc.	Religion.	MALES.																													
				All Ages.					0–9.					10–14.					15–39.					40 and over.					Not stated.				
				Total.	Single.	Married.	Widowed.	Not stated.	Total.	Single.	Married.	Widowed.	Not stated.	Total.	Single.	Married.	Widowed.	Not stated.	Total.	Single.	Married.	Widowed.	Not stated.	Total.	Single.	Married.	Widowed.	Not stated.	Total.	Single.	Married.	Widowed.	Not stated.
1	2	3	4	5	6	7	8	9	10	11	12	13	14	15	16	17	18	19	20	21	22	23	24	25	26	27	28	29	30	31	32	33	34
D.—Artisan and Village Menial—contd.	24.—Washermen.	Agasa	Hindu	715	365	320	29	1	168	165	2	...	1	62	59	3	...	...	369	139	215	15	...	116	2	100	14	...	...	...	...	...	...
		Dhóbi	Do.	7	3	4	...	...	...	...	...	...	...	1	...	1	...	...	4	3	1	...	...	2	...	2	...	...	...	...	...	...	...
		Madivála	Do.	187	104	72	11	...	42	41	...	...	...	23	23	...	...	...	91	40	47	4	...	32	...	25	7	...	...	...	...	...	...
		Total, Group D—24.		909	472	396	40	1	209	206	2	...	1	86	82	4	...	...	464	182	263	19	...	150	2	127	21	...	...	...	...	...	...
	25.—Cotton-cleaners.	Pinjári	Musalman	3	3	...	...	...	2	2	...	...	...	1	1	...	...	...	...	...	...	...	...	...	...	...	...	...	...	...	...	...	...
		Total, Group D—25.		3	3	...	...	...	2	2	...	...	...	1	1	...	...	...	...	...	...	...	...	...	...	...	...	...	...	...	...	...	...
	26.—Shepherds, etc.	Golla	Hindu	475	262	195	18	...	135	134	1	...	...	40	39	1	...	...	212	86	120	6	...	88	3	73	12	...	...	...	...	...	...
		Heggade	Do.	696	364	292	40	...	190	190	...	...	...	78	77	...	1	...	314	97	203	14	...	114	...	89	25	...	...	...	...	...	...
		Kavádi	Do.	2	1	1	...	...	1	1	...	...	...	...	...	...	...	...	...	...	...	...	...	1	...	1	...	...	...	...	...	...	...
		Kurikalu	Do.	1	1	...	...	...	...	...	...	...	...	...	...	...	...	...	1	1	...	...	...	...	...	...	...	...	...	...	...	...	...
		Kuruba	Do.	4,123	2,090	1,887	146	...	947	939	8	...	...	365	365	...	...	...	2,080	768	1,252	60	...	730	18	627	85	...	1	...	...	1	...
		Total, Group D—26.		5,297	2,718	2,375	204	...	1,273	1,264	9	...	...	483	481	1	1	...	2,607	952	1,575	80	...	933	21	790	122	...	1	...	...	1	...
	27.—Oil-pressers.	Gániga	Hindu	290	154	121	15	...	43	43	...	...	...	25	25	...	...	...	170	80	85	5	...	52	6	36	10	...	...	...	...	...	...
		Vániya	Do.	85	30	54	1	...	8	8	...	...	...	6	6	...	...	...	55	15	39	1	...	16	1	15	...	...	...	...	...	...	...
		Total, Group D—27.		375	184	175	16	...	51	51	...	...	...	31	31	...	...	...	225	95	124	6	...	68	7	51	10	...	...	...	...	...	...
	28.—Potters.	Koyava	Hindu	173	104	63	6	...	63	63	...	...	...	17	17	...	...	...	69	24	44	1	...	24	...	19	5	...	...	...	...	...	...
		Kumbára	Do.	495	237	227	31	...	106	100	6	...	...	41	37	4	...	...	257	97	150	10	...	91	3	67	21	...	...	...	...	...	...
		Total, Group D—28.		668	341	290	37	...	169	163	6	...	...	58	54	4	...	...	326	121	194	11	...	115	3	86	26	...	...	...	...	...	...
	29.—Glass workers.	Balegára	Hindu	2	2	...	...	...	...	...	...	...	...	...	...	...	...	...	2	2	...	...	...	...	...	...	...	...	...	...	...	...	...
		Total, Group D—29.		2	2	...	...	...	...	...	...	...	...	...	...	...	...	...	2	2	...	...	...	...	...	...	...	...	...	...	...	...	...
	30.—Salt workers.	Uppara	Hindu	210	120	87	3	...	64	64	...	...	...	37	37	...	...	...	83	18	64	1	...	26	1	23	2	...	...	...	...	...	...
		Total, Group D—30.		210	120	87	3	...	64	64	...	...	...	37	37	...	...	...	83	18	64	1	...	26	1	23	2	...	...	...	...	...	...

Class.	Group.	Caste, Tribe, etc.	Religion.	FEMALES. All Ages. Total.	Single.	Married.	Widowed.	Not stated.	0–9. Total.	Single.	Married.	Widowed.	Not stated.	10–14. Total.	Single.	Married.	Widowed.	Not stated.	15–39. Total.	Single.	Married.	Widowed.	Not stated.	40 and over. Total.	Single.	Married.	Widowed.	Not stated.	Not stated. Total.	Single.	Married.	Widowed.	Not stated.
				35	36	37	38	39	40	41	42	43	44	45	46	47	48	49	50	51	52	53	54	55	56	57	58	59	60	61	62	63	64
D.—ARTISAN AND VILLAGE MENIAL—contd.	24.—Washermen	Agasa	Hindu	652	244	308	100	...	182	179	2	1	...	49	42	7	...	...	323	23	265	35	...	98	...	34	64	...	...	...	...	...	...
		Dhóbi	Do.	8	3	2	3	...	...	...	...	...	...	...	...	...	...	...	6	2	2	2	...	2	1	...	1	...	...	...	...	...	...
		Madivála	Do.	248	60	61	27	...	39	38	1	...	...	14	12	2	...	...	67	10	47	10	...	28	...	11	17	...	...	...	...	...	...
		Total, Group D—24	...	808	307	371	130	...	221	217	3	1	...	63	54	9	...	...	396	35	314	47	...	128	1	45	82	...	...	...	...	...	...
	25.—Cotton-cleaners	Pinjári	Musalman	...	...	...	...	...	...	...	...	...	...	...	...	...	...	...	...	...	...	...	...	...	...	...	...	...	...	...	...	...	...
		Total, Group D—25	...	...	...	...	...	...	...	...	...	...	...	...	...	...	...	...	...	...	...	...	...	...	...	...	...	...	...	...	...	...	...
	26.—Shepherds, etc.	Golla	Hindu	448	186	180	82	...	131	126	5	...	...	52	40	12	...	...	180	19	138	23	...	84	...	25	59	...	1	1	...	...	...
		Heggade	Do.	611	278	250	83	...	182	182	...	...	...	67	60	7	...	...	268	34	210	24	...	93	1	33	59	...	1	1	...	...	...
		Kavádi	Do.	1	...	1	...	...	...	...	...	...	...	...	...	...	...	...	1	...	1	...	...	...	...	...	...	...	...	...	...	...	...
		Kurikalu	Do.	...	...	...	...	...	...	...	...	...	...	...	...	...	...	...	...	...	...	...	...	...	...	...	...	...	...	...	...	...	...
		Kuruba	Do.	3,498	1,493	1,620	384	1	1,009	1,003	5	...	1	292	276	15	1	...	1,749	211	1,381	157	...	448	3	219	226	...	...	...	...	...	...
		Total, Group D—26	...	4,558	1,957	2,051	549	1	1,322	1,311	10	...	2	411	376	34	1	...	2,198	264	1,730	204	...	625	4	277	344	...	2	2	...	...	...
	27.—Oil-pressers	Gániga	Hindu	195	85	71	39	...	57	57	...	...	...	16	16	...	...	...	85	12	59	14	...	37	...	12	25	...	...	...	...	...	...
		Vániya	Do.	4	3	1	...	...	3	3	...	...	...	...	...	...	...	...	1	...	1	...	...	...	...	...	...	...	...	...	...	...	...
		Total, Group D—27	...	199	88	72	39	...	60	60	...	...	...	16	16	...	...	...	86	12	60	14	...	37	...	12	25	...	...	...	...	...	...
	28.—Potters	Koyava	Hindu	150	72	64	14	...	48	48	...	...	...	16	15	1	...	...	69	9	55	5	...	17	...	8	9	...	...	...	...	...	...
		Kumbára	Do.	413	154	184	75	...	119	100	19	...	...	47	37	10	...	...	177	16	135	26	...	70	1	20	49	...	...	...	...	...	...
		Total, Group D—28	...	563	226	248	89	...	167	148	19	...	...	63	52	11	...	...	246	25	190	31	...	87	1	28	58	...	...	...	...	...	...
	29.—Glass Workers	Balegára	Hindu	6	3	1	2	...	1	1	...	...	...	...	...	...	...	...	3	2	1	...	...	2	...	...	2	...	...	...	...	...	...
		Total, Group D—29	...	6	3	1	2	...	1	1	...	...	...	...	...	...	...	...	3	2	1	...	...	2	...	...	2	...	...	...	...	...	...
	30.—Salt Workers	Uppara	Hindu	129	45	46	38	...	22	22	...	...	...	11	11	...	...	...	72	12	44	16	...	24	...	2	22	...	...	...	...	...	...
		Total, Group D—30	...	129	45	46	38	...	22	22	...	...	...	11	11	...	...	...	72	12	44	16	...	24	...	2	22	...	...	...	...	...	...

TABLE E.—Castes, Tribes and Races by Civil Condition—*contd.*

Class.	Group.	Caste, Tribe, etc.	Religion.	MALES. All Ages. Total.	All Ages. Single.	All Ages. Married.	All Ages. Widowed.	All Ages. Not stated.	0—9. Total.	0—9. Single.	0—9. Married.	0—9. Widowed.	0—9. Not stated.	10—14. Total.	10—14. Single.	10—14. Married.	10—14. Widowed.	10—14. Not stated.	15—39. Total.	15—39. Single.	15—39. Married.	15—39. Widowed.	15—39. Not stated.	40 and over. Total.	40 and over. Single.	40 and over. Married.	40 and over. Widowed.	40 and over. Not stated.	Not stated. Total.	Not stated. Single.	Not stated. Married.	Not stated. Widowed.	Not stated. Not stated.
1	2	3	4	5	6	7	8	9	10	11	12	13	14	15	16	17	18	19	20	21	22	23	24	25	26	27	28	29	30	31	32	33	34
D.—Artisan and Village Menial—*contd.*	35.—Fishermen, Boatmen, Palki-bearers, Cooks, etc.	Besta	Hindu	329	140	173	16	...	54	54	...	...	...	18	17	1	...	...	208	69	134	5	...	49	...	38	11	...	...	...	...	...	...
		Béyi	Do.	482	276	184	22	...	125	124	1	...	...	52	50	2	...	...	215	98	111	6	...	90	4	70	16	...	...	...	...	...	...
		Kabbéra	Do.	3	2	1	...	...	...	...	...	...	...	2	2	...	...	...	1	...	1	...	...	...	...	...	...	...	...	...	...	...	...
		Mogér	Do.	1	...	1	...	...	...	...	...	...	...	...	...	...	...	...	...	...	...	...	...	1	...	1	...	...	...	...	...	...	...
		Toreya	Do.	249	112	134	3	...	44	44	...	...	...	14	12	2	...	...	156	54	102	...	...	35	2	30	3	...	...	...	...	...	...
		Total, Group D—35	...	1,064	530	493	41	...	223	222	1	...	...	86	81	5	...	...	580	221	348	11	...	175	6	139	30	...	...	...	...	...	...
	35(a).—Personal Service	Mukkári	Hindu	8	3	5	...	...	...	...	...	...	...	...	...	...	...	...	7	3	4	...	...	1	...	1	...	...	...	...	...	...	...
		Total, Group D—35 (a)	...	8	3	5	...	...	...	...	...	...	...	...	...	...	...	...	7	3	4	...	...	1	...	1	...	...	...	...	...	...	...
	36.—Distillers and Toddy-drawers.	Billava	Hindu	998	468	494	36	...	99	99	...	...	...	59	59	...	...	...	690	306	372	12	...	150	4	122	24	...	...	...	...	...	...
		Biruva	Do.	10	1	7	2	...	...	...	...	...	...	...	...	...	...	...	4	1	3	...	...	6	...	4	2	...	...	...	...	...	...
		Divar	Do.	377	209	146	22	...	84	84	...	...	...	39	36	3	...	...	183	84	90	9	...	71	5	53	13	...	...	...	...	...	...
		Halepaik	Do.	16	6	9	1	...	3	3	...	...	...	1	1	...	...	...	7	2	4	1	...	5	...	5	...	...	...	...	...	...	...
		Hummaliga	Do.	9	4	5	...	...	...	...	...	...	...	1	1	...	...	...	7	3	4	...	...	1	...	1	...	...	...	...	...	...	...
		Idiga	Do.	17	11	6	...	...	1	1	...	...	...	...	...	...	...	...	14	10	4	...	...	2	...	2	...	...	...	...	...	...	...
		Tiyyan	Do.	814	259	525	30	...	20	20	...	...	...	17	15	2	...	...	630	220	395	15	...	146	3	128	15	...	1	1	...	...	...
		Total, Group D—36	...	2,241	958	1,192	91	...	207	207	...	...	...	117	112	5	...	...	1,535	626	872	37	...	381	12	315	54	...	1	1	...	...	...
	37.—Butchers	Kasáyi	Hindu	5	2	3	...	...	...	...	...	...	...	...	...	...	...	...	5	2	3	...	...	...	...	...	...	...	...	...	...	...	...
		Total, Group D—37	...	5	2	3	...	...	...	...	...	...	...	...	...	...	...	...	5	2	3	...	...	...	...	...	...	...	...	...	...	...	...
	38.—Leather Workers	Mádiga	Hindu	920	446	438	36	...	155	155	...	...	...	67	67	...	...	...	574	215	341	18	...	124	9	97	18	...	...	...	...	...	...
		Mucchi	Do.	8	2	6	...	...	2	2	...	...	...	...	...	...	...	...	4	...	4	...	...	2	...	2	...	...	...	...	...	...	...
		Total, Group D—38	...	928	448	444	36	...	157	157	...	...	...	67	67	...	...	...	578	215	345	18	...	126	9	99	18	...	...	...	...	...	...
		Total, Class D.	...	16,973	8,448	7,836	687	2	3,444	3,420	22	...	2	1,460	1,426	32	2	...	9,127	3,506	5,346	275	...	2,940	95	2.436	409	...	2	1	...	1	...
E.—Vagrants, Minor Artisans and Performers, etc.	41.—Earth Workers	Odde	Hindu	260	137	115	8	...	32	31	...	...	...	63	61	2	...	...	123	44	76	3	...	43	1	37	5	...	...	...	...	...	...
		Total, Group E—41	...	260	137	115	8	...	32	32	...	...	...	63	61	2	...	...	123	44	76	3	...	43	1	37	5	...	...	...	...	...	...
	42.—Knife Grinders	Sikligára	Hindu	1	...	1	...	...	...	...	...	...	...	...	...	...	...	...	1	...	1	...	...	...	...	...	...	...	...	...	...	...	...
		Total, Group E—42	...	1	...	1	...	...	...	...	...	...	...	...	...	...	...	...	1	...	1	...	...	...	...	...	...	...	...	...	...	...	...

Table E.—Castes by Civil Condition and Age—Coorg.

Class.	Group.	Caste, Tribe, etc.	Religion.	FEMALES.																													
				All Ages.					0–9.					10–14.					15–39.					40 and over.					Not stated.				
				Total.	Single.	Married.	Widowed.	Not stated.	Total.	Single.	Married.	Widowed.	Not stated.	Total.	Single.	Married.	Widowed.	Not stated.	Total.	Single.	Married.	Widowed.	Not stated.	Total.	Single.	Married.	Widowed.	Not stated.	Total.	Single.	Married.	Widowed.	Not stated.
				35	36	37	38	39	40	41	42	43	44	45	46	47	48	49	50	51	52	53	54	55	56	57	58	59	60	61	62	63	64
D.—Artisan and Village Menial—contd.	35.—Fishermen, Boatmen, Palki Bearers, etc.	Besta	Hindu	298	104	141	53	...	69	63	6	...	...	22	17	5	...	...	165	21	120	24	...	42	3	10	29	...	...	...	...	...	...
		Bóyi	Do.	476	200	181	95	...	137	137	...	...	...	45	38	7	...	...	221	24	152	45	...	73	1	22	50	...	...	...	...	...	...
		Kabbéra	Do.	...	...	...	...	...	...	...	...	...	...	...	...	...	...	...	...	...	...	...	...	...	...	...	...	...	...	...	...	...	...
		Mogér	Do.	...	...	...	...	...	...	...	...	...	...	...	...	...	...	...	...	...	...	...	...	...	...	...	...	...	...	...	...	...	...
		Toreya	Do.	179	62	98	19	...	46	45	1	...	...	8	7	1	...	...	106	7	90	9	...	19	3	6	10	...	...	...	...	...	...
		Total, Group D—35		953	366	420	167	...	252	245	7	...	...	75	62	13	...	...	492	52	362	78	...	134	7	38	89	...	...	...	...	...	...
	35(a).—Personal Service	Mukkári	Hindu	...	...	...	...	...	...	...	...	...	...	...	...	...	...	...	...	...	...	...	...	...	...	...	...	...	...	...	...	...	...
		Total, Group D—35(a)	...	...	...	...	...	...	...	...	...	...	...	...	...	...	...	...	...	...	...	...	...	...	...	...	...	...	...	...	...	...	...
	36.—Distillers and Toddy-drawers.	Billava	Hindu	368	138	166	64	...	204	104	...	...	...	18	18	...	...	...	182	16	154	12	...	64	...	12	52	...	...	...	...	...	...
		Biruva	Do.	2	...	1	1	...	...	...	...	...	...	...	...	...	...	...	2	...	1	1	...	...	...	...	...	...	...	...	...	...	...
		Dívar	Do.	326	147	114	65	...	96	94	...	2	...	44	34	6	4	...	146	18	99	29	...	40	1	9	30	...	...	...	...	...	...
		Halepaik	Do.	12	4	6	2	...	4	4	...	...	...	...	...	...	...	...	6	...	5	1	...	2	...	1	1	...	...	...	...	...	...
		Hummaliga	Do.	...	...	...	...	...	...	...	...	...	...	...	...	...	...	...	...	...	...	...	...	...	...	...	...	...	...	...	...	...	...
		Ídiga	Do.	6	1	2	3	...	...	...	...	...	...	...	...	...	...	...	4	1	2	1	...	2	...	...	2	...	...	...	...	...	...
		Tiyyan	Do.	118	43	61	14	...	27	27	...	...	...	5	5	...	...	...	63	9	54	...	...	23	2	7	14	...	...	...	...	...	...
		Total, Group D—36	...	832	333	350	149	...	231	229	...	2	...	67	57	6	4	...	403	44	315	44	...	131	3	29	99	...	...	...	...	...	...
	37.—Butchers	Kasáyi	Hindu	3	...	1	2	...	...	...	...	...	...	...	...	...	...	...	1	...	1	...	...	2	...	...	2	...	...	...	...	...	...
		Total, Group D—37	...	3	...	1	2	...	...	...	...	...	...	...	...	...	...	...	1	...	1	...	...	2	...	...	2	...	...	...	...	...	...
	38.—Leather Workers	Mádiga	Hindu	629	218	304	107	...	145	143	2	...	...	47	38	8	1	...	345	33	262	50	...	92	4	32	56	...	...	...	...	...	...
		Muc'chi	Do.	6	2	2	2	...	1	1	...	...	...	1	1	...	...	...	2	...	1	1	...	2	...	1	1	...	...	...	...	...	...
		Total, Group D—38	...	635	220	306	109	...	146	144	2	...	...	48	39	8	1	...	347	33	263	51	...	94	4	33	57	...	...	...	...	...	...
		Total, Class D.	...	12,895	5,159	5,606	2,127	3	3,487	3,432	49	4	2	1,223	1,069	144	10	...	6,135	632	4,695	808	...	2,048	24	718	1,306	1	2	2	...	...	...
E.—Vagrants, Minor Artisans and Performers, etc.	41.—Earth Workers	Odde	Hindu	181	70	84	27	...	33	33	...	...	...	34	29	5	...	...	84	8	71	5	...	30	...	8	22	...	...	...	...	...	...
		Total, Group E—41	...	181	70	84	27	...	33	33	...	...	...	34	29	5	...	...	84	8	71	5	...	30	...	8	22	...	...	...	...	...	...
	42.—Knife Grinders	Sikligára	Hindu	...	...	...	...	...	...	...	...	...	...	...	...	...	...	...	...	...	...	...	...	...	...	...	...	...	...	...	...	...	...
		Total, Group E—42	...	...	...	...	...	...	...	...	...	...	...	...	...	...	...	...	...	...	...	...	...	...	...	...	...	...	...	...	...	...	...

Table E.—Castes by Civil Condition and Age.—Coorg.

TABLE E.—Castes, Tribes and Races by Civil Condition—*contd.*

Class.	Group.	Caste, Tribe, etc.	Religion.	MALES. All Ages.					0–9.					10–14.					15–39.					40 and over.					Not stated.				
				Total.	Single.	Married.	Widowed.	Not stated.	Total.	Single.	Married.	Widowed.	Not stated.	Total.	Single.	Married.	Widowed.	Not stated.	Total.	Single.	Married.	Widowed.	Not stated.	Total.	Single.	Married.	Widowed.	Not stated.	Total.	Single.	Married.	Widowed.	Not stated.
1	2	3	4	5	6	7	8	9	10	11	12	13	14	15	16	17	18	19	20	21	22	23	24	25	26	27	28	29	30	31	32	33	34
E.—Vagrants, Minor Artisans and Performers, etc.—*contd.*	43.—Mat-makers, Cane-splitters, etc.	Gauriga	Hindu	186	110	65	11	...	40	40	...	...	...	18	18	...	...	...	82	51	30	1	...	46	1	35	10	...	...	...	...	...	...
		Korama	Do.	154	77	73	4	...	31	31	...	...	...	11	11	...	...	...	88	35	51	2	...	24	...	22	2	...	...	...	...	...	...
		Méda	Do.	134	72	56	6	...	29	29	...	...	...	20	20	...	...	...	59	19	35	5	...	26	4	21	1	...	...	...	...	...	...
		Total, Group E.—43	...	474	259	194	21	...	100	100	...	...	...	49	49	...	...	...	229	105	116	8	...	96	5	78	13	...	...	...	...	...	...
	44.—Hunters, etc.	Bédar	Hindu	129	67	57	5	...	24	24	...	...	...	7	7	...	...	...	71	35	34	2	...	27	1	23	3	...	...	...	...	...	...
		Total, Group E—44	...	129	67	57	5	...	24	24	...	...	...	7	7	...	...	...	71	35	34	2	...	27	1	23	3	...	...	...	...	...	...
	45.—Miscellaneous and Disreputable Vagrants.	Mále or Maleya	Hindu	107	41	60	6	...	15	15	...	...	...	8	7	1	...	...	62	18	41	3	...	22	1	18	3	...	...	...	...	...	...
		Sále	Do.	1	1	...	...	...	1	1	...	...	...	...	...	...	...	...	...	...	...	...	...	...	...	...	...	...	...	...	...	...	...
		Total, Group E—45	...	108	42	60	6	...	16	16	...	...	...	8	7	1	...	...	62	18	41	3	...	22	1	18	3	...	...	...	...	...	...
	45(a).—Beggars, etc.	Banni	Hindu	81	25	54	2	...	8	8	...	...	...	6	6	...	...	...	49	9	39	1	...	18	2	15	1	...	...	...	...	...	...
		Dásari	Do.	10	4	5	1	...	3	3	...	...	...	...	...	...	...	...	5	1	3	1	...	2	...	2	...	...	...	...	...	...	...
		Helava	Do.	1	1	...	...	...	...	...	...	...	...	...	...	...	...	...	1	1	...	...	...	...	...	...	...	...	...	...	...	...	...
		Jógi	Do.	66	29	36	1	...	9	9	...	...	...	8	8	...	...	...	33	11	22	...	...	16	1	14	1	...	...	...	...	...	...
		Kutuma	Do.	34	17	15	2	...	10	10	...	...	...	1	1	...	...	...	11	5	6	...	...	12	1	9	2	...	...	...	...	...	...
		Paradési	Do.	2	...	2	...	...	...	...	...	...	...	...	...	...	...	...	...	...	...	...	...	2	...	2	...	...	...	...	...	...	...
		Siddha	Do.	10	5	5	...	...	2	2	...	...	...	...	...	...	...	...	8	3	5	...	...	...	...	...	...	...	...	...	...	...	...
		Total, Group E—45(a)	...	204	81	117	6	...	32	32	...	...	...	15	15	...	...	...	107	30	75	2	...	50	4	42	4	...	...	...	...	...	...
	46.—Tumblers and Acrobats.	Domba	Hindu	17	2	14	1	...	2	2	...	...	...	...	...	...	...	...	13	...	12	1	...	2	...	2	...	...	...	...	...	...	...
		Jetti	Do.	1	...	1	...	...	...	...	...	...	...	...	...	...	...	...	...	...	...	...	...	1	...	1	...	...	...	...	...	...	...
		Total, Group E—46	...	18	2	15	1	...	2	2	...	...	...	...	...	...	...	...	13	...	12	1	...	3	...	3	...	...	...	...	...	...	...
		Total, Class E.	...	1,194	588	559	47	...	205	205	...	...	...	142	139	3	...	...	606	232	355	19	...	241	12	207	22	...	...	...	...	...	...
F.—Races and Nationalities.	48.—Non-Indian Asiatic Races.	Armenian	Christian	9	6	3	...	...	3	3	...	...	...	...	...	...	...	...	3	2	1	...	...	3	1	2	...	...	...	...	...	...	...
		Duráni	Musalman	6	1	5	...	...	...	...	...	...	...	...	...	...	...	...	3	1	2	...	...	3	...	3	...	...	...	...	...	...	...
		Ebóda	Christian	1	...	1	...	...	...	...	...	...	...	...	...	...	...	...	...	...	...	...	...	1	...	1	...	...	...	...	...	...	...
		Khurési	Musalman	2	1	1	...	...	...	...	...	...	...	...	...	...	...	...	2	1	1	...	...	...	...	...	...	...	...	...	...	...	...
		Lódi Pathán	Do.	2	...	2	...	...	...	...	...	...	...	...	...	...	...	...	2	...	2	...	...	...	...	...	...	...	...	...	...	...	...
		Moghal	Do.	58	33	21	4	...	7	7	...	...	...	9	9	...	...	...	28	17	11	...	...	14	...	10	4	...	...	...	...	...	...
		Pársi	Parsi	24	15	7	2	...	13	13	...	...	...	...	...	...	...	...	6	2	3	1	...	5	...	4	1	...	...	...	...	...	...
		Pathán	Musalman	465	249	195	21	...	83	83	...	...	...	47	44	3	...	...	257	117	132	8	...	77	5	59	13	...	1	...	1	...	...
		Saiyad	Do.	411	208	194	9	...	74	74	...	...	...	32	32	...	...	...	215	95	116	4	...	90	7	78	5	...	...	...	...	...	...
		Sheik	Do.	1,889	996	835	58	...	369	366	3	...	...	158	156	2	...	...	984	459	508	17	...	378	15	322	41	...	...	...	...	...	...
		Total, Group F—48	...	2,867	1,509	1,264	94	...	549	546	3	...	...	246	241	5	...	...	1,500	694	776	30	...	572	28	479	64	...	2	...	2	...	...

Table B.—Castes by Civil Condition and Age.—Coorg.

FEMALES.

Class.	Group.	Caste, Tribe, etc.	Religion.	All Ages. Total.	All Ages. Single.	All Ages. Married.	All Ages. Widowed.	All Ages. Not stated.	0—9. Total.	0—9. Single.	0—9. Married.	0—9. Widowed.	0—9. Not stated.	10—14. Total.	10—14. Single.	10—14. Married.	10—14. Widowed.	10—14. Not stated.	15—20. Total.	15—20. Single.	15—20. Married.	15—20. Widowed.	15—20. Not stated.	20 and over. Total.	20 and over. Single.	20 and over. Married.	20 and over. Widowed.	20 and over. Not stated.	Not stated. Total.	Not stated. Single.	Not stated. Married.	Not stated. Widowed.	Not stated. Not stated.
				35	36	37	38	39	40	41	42	43	44	45	46	47	48	49	50	51	52	53	54	55	56	57	58	59	60	61	62	63	64
E.—VAGRANTS, MINOR ARTISANS AND PERFORMERS, ETC.—contd.	43.—Mat-Makers, Cane-Splitters, etc.	Gauriga	Hindu	276	72	69	35	...	48	45	...	3	...	18	15	1	2	...	80	10	60	10	...	30	2	8	20	...	...	...	...	...	...
		Korama	Do.	170	71	64	35	...	44	43	1	...	...	22	19	2	...	...	71	9	49	13	...	34	...	12	22	...	...	...	...	...	...
		Méda	Do.	127	45	64	18	...	33	31	2	...	...	11	10	1	...	...	63	4	52	7	...	20	...	9	11	...	...	...	...	...	...
		Total, Group E—43.		473	188	197	88	...	125	119	3	3	...	50	44	4	2	...	214	23	161	30	...	84	2	29	53	...	...	...	...	...	...
	44.—Hunters, etc.	Bédar	Hindu	94	34	40	20	...	20	20	...	...	...	10	8	1	1	...	50	6	34	10	...	14	...	5	9	...	...	...	...	...	...
		Total, Group E—44		94	34	40	20	...	20	20	...	...	...	10	8	1	1	...	50	6	34	10	...	14	...	5	9	...	...	...	...	...	...
	45.—Miscellaneous and Disreputable Vagrants.	Mále or Maleya	Hindu	88	29	36	23	...	16	16	...	...	...	9	7	1	1	...	48	6	32	10	...	15	...	3	12	...	...	...	...	...	...
		Súle	Do.	...	...	...	...	...	...	...	...	...	...	...	...	...	...	...	...	...	...	...	...	...	...	...	...	...	...	...	...	...	...
		Total, Group E—45		88	29	36	23	...	16	16	...	...	...	9	7	1	1	...	48	6	32	10	...	15	...	3	12	...	...	...	...	...	...
	45 (a).—Beggars, etc.	Banna	Hindu	66	15	44	7	...	13	12	1	...	...	4	2	2	...	...	34	1	32	1	...	15	...	9	6	...	...	...	...	...	...
		Dásari	Do.	8	3	4	1	...	2	2	...	...	...	1	1	...	...	...	4	...	4	...	...	1	...	...	1	...	...	...	...	...	...
		Helava	Do.	...	...	...	...	...	...	...	...	...	...	...	...	...	...	...	...	...	...	...	...	...	...	...	...	...	...	...	...	...	...
		Jógi	Do.	38	13	19	6	...	12	12	...	...	...	...	...	...	...	...	13	...	13	...	...	12	...	6	6	...	...	...	...	...	...
		Kutuma	Do.	40	11	20	9	...	10	10	...	...	...	1	1	...	...	...	11	...	11	...	...	14	...	5	9	...	...	...	...	...	...
		Paradési	Do.	1	...	1	...	...	...	...	...	...	...	5	1	4	...	...	1	...	1	...	...	...	...	...	...	...	...	...	...	...	...
		Siddha	Do.	10	2	3	5	...	1	1	...	...	...	...	...	...	...	...	6	1	3	2	...	3	...	...	3	...	...	...	...	...	...
		Total, Group E—45(a)		163	44	91	28	...	38	37	1	...	...	11	5	6	...	...	69	2	64	3	...	45	...	20	25	...	...	...	...	...	...
	46.—Tumblers and Acrobats.	Domba	Hindu	12	3	8	1	...	1	1	...	...	...	...	...	...	...	...	9	1	8	...	...	2	1	...	1	...	...	...	...	...	...
		Jetti	Do.	2	1	1	...	...	...	...	...	...	...	...	...	...	...	...	2	1	1	...	...	...	...	...	...	...	...	...	...	...	...
		Total, Group E—46		14	4	9	1	...	1	1	...	...	...	...	...	...	...	...	11	2	9	...	...	2	1	...	1	...	...	...	...	...	...
		Total, Class E		1,013	389	457	167	...	233	228	4	3	...	114	93	17	4	...	476	47	371	58	...	190	8	65	122	...	...	...	...	...	...
F.—RACES AND NATIONALITIES.	48.—Non-Indian Asiatic Races.	Armenian	Christian	11	9	2	...	...	5	5	...	...	...	3	3	...	...	...	3	1	2	...	...	...	...	...	...	...	...	...	...	...	...
		Duráni	Musalman	2	1	1	...	...	...	...	...	...	...	...	...	...	...	...	2	1	1	...	...	...	...	...	...	...	...	...	...	...	...
		Ebóda	Christian	...	...	...	...	...	...	...	...	...	...	...	...	...	...	...	...	...	...	...	...	...	...	...	...	...	...	...	...	...	...
		Khurési	Musalman	5	2	1	2	...	2	2	...	...	...	...	...	...	...	...	1	...	1	...	...	2	...	...	2	...	...	...	...	...	...
		Lódi Pathán	Do.	1	...	...	1	...	...	...	...	...	...	...	...	...	...	...	...	...	...	...	...	1	...	...	1	...	...	...	...	...	...
		Moghal	Do.	43	15	20	8	...	9	9	...	...	...	4	4	...	...	...	21	2	17	2	...	9	...	3	6	...	...	...	...	...	...
		Pársi	Parsi	15	5	7	3	...	4	4	...	...	...	1	1	...	...	...	8	...	7	1	...	2	...	...	2	...	...	...	...	...	...
		Pathán	Musalman	408	159	160	89	...	108	107	1	...	...	31	27	4	...	...	188	25	137	26	...	81	...	18	63	...	...	...	...	...	...
		Saiyad	Do.	314	112	140	62	...	82	82	...	...	...	24	19	5	...	...	134	11	102	21	...	74	...	33	41	...	...	...	...	...	...
		Sheik	Do.	1,484	504	670	310	...	366	364	2	...	...	124	103	21	...	...	694	35	576	83	...	300	2	71	227	...	...	...	...	...	...
		Total, Group F—48		2,283	807	1,001	475	...	576	573	3	...	...	187	157	30	...	...	1,051	75	843	133	...	469	2	125	342	...	...	...	...	...	...

TABLE E.—Castes, Tribes and Races by Civil Condition.

Table E.—Castes by Civil Condition and Age.—Coorg.

Class.	Group.	Caste, Tribe, etc.	Religion.	Males. All Ages. Total.	All Ages. Single.	All Ages. Married.	All Ages. Widowed.	All Ages. Not stated.	0–9. Total.	0–9. Single.	0–9. Married.	0–9. Widowed.	0–9. Not stated.	10–14. Total.	10–14. Single.	10–14. Married.	10–14. Widowed.	10–14. Not stated.	15–39. Total.	15–39. Single.	15–39. Married.	15–39. Widowed.	15–39. Not stated.	40 and over. Total.	40 and over. Single.	40 and over. Married.	40 and over. Widowed.	40 and over. Not stated.	Not stated. Total.	Not stated. Single.	Not stated. Married.	Not stated. Widowed.	Not stated. Not stated.
1	2	3	4	5	6	7	8	9	10	11	12	13	14	15	16	17	18	19	20	21	22	23	24	25	26	27	28	29	30	31	32	33	34
F.—Races and Nationalities—contd.	50.—Non-Asiatic Races	Celtic	Christian	...	...	...	...	...	...	...	...	...	...	...	...	...	...	...	...	...	...	...	...	...	...	...	...	...	...	...	...	...	...
		English	Do.	3	1	2	...	...	1	1	...	...	...	...	...	...	...	...	2	...	2	...	...	...	...	...	...	...	...	...	...	...	...
		European	Do.	163	91	62	10	...	24	23	1	...	...	7	7	...	...	...	95	52	39	4	...	37	9	22	6	...	...	...	...	...	...
		Portuguese	Do.	13	6	5	2	...	2	2	...	...	...	1	1	...	...	...	5	3	2	...	...	5	...	3	2	...	...	...	...	...	...
		Scotch	Do.	1	1	...	...	...	...	...	...	...	...	...	...	...	...	...	1	1	...	...	...	...	...	...	...	...	...	...	...	...	...
		Total, Group F—50.	...	180	99	69	12	...	27	26	1	...	...	8	8	...	...	...	103	56	43	4	...	42	9	25	8	...	...	...	...	...	...
	51.—Eurasians	Eurasian	Christian	114	57	44	11	2	33	32	...	...	1	1	...	...	...	1	53	19	29	5	...	27	6	15	6	...	...	...	...	...	...
		Total, Group F—51.	...	114	57	44	11	2	33	32	...	...	1	1	...	...	...	1	53	19	29	5	...	27	6	15	6	...	...	...	...	...	...
	52.—Christian Converts	Native Christian	Christian	1,460	783	629	45	3	319	316	1	...	2	104	104	...	...	...	787	353	418	16	...	249	10	220	29	...	1	...	...	...	1
		Total, Group F-52.	...	1,460	783	629	45	3	319	316	1	...	2	104	104	...	...	...	787	353	418	16	...	249	10	220	29	...	1	...	...	...	1
		Total, Class F.	...	4,621	2,448	2,006	162	5	928	920	5	...	3	359	353	5	...	1	2,443	1,122	1,266	55	...	889	53	729	107	...	2	...	1	...	1
G.—Indefinite and Unknown.	53.—Titular Names	Mudali	Hindu	19	7	10	2	...	3	3	...	...	...	2	2	...	...	...	8	2	5	1	...	6	...	5	1	...	...	...	...	...	...
		Náyaka	Do.	57	28	27	2	...	6	6	...	...	...	1	1	...	...	...	38	18	19	1	...	12	3	8	1	...	...	...	...	...	...
		Náyudu	Do	9	5	3	1	...	4	4	...	...	...	...	...	...	...	...	3	1	2	...	...	2	...	1	1	...	...	...	...	...	...
		Pillai	Do.	6	3	3	...	...	...	...	...	...	...	1	...	1	...	...	4	3	1	...	...	1	...	1	...	...	...	...	...	...	...
		Total, Group G—53.	...	91	43	43	5	...	13	13	...	...	...	4	3	1	...	...	53	24	27	2	...	21	3	15	3	...	...	...	...	...	...
	54.—Territorial, Linguistic and Sectarian Names.	Ándhra	Hindu	3	1	2	...	...	1	1	...	...	...	...	...	...	...	...	1	...	1	...	...	1	...	1	...	...	...	...	...	...	...
		Cháptia Sunní	Musalman	2	2	...	...	...	1	1	...	...	...	...	...	...	...	...	1	1	...	...	...	...	...	...	...	...	...	...	...	...	...
		Hanafi	Do.	39	21	16	2	...	9	9	...	...	...	3	3	...	...	...	18	9	8	1	...	9	...	8	1	...	...	...	...	...	...
		Islám	Do.	6	5	1	...	...	3	3	...	...	...	...	...	...	...	...	3	2	1	...	...	...	...	...	...	...	...	...	...	...	...
		Karnátaka	Hindu	18	8	10	...	...	2	2	...	...	...	2	2	...	...	...	10	4	6	...	...	4	...	4	...	...	...	...	...	...	...
		Konga	Do	51	27	22	2	...	13	13	...	...	...	8	8	...	...	...	20	6	12	2	...	10	...	10	...	...	...	...	...	...	...
		Konkani	Do.	364	189	156	19	...	57	56	1	...	...	39	37	2	...	...	200	92	103	5	...	67	3	50	14	...	1	1	...	...	...
			Christian	73	50	18	5	...	24	23	1	...	...	5	5	...	...	...	33	22	10	1	...	11	...	7	4	...	...	...	...	...	...
		Krishnamata	Hindu	1	...	1	...	...	...	...	...	...	...	...	...	...	...	...	1	...	1	...	...	...	...	...	...	...	...	...	...	...	...
		Lingáyat	Do.	1,785	1,003	675	107	...	438	437	1	...	...	177	171	6	...	...	868	383	449	36	...	301	11	219	71	...	1	1	...	...	...
		Malayáli	Do.	143	32	110	1	...	3	3	...	...	...	2	2	...	...	...	101	24	76	1	...	37	3	34	...	...	...	...	...	...	...
		Multáni	Do	3	...	3	...	...	...	...	...	...	...	...	...	...	...	...	1	...	1	...	...	2	...	2	...	...	...	...	...	...	...
		Musalman	Musalman	770	408	332	29	1	127	126	1	...	...	58	58	...	...	...	445	216	219	10	...	138	7	112	19	...	2	1	...	...	1
		Panchháchára	Hindu	244	157	71	16	...	74	74	...	...	...	21	21	...	...	...	111	60	45	6	...	38	2	26	10	...	...	...	...	...	...
		Rámánuja	Do.	2	1	1	...	...	1	1	...	...	...	...	...	...	...	...	1	...	1	...	...	...	...	...	...	...	...	...	...	...	...
		Saiva	Do.	115	44	66	5	...	25	25	...	...	...	7	7	...	...	...	73	11	60	2	...	10	1	6	3	...	...	...	...	...	...
		Sháfi	Musalman	14	3	10	1	...	1	1	...	...	...	...	...	...	...	...	9	2	7	...	...	4	...	3	1	...	...	...	...	...	...
		Sunni	Do.	12	1	10	1	...	...	...	...	...	...	...	...	...	...	...	7	1	6	...	...	5	...	4	1	...	...	...	...	...	...
		Tamil	Hindu	14	8	4	2	...	...	...	...	...	...	...	...	...	...	...	10	6	3	1	...	4	2	1	1	...	...	...	...	...	...
		Telugu	Do.	597	348	220	28	1	147	146	...	...	1	63	63	...	...	...	284	137	136	11	...	103	2	84	17	...	...	...	...	...	...
		Tulava	Do.	31	18	10	3	...	4	4	...	...	...	2	2	...	...	...	22	11	8	3	...	3	1	2	...	...	...	...	...	...	...
		Turakaru	Musalman	5	2	3	...	...	...	...	...	...	...	...	...	...	...	...	2	2	...	...	...	3	...	3	...	...	...	...	...	...	...
		Vaishnava	Hindu	75	36	36	3	...	13	13	...	...	...	4	4	...	...	...	50	18	30	2	...	8	1	6	1	...	...	...	...	...	...
		Vírasaiva	Do.	709	376	277	56	...	169	164	5	...	...	97	93	4	...	...	320	114	185	21	...	123	5	83	35	...	...	...	...	...	...
		Total, Group G—54.	...	5,076	2,740	2,054	280	2	1,112	1,102	9	...	1	488	476	12	...	...	2,591	1,121	1,368	102	...	881	38	665	178	...	4	3	...	...	1

Table E.—Castes by Civil Condition and Age.—Coorg.

Class.	Group.	Caste, Tribe, etc.	Religion.	FEMALES. All Ages. Total.	Single.	Married.	Widowed.	Not stated.	0–9. Total.	Single.	Married.	Widowed.	Not stated.	10–14. Total.	Single.	Married.	Widowed.	Not stated.	15–39. Total.	Single.	Married.	Widowed.	Not stated.	40 and over. Total.	Single.	Married.	Widowed.	Not stated.	Not stated. Total.	Single.	Married.	Widowed.	Not stated.
				35	36	37	38	39	40	41	42	43	44	45	46	47	48	49	50	51	52	53	54	55	56	57	58	59	60	61	62	63	64
F.—Races and Nationalities—*contd.*	50.—Non-Asiatic Races	Celtic	Christian	1	1	...	...	...	...	...	...	...	...	...	...	...	...	...	1	1	...	...	...	...	...	...	...	...	...	...	...	...	...
		English	Do.	1	...	1	...	...	...	...	...	...	...	...	...	...	...	...	1	...	1	...	...	...	...	...	...	...	...	...	...	...	...
		European	Do.	79	40	35	4	...	24	24	...	...	...	3	3	...	...	...	45	11	33	1	...	7	2	2	3	...	...	...	...	...	...
		Portuguese	Do.	8	7	...	1	...	2	2	...	...	...	1	1	...	...	...	4	4	...	...	...	1	...	...	1	...	...	...	...	...	...
		Scotch	Do.	1	1	...	...	...	...	...	...	...	...	...	...	...	...	...		1	...	...	...	...	...	...	...	...	...	...	...	...	...
		Total, Group F—50	...	90	49	36	5	...	26	26	...	...	...	4	4	...	...	...	52	17	34	1	...	8	2	2	4	...	...	...	...	...	...
	51.—Eurasians	Eurasian	Christian	98	53	35	8	2	32	30	...	...	2	11	10	1	...	...	42	12	28	2	...	13	1	6	6	...	...	...	...	...	...
		Total, Group F—51	...	98	53	35	8	2	32	30	...	...	2	11	10	1	...	...	42	12	28	2	...	13	1	6	6	...	...	...	...	...	...
	52.—Christian Converts	Native Christian	Christian	1,245	488	500	253	4	307	302	2	...	3	121	114	7	...	...	611	70	442	99	...	206	2	49	154	1	...	...	...	...	...
		Total, Group F—52	...	1,245	488	500	253	4	307	302	2	...	3	121	114	7	...	...	611	70	442	99	...	206	2	49	154	1	...	...	...	...	...
		Total, Class F	...	**3,716**	**1,397**	**1,572**	**741**	**6**	**941**	**931**	**5**	...	**5**	**323**	**285**	**38**	...	...	**1,756**	**174**	**1,347**	**235**	...	**696**	**7**	**182**	**506**	**1**	...	...	...	...	...
G.—Indefinite and Unknown	53.—Titular names	Mudali	Hindu	19	6	9	4	...	4	4	...	...	...	2	2	...	...	...	9	...	9	...	...	4	...	...	4	...	...	...	...	...	...
		Náyaka	Do.	23	6	12	5	...	2	2	...	...	...	4	3	1	...	...	12	...	11	1	...	5	1	...	4	...	...	...	...	...	...
		Náyudu	Do.	3	1	2	...	...	...	...	...	...	...	1	1	...	...	...	2	...	2	...	...	...	...	...	...	...	...	...	...	...	...
		Pillai	Do.	8	4	2	2	...	1	...	1	...	...	1	...	1	...	...	5	4	...	1	...	1	...	...	1	...	...	...	...	...	...
		Total, Group G—53	...	53	17	25	11	...	7	6	1	...	...	8	6	2	...	...	28	4	22	2	...	10	1	...	9	...	...	...	...	...	...
	54.—Territorial, Linguistic and Sectarian names	Ándhra	Hindu	2	...	2	...	...	...	...	...	...	...	...	...	...	...	...	1	...	1	...	...	1	...	1	...	...	...	...	...	...	...
		Cháptia Sunni	Musalman	1	1	...	...	...	1	1	...	...	...	...	...	...	...	...	...	...	...	...	...	...	...	...	...	...	...	...	...	...	...
		Hanafi	Do.	50	19	19	12	...	15	15	...	...	...	3	2	1	...	...	21	2	17	2	...	11	...	1	10	...	...	...	...	...	...
		Islám	Do.	7	3	1	3	...	1	1	...	...	...	...	...	...	...	...	3	2	1	...	...	3	...	...	3	...	...	...	...	...	...
		Karnátaka	Hindu	19	8	7	4	...	6	6	...	...	...	3	2	1	...	...	8	...	5	3	...	2	...	1	1	...	...	...	...	...	...
		Kouga	Do.	35	12	15	8	...	9	9	...	...	...	2	2	...	...	...	16	1	11	4	...	8	...	4	4	...	...	...	...	...	...
		Konkani	Do.	248	70	84	94	...	43	43	...	...	...	28	19	9	...	...	113	8	66	39	...	64	...	9	55	...	...	...	...	...	...
		Konkani	Christian	45	24	12	9	...	19	19	...	...	...	2	2	...	...	...	15	3	10	2	...	9	...	2	7	...	...	...	...	...	...
		Krishnamata	Hindu	...	...	...	...	...	...	...	...	...	...	...	...	...	...	...	...	...	...	...	...	...	...	...	...	...	...	...	...	...	...
		Lingáyat	Do.	1,754	737	584	433	...	477	474	2	1	...	193	176	16	1	...	785	86	519	180	...	299	1	47	251	...	...	...	...	...	...
		Malayáli	Do.	8	7	1	...	...	3	3	...	...	...	4	4	...	...	...	1	...	1	...	...	...	...	...	...	...	...	...	...	...	...
		Multáni	Do.	...	...	...	...	...	...	...	...	...	...	...	...	...	...	...	...	...	...	...	...	...	...	...	...	...	...	...	...	...	...
		Musalman	Musalman	555	177	243	135	...	129	127	2	...	...	42	33	9	...	...	273	17	208	48	...	111	...	24	87	...	...	...	...	...	...
		Panchāchára	Hindu	259	105	80	74	...	76	76	...	...	...	25	25	...	...	...	109	4	67	38	...	49	...	13	36	...	...	...	...	...	...
		Rámánuja	Do.	3	2	1	...	...	2	2	...	...	...	...	...	...	...	...	1	...	1	...	...	...	...	...	...	...	...	...	...	...	...
		Saiva	Do.	141	84	41	16	...	64	64	...	...	...	17	17	...	...	...	50	3	41	6	...	10	...	...	10	...	...	...	...	...	...
		Sháfi	Musalman	1	...	1	...	...	...	...	...	...	...	...	...	...	...	...	1	...	1	...	...	...	...	...	...	...	...	...	...	...	...
		Sunni	Do.	2	...	2	...	...	...	...	...	...	...	...	...	...	...	...	2	...	2	...	...	...	...	...	...	...	...	...	...	...	...
		Tamil	Hindu	15	6	5	4	...	2	2	...	...	...	2	2	...	...	...	10	2	4	4	...	1	...	1	...	...	...	...	...	...	...
		Telugu	Do.	563	231	219	113	...	151	150	1	...	...	58	51	7	...	...	256	27	195	34	...	98	3	16	79	...	...	...	...	...	...
		Tuluva	Do.	14	8	5	1	...	6	6	...	...	...	1	1	...	...	...	5	1	4	...	...	2	...	1	1	...	...	...	...	...	...
		Turakaru	Musalman	...	...	...	...	...	...	...	...	...	...	...	...	...	...	...	...	...	...	...	...	...	...	...	...	...	...	...	...	...	...
		Vaishnava	Hindu	49	12	21	16	...	9	9	...	...	...	...	...	...	...	...	29	3	21	5	...	11	...	...	11	...	...	...	...	...	...
		Vírasaiva	Do.	871	326	276	269	...	198	197	...	1	...	107	97	8	2	...	378	31	225	122	...	188	1	43	144	...	...	...	...	...	...
		Total, Group G—54	...	4,642	1,832	1,619	1,191	...	1,211	1,204	5	2	...	487	433	51	3	...	2,077	190	1,400	487	...	867	5	163	699	...	...	...	...	...	...

Table E.—Castes by Civil Condition and Age.—Coorg.

TABLE E.—Castes, Tribes and Races by Civil Condition—*contd.*

Class.	Group.	Caste, Tribe, etc.	Religion.	MALES. All Ages. Total.	All Ages. Single.	All Ages. Married.	All Ages. Widowed.	All Ages. Not stated.	0–9. Total.	0–9. Single.	0–9. Married.	0–9. Widowed.	0–9. Not stated.	10–14. Total.	10–14. Single.	10–14. Married.	10–14. Widowed.	10–14. Not stated.	15–39. Total.	15–39. Single.	15–39. Married.	15–39. Widowed.	15–39. Not stated.	40 and over. Total.	40 and over. Single.	40 and over. Married.	40 and over. Widowed.	40 and over. Not stated.	Not stated. Total.	Not stated. Single.	Not stated. Married.	Not stated. Widowed.	Not stated. Not stated.
1	2	3	4	5	6	7	8	9	10	11	12	13	14	15	16	17	18	19	20	21	22	23	24	25	26	27	28	29	30	31	32	33	34
G.—Indefinite and Unknown—*contd.*	55.—Unclassified Castes.	Bánava	Hindu	1	...	1	...	...	...	...	...	...	...	...	...	...	...	...	...	...	...	...	...	1	...	1	...	...	...	...	...	...	...
		Bandára	Do.	4	2	2	...	...	...	...	...	...	...	1	1	...	...	...	3	1	2	...	...	...	...	...	...	...	...	...	...	...	...
		Chaniya	Do.	1	...	1	...	...	...	...	...	...	...	...	...	...	...	...	1	...	1	...	...	...	...	...	...	...	...	...	...	...	...
		Chauriya	Do.	1	1	...	...	...	...	...	...	...	...	...	...	...	...	...	1	1	...	...	...	...	...	...	...	...	...	...	...	...	...
		Chipira	Musalmán	...	...	...	...	...	...	...	...	...	...	...	...	...	...	...	...	...	...	...	...	...	...	...	...	...	...	...	...	...	...
		Davala	Hindu	...	...	...	...	...	...	...	...	...	...	...	...	...	...	...	...	...	...	...	...	...	...	...	...	...	...	...	...	...	...
		Gópi	Do.	1	...	1	...	...	...	...	...	...	...	...	...	...	...	...	...	...	...	...	...	1	...	1	...	...	...	...	...	...	...
		Kurchi	Do.	10	2	7	1	...	2	1	...	...	...	1	1	...	...	...	3	...	3	...	...	5	...	4	1	...	...	...	...	...	...
		Low caste	Christian	1	1	...	...	...	...	...	...	...	...	...	...	...	...	...	...	...	...	...	...	1	1	...	...	...	...	...	...	...	...
		Mahale	Hindu	3	3	...	...	...	...	...	...	...	...	...	...	...	...	...	2	2	...	...	...	1	1	...	...	...	...	...	...	...	...
		Malkara	Do.	...	...	...	...	...	...	...	...	...	...	...	...	...	...	...	...	...	...	...	...	...	...	...	...	...	...	...	...	...	...
		Massadi	Musalman	2	1	1	...	...	...	...	...	...	...	...	...	...	...	...	1	1	...	...	...	1	...	1	...	...	...	...	...	...	...
		Native	Hindu	...	...	...	...	...	...	...	...	...	...	...	...	...	...	...	...	...	...	...	...	...	...	...	...	...	...	...	...	...	...
		Palinga	Do.	3	3	...	...	...	1	1	...	...	...	...	...	...	...	...	2	2	...	...	...	...	...	...	...	...	...	...	...	...	...
		Total, Group G—55.		27	13	13	1	...	2	2	...	...	...	2	2	...	...	...	13	7	6	...	...	10	2	7	1	...	...	...	...	...	...
		Total, Class G		5,194	2,796	2,110	286	2	1,127	1,117	9	...	1	494	481	13	...	...	2,657	1,152	1,401	104	...	812	43	667	102	...	4	3	...	...	1
Not stated.	Not stated	Caste—Not returned	Hindu	55	32	22	1	...	6	6	...	...	...	6	6	...	...	...	34	20	14	...	...	9	...	8	1	...	...	...	...	...	...
		GRAND TOTAL		95,907	50,947	41,187	3,724	49	21,663	21,546	94	2	21	9,020	8,851	162	4	3	49,449	20,040	27,901	1,495	13	15,743	494	13,026	2,219	4	32	16	4	4	8

Tabe E.—Castes by Civil Condition and Age.—Coorg.

Class.	Group.	Caste, Tribe, etc.	Religion.	FEMALES. All Ages. Total.	All Ages. Single.	All Ages. Married.	All Ages. Widowed.	All Ages. Not stated.	0—9. Total.	0—9. Single.	0—9. Married.	0—9. Widowed.	0—9. Not stated.	10—14. Total.	10—14. Single.	10—14. Married.	10—14. Widowed.	10—14. Not stated.	15—39. Total.	15—39. Single.	15—39. Married.	15—39. Widowed.	15—39. Not stated.	40 and over. Total.	40 and over. Single.	40 and over. Married.	40 and over. Widowed.	40 and over. Not stated.	Not stated. Total.	Not stated. Single.	Not stated. Married.	Not stated. Widowed.	Not stated. Not stated.
				35	36	37	38	39	40	41	42	43	44	45	46	47	48	49	50	51	52	53	54	55	56	57	58	59	60	61	62	63	64
G.—INDEFINITE AND UNKNOWN—contd.	55.—Unclassified Castes.	Bánava	Hindu	...	...	...	...	...	...	...	...	...	...	...	...	...	...	...	...	...	...	...	...	...	...	...	...	...	...	...	...	...	...
		Bandára	Do.	4	2	2	...	...	2	2	...	...	...	...	...	...	...	...	2	...	2	...	...	...	...	...	...	...	...	...	...	...	...
		Chaniya	Do.	1	...	...	1	...	...	...	...	...	...	...	...	...	...	...	...	...	...	...	...	1	...	...	1	...	...	...	...	...	...
		Chauriya	Do.	...	...	...	...	...	...	...	...	...	...	...	...	...	...	...	...	...	...	...	...	...	...	...	...	...	...	...	...	...	...
		Chipira	Musalman	1	...	...	1	...	...	...	...	...	...	...	...	...	...	...	1	...	...	1	...	...	...	...	...	...	...	...	...	...	...
		Davala	Hindu	1	1	...	...	...	...	...	...	...	...	...	...	...	...	...	1	1	...	...	...	...	...	...	...	...	...	...	...	...	...
		Gópi	Do.	1	...	1	...	...	...	...	...	...	...	1	...	1	...	...	...	...	...	...	...	...	...	...	...	...	...	...	...	...	...
		Kurchi	Do.	2	1	1	...	...	1	1	...	...	...	...	...	...	...	...	1	...	1	...	...	...	...	...	...	...	...	...	...	...	...
		Low caste	Christian	...	...	...	...	...	...	...	...	...	...	...	...	...	...	...	...	...	...	...	...	...	...	...	...	...	...	...	...	...	...
		Mahale	Hindu	...	...	...	...	...	...	...	...	...	...	...	...	...	...	...	...	...	...	...	...	...	...	...	...	...	...	...	...	...	...
		Malkara	Do.	1	1	...	...	...	...	...	...	...	...	...	...	...	...	...	1	1	...	...	...	...	...	...	...	...	...	...	...	...	...
		Massadi	Musalman	2	1	1	...	...	...	...	...	...	...	1	1	...	...	...	1	...	1	...	...	...	...	...	...	...	...	...	...	...	...
		Native	Hindu	1	...	...	1	...	...	...	...	...	...	...	...	...	...	...	...	...	...	...	...	1	...	...	1	...	...	...	...	...	...
		Palinga	Do.	2	2	...	...	...	2	2	...	...	...	...	...	...	...	...	...	...	...	...	...	...	...	...	...	...	...	...	...	...	...
		Total, Group G—55.	...	16	8	5	3	...	5	5	...	...	...	2	1	1	...	...	7	2	4	1	...	2	...	...	2	...	...	...	...	...	...
		Total, Class G	...	4,711	1,857	1,649	1,205	...	1,223	1,215	6	2	...	497	440	54	3	...	2,112	196	1,426	490	...	879	6	163	710	...	...	...	...	...	...
NOT STATED.	Not stated	Caste—Not returned	Hindu	50	28	11	11	...	13	13	...	...	...	2	2	...	...	...	22	3	15	4	...	13	...	6	7	...	...	...	...	...	...
		GRAND TOTAL	...	77,148	32,651	31,622	12,835	40	21,935	21,741	155	13	26	7,619	6,731	853	34	1	35,587	4,044	26,781	4,756	6	11,990	126	3,828	8,032	4	17	9	5	...	3

CASTE INDEX, COORG.

The names of main Castes are printed in **Antique** and those of Sub-divisions in Roman type. The figures denote the full strength of the Caste and Sub-division respectively. In the case of Sub-divisions only the strength of those few which are numerically important has been given.

Adiyán . . 537
- Battya Malayáli.
- Moyila.

Agamudaiyan . 8

Agasa . . 1,367
- Ande.
- Banna.
- Kannada.
- Kodagu.
- Madivála.
- Malayáli.
- Nádu.
- Panneya.
- Telugu.
- Telugu Banajiga.
- Tulu.

Agnáni . . 34

Agraväla . . 2

Ajala . . 1
- Tulu.

Akkasále . . 1,196
- Áchári.
- Badagi.
- Bráhman.
- Byla.
- Chikkamane Sampradáya.
- Drávida.
- Gauda.
- Karnátaka.
- Kollaru.
- Konga.
- Kuláchára.
- Lingáyat.
- Malayáli.
- Panchachára.
- Pánchála.
- Panchánana.
- Panchánga.
- Ponnabáge.
- Siváchára.
- Sonára.
- Takare.
- Tammalu.
- Telugu.
- Tulu.
- Utharáji.
- Visva Bráhmana.
- Visvagna.
- Visvakarma.

Ambalavási . 5
- Stánika.

Ándhra . . 5
- Kartanavíra.

Ánekula . . 9
- Holeya.

Arasu . . 30
- Bada Arasu.
- Rájabanda.
- Rájaputra.
- Siváchára.

Áré . . 74
- Darji.
- Kannada.
- Kshatri.
- Maráthi.
- Námdév.
- Rangári.

Armenian . . 20
- East Indian.

Aruchi . . 1

Ásári . . 160
- Akkasále.
- Badagi.

Ásári—*contd.*
- Malayáli.
- Panchánana.
- Siváchára.
- Tac'chan.
- Tulu.
- Visva Bráhmana.

Ayaskári . . 3
- Pancháná.

Áyiri . . 1,007
- Áchári.
- Badagi.
- Kadamba.
- Kóláyiri.
- Kolla.
- Kubbe.
- Kumri.
- Malayáli.
- Mallari.
- Muváyiri.
- Nyáda.
- Tac'cháyiri.
- Todanáyiri.

Ayyambokkalu 4

Badaga . . 1

Badagi . . 581
- Áchári.
- Áyiri.
- Bhava.
- Bol.
- Bráhman.
- Kada.
- Kadamba Árya.
- Kammara.
- Kannada.
- Karnátaka.
- Kodagu.
- Kuláchára.
- Kulni.
- Pánchála.
- Siváchára.
- Tac'cháyiri.
- Tulu.

Bákuda . . 6
- Pále.

Balegára . . 8
- Banajiga Chetti.

Bálólikára . . 9
- Konkani.

Banajiga . . 1,549
- Badda Lingáyat.
- Balegára.
- Chetti.
- Dása.
- Désasta.
- Gázulu.
- Golla.
- Gurustala.
- Hajám.
- Kallali.
- Lingáyat.
- Mani.
- Naidu.
- Námadári.
- Ráya.
- Siváchára.
- Stala.
- Telugu.
- Vasabanáti.
- Vírasaiva.
- Vurattarattya.
- Yelé.
- Yennaikelasaru.

Bánava . . 1

Bandára . . 8

Baniya . . 22

Banna . . 14
- Jótiphana.
- Peru.

Banta . . 1,117
- Alava.
- Bannagára.
- Bidina.
- Biru.
- Budipa.
- Gutha.
- Kollada.
- Kumbára.
- Mádhva.
- Massádi.
- Parivára.
- Sivalli.
- Toreya.
- Tulu.
- Vakkaliga.

Basavi . . 17

Batta . . 18
- Hogala.
- Karnátaka.

Bédar . . 223
- Besta.
- Gangadikára.
- Gauda.
- Hálu.
- Kádu.
- Náyaka.
- Náyar.
- Para.
- Parikári Náyak.
- Pútalóllu.
- Telaga.
- Úru.
- Uttama.
- Valmíka.

Besta . . 627
- Balai.
- Bóyi.
- Bunda.
- Buruda.
- Gangimakkalu.
- Kannada.
- Mínu.
- Mullu.
- Pallaki.
- Parava.
- Parivára.
- Sunna.
- Toreya.
- Totiyaru.

Betta . . 3

Bhaira . . 58
- Álavanta.
- Balagai.

Bilimagga . . 1,103
- Hirihasube Kumari Chetti.
- Hirihasube Kurivina Chetti.
- Hirihasubina Kóvina Chetti.
- Kurivina Chetti.

Billava . . 1,366
- Baidya.
- Jain.
- Kannada.
- Malai.
- Malayáli.
- Súdra.
- Tiyyan.
- Tulu.

Binepatta . . 101

Biruva . . 12
- Tulu.

Bóyi . . 958
- Alli.
- Besta.
- Gangimakkalu.
- Kattu.
- Malai.
- Pallaki.
- Sunna.
- Telugu.
- Toreya.

Bráhman . . 2,541
- Advaita.
- Aitála.
- Ándhra.
- Árádhya.
- Áravattuvakkalu.
- Áruvélu.
- Babbúru Kamme.
- Badaganádu.
- Bettadapurada Sankéti.
- Brahacharanam.
- Bráhman.
- Chittapávana.
- Chólamandala.
- Désasta.
- Drávida.
- Gauda.
- Golkonda.
- Hale Kannadiga.
- Hale Karnátaka.
- Havig.
- Hebbára.
- Hemmige.
- Hoisala Karnátaka.
- Hosánádu Karnátaka.
- Kamme.
- Kanauj
- Kandavara.
- Kannada.
- Karnátaka.
- Kóna Símai Drávida.
- Konkanasta.
- Kóta.
- Kudlukára.
- Mádhva.
- Maharáshtra.
- Malanádu Kamme.
- Malanádu Karnátaka.
- Márvádi.
- Pralákaiyanavamsa.
- Rámánujamatam.
- Sankéti.
- Sárasvata.
- Shivalli.
- Smárta.
- Smárta Karnátaka.
- Srívaishnava.
- Tengalai.
- Tulu.
- Ulucha Kamone.
- Uttaráji.
- Vadagalai.
- Vadama.
- Vaidíki.
- Vaishnava.
- Vélanádu Ándhra.

Celtic . . 1

Cháliya . . 129
- Nagarada.
- Yadanga.
- Yeda.

Chaniya . . 2

Cháptia Sunni . 3

Cháródi . . 4
- Cháródivarga.

Chauriya . . 1

Chembukutti . 23

Cheptégára . 54
Konkani.
Náyar.

Chetti . . 87
Balija.
Jáda.
Pappada.
Telugu.
Vellála.

Chinnavára . 2

Chipira . 1

Darji . 58
Maráthi.
Námdév.

Dásari . 18
Karnátaka.
Telugu.

Davala . 1

Désiyatvani . 9

Dévadiga . 3

Dévánga . 2,361
Bedara.
Bilimagga.
Chetti.
Déva Bráhmana.
Dévánga Smárta.
Hirihasube.
Kannada.
Karimaggada.
Mudina.
Panchabana.
Telugu.

Dhóbi . 15
Agasa.
Karnátaka.

Dívar . 703
Billava.
Halepaik.
Kannada.
Kshatriya.
Makkalu.
Parivára.

Domba . 29
Karnátaka.
Telugu.

Durání . 8
Kándáre.

Ehóda . 1

English . 4

Eurasian . 212
Armenian.
East Indian.
Scotch.

European . 242
English.
Eurasian.
French.
German.
Indian.
Irish.
Scotch.
Swiss.
Welsh.

Gandhári . 3

Gániga . . 485
Bokebannadava.
Chetti.
Gázulu.
Heggániga.
Jótiphana.
Kirigániga.
Konga.
Malayáli.
Rébádi.
Tulu.
Yemme.

Gauda . . 13,325
Akkisor.
Gangadikára.
Gaudálike.
Hálu.
Karnátaka.
Kodagu.
Mulu.
Siváchára.
Tigala.
Tulu, 3,431.
Tulukumbára.
Vakkaliga.

Gauliga . . 179
Krishna Golla.
Yemme.

Gauriga . . 362
Biliyale Chetti.
Bóyi.
Karnátaka.
Kukke.
Myása.
Myása Batti.

Gejjegára . 4

Golla . . 923
Bákula.
Bare.
Dhóniga.
Gauli.
Gondalu.
Hálu.
Kádu.
Kengolla.
Kristna.
Kshatriya.
Mári.
Nagarattu.
Púja.
Telugu.
Úru.
Vakkaliga.
Yerra.

Gópi . . 2

Gósáyi . . 7
Maharáshtra.

Gudigára . . 2

Hajám . . 886
Banajiga.
Gangadikára.
Kannada.
Karnátaka.
Kelasi.
Malaparu.
Nádu.
Náyinda.
Siváchára.
Tamil.
Telugu.
Tulu.

Halepaik . 28

Hallikára . 2

Hanafi . 89
Pathán.
Saiyad.
Sheik.

Heggade . 1,307
Hálukuruba.
Hanikallu.
Kálu.
Koruvakatti.
Kuruba.

Helava . 1
Balegára.

Holeya . 24,085
Agnáni.
Álavanta.
Ande.
Badagi.
Balagai.
Balamari.
Baligonda.
Bellikula.
Bháira.
Chetti.
Dása.

Holeya—*contd.*
Déva.
Gangadikára.
Gázula.
Jógi.
Kannada.
Kannadapattu.
Karnátaka.
Kembatti.
Konga.
Kukka.
Mádiga.
Maggada.
Mahiyana.
Mailára.
Maluvamane.
Márangi.
Maráthi.
Mári.
Méda.
Mundála.
Palla.
Pallai.
Sále.
Tamil.
Telugu.
Tengalai.
Tigala.
Tulu.
Uppara.
Uppukorava.
Vakkaliga.
Yedagai.

Hummaliga . 9
Chetti.

Huvvadiga . 2

I'diga . 23

Islám . 13

Jáda . 10

Jain . 62
Agasa.
Digambara.
Kshatriya.
Tírtha Kshatriya.

Jangam . 981

Jetti . 3

Jógi . 104
Barabar.
Kadri.
Kannada.
Kara.
Kshatri.
Kulabalagai.

Kabbéra . 3

Kaikólan . 2
Sengunda Mudali.

Káládi . 5

Kallan . 1

Kallukkutti . 78
Kallutiga.

Kammara . 2

Kanchugára . 9
Karna.
Koshaka.

Kaniya . 206
Malayáli.

Kápála . 150

Kárgóll . 7

Karnátaka . 37
Balagai Holeya.
Holeya.
Kannada.
Kodagu.

Kasáyi . 8
Linga.

Kavádi . 8

Kavarai . 32
Jaiva Pancha.
Musang.
Nádár.
Náyudu.
Telugu Banajiga.
Uppadu.

Kávudi . 37

Khuréśi . 7

Kodagu . 32,611
Amma, 393.
Boda.
Gangadi.
Heggade.
Jammada.
Jandu.
Nági.
Sanna, 1,081.

Kóláyiri . 392
Antráyi.
Baduva.
Maniyáni.
Náyar.
Tulu.

Kollan . 96
Agattu Náyar.
Badigi.
Kuruva Náyar.
Malayáli.

Kómati . 17

Konga . 86
Agasa.
Agnáni.
Holeya.

Konkani . . 730
Angadi.
Balavali.
Balegára.
Ballu.
Bálólikára.
Baralikára.
Bráhmana.
Chaptegára.
Chetti.
Désinandavarája.
Gauda Sárasvata.
Gaula.
Hálukuruba Chetti.
Kádu.
Maráthi.
Modlakára.
Native Christian.
Potikaru.
Pyáde.
Rájápuri.
Sonegára.
Visvakarma Badigi.

Koraga . . 11
Holeya.

Korama or Korcha 324
Ashta.
Chetti.
Dásavaktaka.
Kávadi.
Kondakorava.
Korava Naik.
Kuge.
Kukke.
Mandragatti.
Méldadi.
Náyar.
Sátvádi.
Uppu.
Víravára.
Yentumale Chetti.
Yettina.

Kóvinajáti . . 8

Koyava . . 323
Kumbára.
Náyak.
Náyar.

Krishnamata . 1

Kshatriya . . 223
Belivamsa.
Bráhmana.
Chettikula.
Chitragára.
Konkani.
Kulóni.
Maráthi.
Náyar.
Rájah.
Rájaputra.
Rájavára.
Sanna Kodagu.
Sindhu.
Telugu Banijiga.

Kshauraka . . 2

Kudiya . . 642
Adeke.
Áre.
Male.
Púmale.

Kuláchári . . 2
Akkasále.

Kumbára . . 908
Bóyi.
Chetti.
Gunda Bráhmana.
Kannada.
Karnátaka.
Konkani.
Koyava.
Madekemadura.
Telaga.
Tulu.
Vádári.

Kunchiga . . 24

Kurchi . . 12

Kurikalu . . 1

Kurumba or **Kuruba**, 7,621
Anda.
Betta.
Gauda.
Hálu.
Heggade.
Jénu.
Kambali.
Kanna.
Kuri.
Reddi.
Tulu.

Kuttuma . . 74

Labbai . . 513
Hanafi.
Sheik.

Ládar . . 7
Kshatri.

Lambádi . 156
Májamman.
Sugáli.

Lingáyat . 3,539
Akkásála.
Árádhya Jangam.
Badagala.
Banajiga.
Chetti.
Gangadikára.
Gaudálike.
Gauda.
Gaudamane.
Gurustala.
Hirihasubi.
Jangam.
Jangamárádya.
Kannadi.
Kshauraka.
Kumbára.
Kunchigauda.
Kunchitiga.
Nagarattu.
Nonabaru
Pancháchára.
Panchácharada Gauda.
Panchamasále Banajiga.
Rájabanna.
Sádugalu.

Lingáyat—*contd.*
Sajjana.
Sankéta.
Sílavanta.
Síva Bráhman.
Siváchará.
Staladavaru.
Stánika.
Subbanaru.
Telugu.
Vaisya.
Vírasaiva.

Lódí Pathán . 3

Low Caste . 1

Mádiga . 1,549
Adijámbuvana Makkalu.
Kannada.
Karnátaka.
Saja.
Yedagai Holeya.

Madivála . 335
Agasa.
Banna.
Besta.
Bettavageyava.
Chetti.
Kannada.
Karnátaka.
Kodagu.
Tulu.
Vírasaiva.

Maggadava . 15
Billi.

Mahale . 3

Malasar . 16

Malayáli . 151
Ayari.
Cháliya.
Kolári.
Maráta.
Náyar.
Tiyya.

Mále or **Maleya** 195
Banna.
Heggade.
Náyar.
Tiyya.

Malkara . 1
Pancha Gauda.

Maniyáni . 107
Eruman.
Holeya.
Kuléya.

Máppilla . 5,170
Jónaka.
Návi.
Saiyad.
Shafi.

Maráthi . 2,384
Andéravuta.
Ande.
Arasa.
Áre, 655.
Áre Kshatri.
Ávulaguvári.
Baniya.
Budabudike.
Darji.
Désasta.
Gauda Déva.
Hale.
Hálu.
Holeya, 176.
Jinigára.
Kádu.
Kaláyi.
Kalluvadda.
Kannada.
Kannada Billi.
Karuva.
Killékyáta.
Kolári.
Kóli.
Kombe.
Konkani.
Kshatriya.

Maráthi—*contd.*
Kudure.
Kumri, 384.
Kurubi.
Ládaru.
Lála.
Móchi.
Nádu.
Nalle.
Námdév.
Náyaka.
Rájaputra.
Rangadév.
Rangári.
Ráyarávata.
Sálunka Rau Yenkóji Rau.
Sulabhi.
Tambra.
Telaga.
Tulu.
Yennavaru.

Massadi . 4

Máyava . 1

Máyila . 130
Adiyán.
Bettava.
Kádu.
Kukka.
Pále.
Tulu.

Méda . 261
Chetti.
Kodagu.
Kosa.

Méman . 42
Hanafi.

Méra . 12

Mogér . 1

Moghal . 101
Hanafi.
Saiyad.
Sheik.

Moyili . 8

Muc'chi . 14

Mudali . 38

Mukkári . 8

Mukkáti . 23
Ambalavási.
Stánika.

Múltáni . 3

Musalman . 1,325
Batkali.
Gauliga.
Kakari.
Kandata.
Labbai.
Máppila.
Moghal.
Pathán.
Pindári.
Saiyad.
Sháfi.
Sheik.
Yenne Gauliga.

Muyáyiri . 4

Námdév . 27
Rangári.

Native . 1

Native Christian 2,705
Agnáni.
Balagai.
Basel Mission.
British Indian.
East Indian.
Gauda.
Holeya.

Native Christian—*contd.*
Karnátaka.
Konkani.
Nazráni.
Pariah.
Roman Catholic.
Tamil.
Vellála.

Naváyat . 325
Batkali.
Sheik.

Náyaka . 80
Agatta Náyaka.
Bédaru.
Besta.
Hálu Bédru
Malai.
Mallara.

Náyar . 1,097
Agatta Náyar.
Baniya.
Béda.
Chárna.
Chelet.
Chembukutti.
Doratta.
Kande.
Kartakanmár.
Kiriyattil.
Kodagu.
Kólayan.
Malayáli.
Marátojári.
Marutta.
Meraka.
Nálupabbu.
Nambiyár.
Padiváda.
Poda.
Porattuchárna.
Sudra.
Suratta.
Tíyavakta.
Vallavada Sudra.
Valita.
Vantivada.
Velláji.

Náyinda . 54
Hajám.

Náyudu . 12
Balija.
Kavarai.

Odde . 441
Bóyi.
Gádiga.
Kallu.
Mannu.
Mári.
Telaga.
Tulu Kallu.

Padárti . . 205
Aliyakattuva vamsam.
Tulu.

Pále . . 4,045
Agasa.
Ajala.
Aramane.
Arati.
Bákuda, 159.
Belu.
Boluméra.
Dora.
Hobbela.
Holeya.
Kari.
Kukka.
Madi.
Malayáli.
Maráti.
Mata, 196.
Matta.
Mávu, 367.
Méra, 519.
Mundála.
Nidra.
Nyápuda.
Rudra.
Súrya.
Tulu.
Yeliya.

Velláia—*contd.*
Kudakyára.
Mudali.
Palli.
Pándiya.
Paraka.
Pillai.
Ponna.
Ponnéri.
Punamalli.
Sále.
Sérvégára.
Sólai.
Sóliya.
Tamil.
Telaga Banajiga.

Velláia—*concld.*
Tondamandala.
Tóta.
Vakkaliga.
Vannian.
Yalai.

Vírasaiva . . 1,580
Badagala.
Banajiga.
Gaudagalu.
Gurustala.
Hiri Hasube Banajiga.
Jangama.
Jangama Gaudálike.
Jangamárádhya.

Vírasaiva—*contd.*
Kallali Banajiga.
Kunchiga.
Lingáyat.
Lingayat Siváchára.
Panchháchára.
Pancháchára Gauda.
Panchánana.
Shadá Kshatri.
Siva Brahman.
Siváchára.
Siváchára Banajiga.
Siváchára Jangam.
Siváchára Kalgale Jangam.
Siváchára Kumbára.
Siváchárada Gaudálike.

Visvakarma . . 235
Akkasále.
Badagi.
Pánchála.
Panchánana.
Telugu.
Tulu Áchári.
Visvagna.

Yerava . . 14,209
Badaga.
Badagi.
Kembatti.
Malayáli.
Paniya, 10,003
Panjiri, 3,345